SCM CORE

Sociology of Religion

Andrew Dawson

scm press

Published in 2011 by SCM Press
Editorial office
13–17 Long Lane,
London, ECIA 9PN, UK

SCM Press is an imprint of Hymns Ancient and Modern Ltd
(a registered charity)
13A Hellesdon Park Road
Norwich NR6 5DR, UK

www.scm-canterburypress.co.uk

British Library Cataloguing in Publication data

A catalogue record for this book is available
from the British Library

978-0-334-04336-2

Typeset by Manila Typesetting Company
Printed and bound by
CPI Antony Rowe, Chippenham, Wiltshire

Contents

Acknowledgements

I am grateful to Natalie Watson of SCM Press for her kind invitation to write this book. The unstinting support and patience of friends and family is also much appreciated. Friends from the 'Greggie' – to whom this book is dedicated – have proved a special source of refreshment and welcome distraction through the course of its writing. As with all of my projects, the unqualified positivity and implacable encouragement of my wife, Debbie, leaves me with debts I can never pay. Mention should also be made of the undergraduate and postgraduate students whose engagement with my teaching of the sociology of religion has both informed its development and refined its focus. While the words and responsibility are mine, many of the questions this book addresses are theirs.

Introduction

When asked by SCM Press to write this book, my initial thoughts turned to whether the sociology of religion really needed another introductory work to what is an already well-provisioned area of study. Accustomed to teaching both under- and postgraduate modules in this particular sub-discipline of sociology, I have never had difficulty filling introductory reading lists from the many companions, handbooks and introductions currently available. Two issues arising from this current abundance of student-orientated works are worthy of note. First, the upsurge in sociological interest in religion is historically recent. Although at the heart of the discipline when founded in the late 1800s (see Chapter 3), by the second half of the twentieth century sociological interest in religion was regarded as little more than an exotic appendage – if not, for some, a complete irrelevance – to the overarching disciplinary paradigm. While not rectified across all aspects of the discipline, ongoing changes in theoretical focus and concrete developments on the ground have combined to pique, once again, sociological interest in the religious landscape.

In respect of changes to the theoretical focus of the discipline, sociology's long-standing preoccupation with overarching structures and large-scale institutional dynamics has steadily been complemented by interest in the everyday interactions, associational contexts and organizational processes through which individuals and communities live their lives and render their experiences meaningful. Accompanied by sundry other developments, this shift in disciplinary focus gradually opened the way for issues relating to religion to progress incrementally, if not haltingly, onto the mainstream sociological agenda. As noted in Chapter 2, academic engagement with the various dimensions of religious belief and practice furnishes insight into a range of issues and themes of direct relevance to the contemporary sociological community – from meaning-making and identity formation, through associational dynamics and organizational processes, to class, race and sex.

Regarding concrete events on the ground, sociological interest in religion has been reignited by a number of developments. Exemplified by the Christian right of the USA, the Shi'ite revolution in Iran and religious nationalism in Asia and Europe, the rise of fundamentalist religiosity has heightened religion's profile both in popular media coverage and academic policy forums (see Chapter 9). At the same time, the growth and internationalization

of Pentecostal, evangelical and charismatic movements have further reinforced the now global profile of conservative religion (see Chapter 10). The
emergence and spread of new religious movements and alternative spiritualities has likewise piqued academic interest in what is fast becoming both
a progressively fluid terrain and vibrant field of study (see Chapters 5 and
7). In combination, developments such as these have challenged prevailing academic assumptions about religion's irrelevance to modern life, and
called for heightened sociological engagement with the dynamics, processes
and structures through which contemporary belief and practice are manifest. Complemented by the aforementioned theoretical shift in disciplinary
focus, the calls and challenges issued by developments on the ground have
resulted in a veritable renaissance of sociological interest in religion – a renaissance evidenced by the current abundance of introductory works in the
sociology of religion.

The second issue raised by this abundance of introductory works relates
to the book that you have before you. If the sociology of religion is so well-
provisioned, why the need for another introduction such as this? The answer to this question resides chiefly in the nature of the introductory works
currently available. In effect, the overwhelming majority of introductions
assume a familiarity with the subject knowledge and skills-base peculiar to
sociology which a great many of their readers simply do not have. Because
of the assumed familiarity of their readership, the bulk of the introductions
available completely skip or superficially pass over a range of basic sociological material the understanding of which is essential to a rounded appreciation of the issues at hand. This particular introduction is a development
of course materials delivered mostly to undergraduate students with little
or no understanding of sociology. While attempting to turn these students
on to the delights of the sociology of religion, this course material does not
require them to be or become full-blown sociologists. It is enough that they
gain a sense of what it means to think sociologically and thereby to engage
religious belief and practice in a manner in keeping with the sociology of
religion. In order to achieve this aspiration, and in addition to the substantive
issues dealt with, students are familiarized throughout with the basics of the
knowledge and skills associated with the sociological treatment of religion.
As a development of these materials, this book is no different.

Such an approach, however, does not prevent this book from making a
useful contribution for those with a degree of sociological learning already
in place. When it comes to the foundations of any discipline, the iteration
of its fundamental components does no one any harm! At the same time,
the distinctive approach of the sociology of religion offers any number of
avenues for developing a more nuanced and broadened understanding of
the overarching sociological paradigm as a whole. Indeed, I have been approached on a number of occasions by undergraduate sociologists who

have commented favourably upon the insights into their discipline gained through their participation in my courses.

Although holding in mind a readership with little or no prior sociological knowledge, this book also serves those who may be coming to religion for the first time. As well as introducing the disciplinary basics of the sociological gaze, what follows offers a foundational treatment of religion both as a concrete socio-cultural phenomenon and a particular field of academic study. In so doing, the book opens with two introductory chapters which outline a range of issues, themes and approaches relating to the academic study of modern society and religion respectively. Chapter 1 delineates the chief characteristics of modern society and the key ways in which sociology both frames and understands these characteristics. Chapter 2 outlines discussions in respect of defining religion and then links what religion is understood to be with questions relating to where it is sought and how it is engaged.

Chapter 3 builds upon these introductory overviews and engages the work of three individuals – Karl Marx, Émile Durkheim and Max Weber – generally recognized as having a major impact upon the foundation and subsequent development of both sociology in general and the sociology of religion in particular. The next three chapters treat a number of issues which revolve immediately around the contributions made by these three foundational thinkers. Chapters 4 and 5 engage discussions and debates about the status and place of religion within modern, urban-industrial society. Chapter 4 addresses a range of arguments relating to the notions of 'secularization' and 'disenchantment' which regard modern society as a less religious environment than what has gone before. In direct contrast, Chapter 5 outlines a number of contrary arguments (such as 'sacralization' and 're-enchantment') which reject the assumed association of modernity with a decline in religious belief and practice. Likewise engaging long-standing sociological discussions, Chapter 6 addresses established understandings of religion as a form of ideology. In so doing, this chapter also deals with the relationship between religion and gender.

What remains of this book addresses some of the most recent developments to which the sociology of religion has turned its attention. Chapter 7 treats the rise and spread of non-traditional forms of religion most commonly categorized as 'new religious movements' (NRMs) and 'alternative spiritualities'. In addition to exploring issues of defining and studying novel religious phenomena, the chapter reflects upon a range of factors which influence the success or failure of new and non-mainstream religiosities. Chapter 8 engages a number of theories and discussions provoked by recent understandings of the religious domain as a kind of economy in which religion functions as an exchange commodity to be marketed and consumed. This chapter looks at the two most influential theoretical frames through which religion's contemporary 'marketization' is understood. Chapter 9 outlines a variety of ways in which sociologists of religion analyse the rise, spread and character of religious fundamentalism. In addition to delineating the various types of religious fundamentalism currently in existence, the chapter focuses upon the analytical approaches employed to explain this characteristically 'modern' phenomenon. Chapter 10 closes the book by treating the contemporary dynamics of globalization and their impact upon modern-day religion. As well as treating the organizational implications of the international spread of traditional religions and new religiosities, the chapter concludes this work by addressing the impact of globalizing modernity upon the contemporary religious landscape.

1

Settling into the Discipline:
Thinking Sociologically

Introduction

What follows introduces the central components of the discipline of sociology. Of course, in a chapter of this length, only the most rudimentary elements of the sociological gaze can be sketched. To this end, the following material aspires only to promote sufficient understanding of the principal concerns, debates and approaches in play within sociology to furnish a suitably informed platform upon which subsequent chapters might build. As the sociology of religion is a sub-discipline of the much broader sociological paradigm, an appreciation of its content, rationale and methods is best achieved through first engaging overarching disciplinary preoccupations and their respective theoretical contentions. Given its thoroughgoingly modern provenance, the discipline of sociology must be understood against the thematic backdrop of 'modernity' (Bilton, Bonnett and Jones, 2002). As such, the chapter opens by outlining the chief characteristics of the modern social landscape which sociology engages. The central importance of society and its constituent dimensions is then treated along with some key theoretical debates in respect of the relationship between individuals and social structures. The chapter closes by sketching a number of the most important themes, theoretical variations and methodological approaches in play across the sociological spectrum.

Modernity

The academic discipline of sociology is inextricably fused with the rise of modern, urban-industrial society. This rise occurred initially in Europe and North America and properly began at the close of the eighteenth and beginning of the nineteenth centuries. As this emergence occurred at a particular historical moment in a particular geographical space, the discipline of sociology bears the marks of a specific time and place. Of course, the twentieth-century globalization of the modern, urban-industrial paradigm has occasioned the socio-cultural pluralization of the sociological gaze. The growth of modernity and spread of urban-industrialization to virtually all parts of the world have resulted in sociology's welcome variegation through the addition of multiple voices speaking with pluriform accents and articulating miscellaneous concerns. However, and for a variety of historical and contemporary reasons, the overwhelming majority of the theory, vocabulary and analytical preoccupations of sociology continue to be those of the modern-day West. Because modernity is 'multiple' and the processes of urban-industrialization multifaceted, it cannot be assumed that theories and concepts which illuminate social dynamics in the West automatically apply to the likes of Brazil, China and India (see Chapter 10). By no means negating the ability of sociology to address matters beyond its traditional Western cradle, this observation nevertheless warrants an element of caution, if not humility, both in respect of sociology in general and the sociology of religion in particular (Cohen and Kennedy, 2007).

Key characteristics of modern society

Like the urban-industrial landscape it seeks to understand, sociology is a modern phenomenon. According to the English social theorist Anthony Giddens:

> modernity is a shorthand term for modern society or industrial civilization
> . . . it is associated with (1) a certain set of attitudes towards the world, the idea of the world as open to transformation by human intervention; (2) a complex of economic institutions, especially industrial production and a market economy; (3) a certain range of political institutions, including the nation-state and mass democracy. Largely as a result of these characteristics, modernity is vastly more dynamic than any previous type of social order. It is a society – more technically, a complex of institutions – which unlike any preceding culture lives in the future rather than the past.
> (1998, p. 94)

In more or less explicit terms, Giddens' definition highlights a number of features which make modern society what it is and thereby distinguish it from what has gone before. Of the most relevant points Giddens makes, first and foremost, modern society is *urban-industrial*. Even rural parts of the modern landscape characterized by agricultural production are in modern society orientated to meeting the needs of the urban-industrial heartlands they ultimately serve. Although by no means evenly achieved across the globe, a typically modern society in any part of the world concentrates the overwhelming majority of its population – understood now as a 'workforce' – within urban environments geared to facilitating mechanized and technologically driven forms of industrial production.

2

Second, modern society is *integrated*. In structural terms, modern societies are characterized by the universal, and usually centralized, application of political, legal, economic, and, at times, linguistic processes which impact upon all aspects of social life. Driven initially by the industrial revolution of the 1800s, structural integration was facilitated through the rapid development of infrastructural networks of transport (e.g. canal, rail, road, air) and communication (e.g. mail, telegraph, telephone, radio, satellite). The social integration characteristic of modernity arises directly from the processes and networks of structural integration. Catalysed by the dynamics of urbanization, social integration is further enhanced by virtue of the modern individual's increased interaction with and mutual reliance upon other human beings. From basic goods (e.g. food, clothing, shelter), through institutional encounter (e.g. education, work, leisure) to mediated interaction (e.g. reading, radio, television, internet), the average member of modern society both interacts with and relies upon a vast array of integrated networks and those who populate them. At the same time, this interaction and dependence relies upon a substantial amount of co-operation enabled by common knowledge and shared values – much of which we take for granted but without which we would be unable to function.

Third, modern society is *highly complex*. Often referred to as 'differentiation', the complexity of modern society is realized through the progressively varied nature of both its structures and population. In structural terms, modern society has an almost vertiginous number of processes, mechanisms, organizations, and institutions through which the day-to-day activities of its members occur. Be they economic, political, legal, employment-related, educational, recreational, communal and familial, the structures of modern society are numerous, variegated and highly specialized. At the same time, modern society exhibits a socio-cultural variety unprecedented in human history. On the one hand, social pluralization occurs in response to structural differentiation. This is the case because variegated kinds of social structures engender progressively diverse life-experiences for the different groups who populate the various parts of the system. The increasing number of 'social categories', 'status groups' or 'classes' evident in modern society responds directly to its structural complexity. On the other hand, social differentiation occurs through migration, as different socio-cultural groups move – or are moved – from one place to another. In addition to adding to the socio-cultural mix by their simple presence, the subsequent interaction of different racial, ethnic and linguistic groups further enhances the socially plural character of modern society.

Fourth, modern society is characterized by *constant, rapid and far-reaching transformation* at both structural and social levels. In combination, for example, the spread of global capitalism and pace of technological innovation necessitate continued revision of economic, political, legal and educational structures. From new means of financial regulation and

3

infrastructural integration through shifting employment patterns and modified modes of civil participation to expanded human rights and extended
access to health care and education, modern societies of every shape and
size are continually remodelling their structures to keep pace with the scale
and rapidity of contemporary change. In socio-cultural terms, for example,
the gap between past and present generations has never been so stark. While
intergenerational differences have long been a feature of human history, the
swift and widespread transformation typical of modernity fundamentally
alters the hold which the traditions and practices of our antecedents are able
to exert. In effect, as the scale and rapidity of change distances contemporary from past experience, current generations find it increasingly hard to
both appreciate the relevance of inherited traditions and willingly perform
received practices. Indeed, for some, this distance is experienced as so great
that the traditions and practices of prior generations are rendered obsolete,
meaningless and irrelevant to today's world.

Fifth, and in contrast to what has gone before, modern society is typically
orientated to the individual. In actuality, of course, society is a variegated
structure comprising a diverse range of more or less formal institutions
(e.g. family, school, peer group, neighbourhood, workplace, leisure network, state apparatus) through which humans live their lives by interacting
with others. What is typical of modern society, though, is the weakening of
the influence which these collective institutions have traditionally exerted
over their individual members. Compared with pre-modern societies, and
allowing for socio-economic variation, modernity furnishes its members
with a degree of individual expression and personal choice which limits
the traditional scope of collective determination. Whether expressed in the
choice of partner, employment or life-style, modernity's enabling of individuality lessens the role played by traditional collectivities (e.g. family,
class, religion) along with their particular refractions of, for example, sex,
race and age.

Modernity is not a fixed phenomenon and did not emerge over 200 years
ago as a finished product with all of its features already in place. In addition to others mentioned throughout this book, each of the characteristics
outlined above has taken time to acquire the features it has today and has
gone through a number of different phases before doing so. For example,
the typically dense urban-industrial landscape which has become such a
feature of modern society has taken many years and experienced a number
of distinct growth spurts to obtain its current profile. Combining inward
migration (from home and abroad) with increased population growth
(aided by improved living conditions), the transition from an overwhelmingly rural to a predominantly urban population is neither an instant nor
even process. Although not necessarily progressing, modernity is certainly
evolving and exists in a permanently transitional, if not fluid state (Urry,
2000).

4

Late modernity

In recent decades, the notion that modernity is now in a new phase of its existence has become increasingly prevalent. Using adjectives such as 'late', 'hyper', 'high' and 'second' to qualify their understanding of 'modernity', certain – mainly European – social theorists argue that modern society is now characterized by a fundamental radicalization of the processes and structures by which it has traditionally been defined (Bauman, 2005; Beck, 1992; Giddens, 1990). Unlike postmodern theorists, however, those advocating the notion of late or second modernity argue that while contemporary society is different in degree from what has gone before, it is not different in kind. Contemporary society is not different in kind from what has gone before because the same kinds of social processes which gave rise to modernity (urban-industrialization, structural differentiation, social pluralization etc.) continue to exist. At the same time, however, and for a variety of reasons, these processes have assumed an intensity which magnifies both the scale and rapidity of their impact upon the structural fabric and social make-up of modern society.

An example often cited by those advocating a late- or second-modernity is the extent to which modern processes of societal integration have been radicalized over the course of the last few decades (Beck, Giddens and Lash, 1994). On the one hand, this radicalization involves the intensification of late-modern integrative processes occurring at a national level. The most influential of such developments is perhaps the 'marketization' of contemporary society engendered by late-capitalist emphases upon economically driven modes of existence. Encompassing far more than financial transactions and commercial activities, the marketization of late modern society impacts upon all walks of life. Through their valorization of competition and inculcation of acquisitive and consumerist lifestyles, the marketizing forces of late modernity engender the progressive commodification of contemporary society as a whole. On the other hand, the radicalization of integrative processes occurs at an unprecedented international level. While the rise of modern society was in many ways predicated on the growth of international exchange – not least in respect of trade and workforce migration – the recent intensification of transnational integration is such that a new term ('globalization') has been adopted to signal the hyper-modern step change in integrative dynamics. The technological advances of the late-modern period (e.g. passenger aircraft, satellite technology, the internet) enable the rapid and large-scale circulation of material goods, people, information, tastes, values and beliefs. Exemplified by the financial crisis of 2008 and subsequent global slump, such is the nature of this worldwide circulation that domestic structures and social dynamics are now inextricably interwoven within a highly integrated network of international processes and flows.

Society

The concept of society is the beating heart of sociological analysis. The word society (from the Latin *societas*) was around long before it was co-opted by early social theorists such as Auguste Comte (1798–1857) and used to designate 'sociology' as the 'science of society' (Seidman, 2004, pp. 11–21). When used sociologically, though, society denotes the totality of the social world whose individual inhabitants occupy any number of collective institutions (family, class, interest-group, religion), whose interactions are structured relative to a range of overarching processes of both a material (economic, political, legal) and symbolic (common knowledge, tradition, morality) kind. Ultimately, what distinguishes one type of society (such as modern/urban-industrial) from another (such as medieval/feudal) is:

- they have different kinds of institutions;
- these institutions interact in different ways; and
- this interaction is orchestrated by different forms of material and symbolic structure.

In respect of different kinds of institutions, the modern family unit, for example, has very different characteristics from feudal kinship structures. Whereas medieval families tended to be extended, tightly knit, categorically heterosexual, and functioning economic units, the modern family is typically nuclear, diffuse, more varied in gender and number, and characterized as principally domestic in character. At the same time, because the economic, legal and political structures of feudal society reflected an aristocratic, religious, agricultural, and strictly hierarchical worldview, the medieval family's interaction with other social institutions was of a very different kind from that of the modern family.

Key dimensions of society

As indicated above, modern society is a complex, multifaceted phenomenon whose constitutive parts (themselves varied and complex) interact in a vertiginous number ways. By way of facilitating sociological analysis of society, its components and their interaction, sociologists often distinguish between what are commonly termed the 'macro', 'meso' and 'micro' dimensions of the social world. Reflecting their derivation from the Greek language, *macro* literally means 'long' or 'large' and refers to the large-scale, overarching structures of society; *meso* means 'middle' and denotes society's mid-range, intermediate parts; and *micro* means 'small' and refers to the, usually face-to-face, interactions between individuals which form the bedrock on which society rests. In their most apparent form, macro-structures take shape as economic (e.g. financial exchange), political (e.g. the state) and juridical (e.g. laws)

6

processes which orchestrate the interaction of social institutions and the individuals who populate them. At the same time, though, macro-structures also exist as value systems (e.g. morality), dominant beliefs (e.g. religion), normative tastes (e.g. humour), and prevailing expectations (gender) which pervade the social world. In so doing, these symbolic structures influence both how individuals act (e.g. dieting, consumption, sexism, racism) and how institutions operate by way of, for example, access and exclusion (e.g. marriage) and reward and sanction (e.g. discrimination).

The intermediate dimension of society is occupied by a wide variety of institutions which, like aforementioned macro-structures, are more or less apparent to the untrained eye. In contemporary urban-industrial society, perhaps the most obvious institutions are those of education (e.g. school and university), employment (e.g. factory and supermarket), finance (e.g. banks and credit agencies), commerce (e.g. business and retail outlets), and state (e.g. local and national government, police, law courts, prisons). Less obviously 'institutional', but no less important because of it, are the institutions of family, interest-group (e.g. union and guild), voluntary association (e.g. uniformed organization) and religion (e.g. Christianity, Islam, Judaism). In sociological terms, institutions are not necessarily made of bricks and mortar, nor need they be constituted by law or have written codes of conduct with clearly defined roles and responsibilities. Rather, and basically put, institutions exist as collective modes of social organization whose members behave and interact in relation to a range of expectations as to, for example, their roles (e.g. lecturer or student, priest or parishioner) and status (e.g. learned or learner, ordained or lay). Different institutions exist in different forms, last different lengths of time and are organized more or less formally.

The micro-dimension of society comprises the myriad interactions which occur between individuals as they go about their daily lives. Sociologically speaking, what is most interesting about the daily interactions which comprise the micro-dimension is that they always involve more than the straightforward exchange between two or more people at any given time or place. In effect, and despite appearances, the everyday interactions from which society springs are influenced by a range of processes and dynamics which frame these social encounters and impact directly upon them to shape, pattern and organize their character in ways which transcend the conscious intentions and immediate awareness of the individuals involved. This is the case because every individual who inhabits society is shaped by a diverse array of influences which are mediated via the institutions through which she moves and the macro-structural processes to which he is exposed. Who we are as selves is, according to Richard Jenkins, 'altogether individual and intrinsically social . . . Even though it is the most individualized of identities . . . selfhood is absolutely social' (1996, p. 50). While a number of academics have contributed greatly to analysing the day-to-day interactions through which human beings construct their social world, what makes this analysis truly sociological is its theoretical linkage with broader concerns relating to the institutions and structures which frame all aspects of interpersonal encounter.

Agency–structure relations

All of the major figures (and most of the minor ones) in the history of sociological thought have understood individuals and society to be intertwined and inextricably fused. Indeed, this is perhaps the founding assumption of sociological thought itself. (Layder, 1994, p. 207)

Framed as the 'agency–structure' or 'self–society' relationship, the interaction between the individual and the social world at large is of central sociological concern. On the one hand, society is self-evidently something created by human beings. Just as there can be no language without those who speak it, there can be no society without the individual agents upon whose actions its existence depends. On the other hand, who we are as human beings is quite clearly influenced by societal dynamics which transcend our immediate consciousness and escape our absolute control. Just as the language we learn structures the very thoughts and words of which we are capable, so too do social processes influence the very persons we are and, indeed, are capable of becoming. While society is produced by human agency, human beings, as social selves, are the products of societal structures and dynamics.

Although it may strike us today as self-evident that society, its structures and institutions are produced by human agency, this insight (itself made available by sociology) has not always been present. Holding that the social order was grounded in a divinely created order (*ordo Dei*) or a biologically determined natural order (*ordo naturalis*), pre-modern thought regarded society and its institutions as fixed entities whose membership and hierarchical ordering reflect unchanging principles and immutable laws. As Pope Pius X put it in 1903: 'It is in conformity with the order established by God in human society that there should be princes and subjects, employers and proletariat, rich and poor, instructed and ignorant' (Houtart and Rousseau, 1971, p. 354). The kind of logic which informed Pope Pius X had implications for the whole of society and its institutions. By divine intent or biological determination, for example, the Western family was regarded as an institution given by nature, to be headed by a male and formed through the monogamous union of two heterosexuals for the purpose of procreation.

The perception of society and its institutions as pre-determined and thereby fixed structures originating beyond the generative processes of human agency is a form of 'reification' (Giddens, 1979, p. 195). Literally meaning 'making a concrete thing (*res*) out of something abstract', the act of

8

reification affords the social world an unchangeable existence independent from the everyday activities of its inhabitants. As Berger and Luckmann maintain:

> The reified world is, by definition, a dehumanized world. It is experienced by man as a strange facticity, an *opus alienum* over which he has no control rather than as the *opus proprium* of his own productive activity . . . Man, the producer of a world, is apprehended as its product, and human activity as an epiphenomenon of non-human processes. (1966, pp. 106–7)

The word 'epiphenomenon' used by Berger and Luckmann refers to something being dependent upon something else for its existence and which has no influence upon that from which it derives. By denoting human beings as dependent and lacking influence upon society, reification undercuts the role of human agency as both giving rise to and continuing to sustain the social world and its structures.

By observing, charting and reflecting upon the myriad social interactions which make up the day-to-day experience of human beings, sociology furnishes an understanding of how everyday human agency both sustains and modifies the institutions and structures within which we live. While engaging *how* agency sustains and modifies structure, some social theorists also reflect upon *why* institutions and structures are such a fundamental part of human existence. Drawing upon other disciplines (such as psychology), the 'why' question is often answered by showing how the stability, safety and predictability which institutions afford human beings address deep-seated needs for security and order (Archer, 2008; Giddens, 1984). Together, sociological insights upon how and why human agency originates and sustains the institutions and structures which populate society shows the individual to be far more than 'a passive entity, determined by external influences'. Rather, emphasis upon the constitutive character of agency underscores the fact that everyday micro-social interactions 'contribute to and directly promote social influences that are global in their consequences and implications' (Giddens, 1991, p. 2).

At the same time, just as the act of reification offers a one-sided reading of actual causal processes, so too does the assertion that society is the simple product of everyday human agency. As Craib notes, if 'we start with social action and see systems as the straightforward product of such action, then we cannot . . . comprehend the very real constraints the social structures and systems place on us' (1992, p. 121). While societal processes and social institutions are, indeed, the unintended by-products of everyday human activity, their ability to structure this everyday activity in ways which both transcend immediate awareness and escape precise control affords them a powerful causal efficacy. Although the understanding of society as artefact (something made by us) is one of sociology's most insightful contributions to modern thought, many would agree with Bauman that:

> it was the incessant effort to solve the puzzle of purposeful action of knowledgeable actors producing 'unintended consequences', or of the evident incapacity of 'free-actors' to exercise their freedom in the course of end-orientated action, or of the stubborn tendency of the multitude of individual actions to sediment into a reality independent of these actions and in its turn making the action dependent on itself which, for all intents and purposes, constituted the history of sociology. (1989, p. 36)

Certainly, the role of agency in generating and sustaining social structures has, by rights, an important place within social theory. However, the 'examination and interpretation of specific compelling forces to which people are exposed in their particular empirically observable societies and groups' has proved a theoretical mainstay of the sociological tradition (Elias, 1978, p. 18).

Social determination

The impact of social structure upon agency has two important and overlapping dimensions. The first, and more abstract, dimension of the social structuring of agency concerns the theoretical issue of determinism. Here, social theory treats the extent to which individual choices, values, beliefs, and tastes originate from voluntary dynamics and subjective freedoms or are the products of social processes and determinative forces exterior to the self. While each extreme of the determinism equation has found adherents within the sociological community, mainstream social theory has traditionally acknowledged elements of both structural determination and subjective freedom as constitutive dimensions of individual agency (Heilbron, 1995). Mainstream opinion remains divided, however, as to which of these two elements deserves most attention and as to how precisely the dimensions of structure and agency interact. For example, while readily acknowledging the importance of individual agency, the French social theorist Pierre Bourdieu affords greater theoretical space to the structuring capacities of social forces (1984, 1993 and 1998). As he remarks, somewhat pessimistically perhaps:

> The true freedom that sociology offers is to give us a small chance of . . . minimizing the ways in which we are manipulated by the forces of the [social] field in which we evolve, as well as by the embodied social forces that operate from within us. (Bourdieu and Wacquant, 1992, p. 198)

On the other hand, while Giddens' 'theory of structuration' gives ample acknowledgment of the 'structural properties of social systems', his analytical emphasis remains squarely upon agency as expressed through 'the reflexively monitored activities of situated actors, having a range of intended and unintended consequences' (1984, p. 212). Although agreeing with Bourdieu and Giddens as to the dual importance of structure and agency, Margaret Archer is critical of their conceptualization of how these two mutually constitutive elements interact. For Archer, both theorists fail to acknowledge that while structural determination may be to the fore in one time or place, in other periods and locales individual agency enjoys heightened efficacy (1996, pp. 72–96). The relationship between structure and agency is, then, often asymmetric in nature.

Wherever they stand on the spectrum of the determinism debate, most sociologists would agree that every individual is a social being whose values and beliefs, preferences and aversions, aspirations, preoccupations and prejudices, are never purely her own. Rather, they stem also from sources outside of ourselves (e.g. family, peer group, schooling, workplace, religion, media) and are internalized by us through our exposure to the processes of socialization particular to each of the institutions through which we pass. As Berger puts it: 'Society does not stop at the surface of our skins. Society penetrates us as much as it envelops us' (1966, p. 140). By virtue of our internalization of them, these exterior influences become integral features of our innermost subjectivity, influencing us in ways which – more often than not – escape our immediate awareness.

The tendency of social processes to influence human beings in ways which escape their immediate notice has sociological implications that go beyond some of the theoretical abstractions of the determinism debate. This is the case because structural determination generates patterns and regularities in human behaviour which impact directly upon the life choices made by and social opportunities available to every individual. As Jonathan Turner notes:

> The symbolic and material resources available to individuals, the placement of people in space, the amount of time people have, the options that are realistically available, and just about everything that is possible in a micro encounter are all dictated by macrostructure. (1988, p. 211)

The macro-determination of micro-possibility generates comparative regularities in individual behaviour which can be mapped against shared characteristics of, for example, class membership, sex or ethnic identity. In respect of class, individuals belonging to poorer socio-economic groups exhibit different patterns of consumption from those from more affluent households. In both the UK and USA, for example, poorer families will spend less of their household income on fruit and vegetables than families from more affluent professional backgrounds. At the same time, more affluent families are more likely to purchase their groceries at supermarkets, where prices are generally cheaper and money goes further, while poorer families are more likely to shop at local stores where prices are generally higher. In the same vein, while those from poorer socio-economic groups are more likely than those from more affluent backgrounds to smoke, have a poorer diet, die sooner, suffer more illness, and recover more slowly from these illnesses, they are less likely to consult a dentist, optician and chiropodist and to make use of preventative facilities such as cervical screening and routine medical examination (Butler and Watt, 2007; Gilbert, 2008).

Where race and ethnicity are concerned, UK figures released in 2003 show different patterns of employment relative to differences in racial-ethnic status. For example, the data indicate that one in 20 Indian men is a doctor, compared with one in 200 white men, 45 per cent of Chinese men are in professional or managerial jobs compared with 25 per cent of white and Indian men, and members of the Hindu community are four times less likely to be unemployed than Pakistani and Bangladeshi Muslims. At the same time, while Black Caribbean women earn £30 more than white women, Pakistani and Bangladeshi women earn £34 less than their white counterparts (Cabinet Office, 2003).

In respect of sex, statistics from the USA clearly demonstrate societal patterning of female agency relative to that of men. For example, the annual income of American women in full-time employment is three-quarters of that of their male counterparts. In the same vein, while a man with a bachelor's degree will earn approximately $25,000 more than a man with a high-school diploma, a woman with a bachelor's degree will earn around only $5,000 more than a man with a high-school diploma. At the same time, whereas female professional employment is concentrated in the social and health sciences, male professional employment is concentrated in engineering and new technologies. Furthermore, during the course of their working lives women will enjoy substantially less leisure time than male workers, while subsequent to retiring from the workforce women are far more likely than men to suffer some form of socio-economic impoverishment (McCall, 2001; Ore, 2008; Rothenberg, 2006).

In terms of explaining the above modes of societal patterning, popular myths, ill-informed bigotries or simple ignorance point readily to the fecklessness or determination of the different classes, the idleness or industry of particular racial-ethnic groups and the respective inclinations of the sexes. In addition to perpetuating classist, racist and sexist prejudices, such poorly judged opinion commits the reductionist error of explaining overarching societal processes through reference to singular causes or unrelated phenomena which function in isolation from the complex systems they purport to explain. For example, while the biological differences between men and women are clearly relevant, they do not in themselves account for the processes of socialization and discrimination which sustain patriarchal structures and their gendered inequalities. In contrast, diligent sociological analysis of differential social outcomes takes due account of the macro-structural dynamics, institutional processes and micro-interactions which provide, ration or deny symbolic and material resources to individuals of differing sex, socio-economic standing or ethnic-racial origins.

The sociological gaze

By way of engaging society, the discipline of sociology turns its gaze upon a variety of domains, dimensions and dynamics which manifest and contribute to the social world as both a 'structuring structure' (through societal determination) and a 'structured structure' (arising from human agency).[1] Sociology, then, concerns itself with analysing societal structures and social institutions which both mould their human inhabitants and shape society's reproduction from one generation to the next. Here, the sociological gaze alights upon the properties and processes of, for example, state, education, employment and family, with particular attention, perhaps, to their variegated mediations of power, privilege, conformity and inequality. At the same time, sociology analyses the dynamics and outcomes of these variegated mediations, not least as they relate to biological characteristics of sex, race and age or the socio-cultural categories of gender, class or caste. In combination, these multiple and variable factors generate a stratified social landscape whose hierarchies of status and authority have direct but differentiated implications for the physical (e.g. health) and social (e.g. mobility) wellbeing of its members.

Traditionally treated through the oppositional themes of 'integration' and 'deviance', sociology also concerns itself with understanding the ways in which macro-processes and institutional dynamics engender the social conformity or manage the nonconformity of individuals and the groups to which they belong. In addition to analysing the concrete mechanisms of reward and punishment, sociology looks also to grasp the impact of prevailing values, conventional beliefs and common knowledges upon individual and collective behaviour. Exemplified by the recent prominence of cultural sociology, analysis of the socializing processes through which normative behaviour is inculcated has been increasingly complemented by critical attention to popular modes of symbolic expression and aesthetic production. Today, analysis of previously neglected modes of cultural production and everyday expression (e.g. television and popular humour) accompanies established critiques of 'high' culture, religious systems and civic traditions. In combination, the values, tastes, practices and conventions of the cultural domain furnish the means – material and symbolic – through which life (both individual and collective) is

13

celebrated and rendered meaningful and its latent possibilities explored and expressed.

The way in which societies change over time is also an important object of sociological scrutiny. As noted above, modern society can be distinguished from earlier (for example feudal) societies through reference both to its typical institutional features and the way these institutions interact relative to the orchestration of particular macro-structural dynamics. As both institutions and macro-structures evolve over time, so too does their interaction and the implications it has for individual members of society. Whether analysing the transition from feudal through pre-modern to modern society or engaging the successive phases of modern society itself, sociology reflects upon the causes, consequences, continuities and ruptures involved in societal transformation. In addition to its concerns with longitudinal change, sociology has an international perspective as it compares or analyses the interaction between the different kinds and versions of society in existence across the world. For example, in recent decades the radicalization of globalizing processes has provided ample opportunity to study the tensions and transformations provoked by the interaction of modern, techno-industrial systems with nations and cultures that, at least until now, have existed in relative isolation from the particular socio-economic structures spawned by the industrial revolution. At the same time, the geographical spread of modernity is giving rise to different versions of modern society ('multiple modernities') as the original Western model is modified subsequent to its interaction with non-Western structures, institutions and cultures (see Chapter 10).

Variations on a sociological theme

While understanding society and our relationship with it is at the heart of the sociological endeavour, there is widespread disagreement among sociologists as to the best manner of undertaking its disciplinary labours. First of all, sociologists disagree about the most appropriate way of conceptualizing society and the interrelationship of its constitutive macro-structures, mid-range institutions and micro-social encounters. Second, sociologists disagree about the character and purpose of their chosen academic discipline.

Theoretical variations

Two of the most prevailing, but contrasting, ways of conceptualizing society will suffice as examples. Traditionally, the most dominant way of conceptualizing society has concentrated upon the dynamics of social order and systemic integration. The French sociologist Émile Durkheim (1858–1917) is generally credited with establishing this model as a theoretical mainstay of the sociological tradition. Often using biological analogies, society is here viewed as an organism which, like other living things, functions best when its constituent parts work harmoniously together. In the same vein, as with any biological entity, society has needs which must be met if it is not only to survive but to flourish and ultimately evolve. Furthermore, just as a living organism has inbuilt mechanisms to adjust in times of change and heal itself in times of need, so too does society have a range of processes and mechanisms which enable it to correct temporary disorders and partial imbalances.

Known as 'functionalism' in its most influential manifestation, this way of conceptualizing society focuses upon the manner in which social cohesion is achieved through the harmonious integration of the various structures, institutions and individuals who make up the social world. At the same time, this approach concerns itself with the ways in which society both optimizes its functionality and maintains its integrative harmony. In respect of optimizing functionality, this is achieved, for example, by society evaluating its various components relative to their overall systemic importance. Consequently, while the most important ('imperative') features of society are promoted through their prioritization, others occupy subordinate positions and justify their existence in respect of the service they offer to the more significant elements of the social order. The maintenance of integrative harmony is undertaken in both a general and specific fashion. Generally, social integration is achieved through the propagation of norms, values and beliefs which underwrite the social system by way of, for example, rationalizing both its hierarchical structures and the differential distribution of roles, status and benefits which they entail. Specifically, integrative harmony may be ensured through the active correction of 'dysfunctional' components (criminals and other 'deviant' elements) through their punishment, censure and, where possible, rehabilitation.

In stark contrast to the conceptualization of society as an organic whole which functions best when its component parts work harmoniously together, conflict models of the social world offer a very different picture. Popularized by the German social-philosopher Karl Marx (1818–83) and developed by his theoretical descendants, conflict models assume a wide variety of conceptual forms and analytical concerns both within and outwith the Marxist tradition. Whereas functionalist thought, for example, sees the hierarchical ordering of society as a necessary and thereby unproblematic condition of its existence, conflict models regard social hierarchies with deep suspicion. This is the case because existing social hierarchies are seen as the outcome of historical struggles in which one or a number of parties have achieved dominance over others. Rather than serving the good of the whole, social hierarchies actually serve the interests of those dominant groups which, for multiple reasons, enjoy the greatest influence in respect of, for example, their distribution of symbolic and practical resources. In effect, then, the macro-structures, mid-range institutions and micro-social encounters which comprise society are not neutral components but actively serve the interests of some to the detriment of others.

Complementing this picture, conflict theories have particular interpretations of the ways in which society goes about integrating its members and maintaining social order. In respect of the norms, values and beliefs underwriting social integration, for example, conflict theories identify a range of processes which both ensure and rationalize the unequal integration of individuals within societal structures. While Marxist approaches have traditionally used the term 'ideology' to emphasize the biased nature of these processes – particularly, but not solely, as they relate to socioeconomic categories such as class – other conflict approaches employ the concepts of patriarchy (feminist theory) and heterosexism (queer theory) (see Chapter 6). In the same vein, conflict models also identify a range of corrective practices and disciplinary regimes which serve to maintain social inequality through the labelling, admonition and punishment of those who transgress the roles and identities given to them. Consequently, while the likes of functionalist theory speak of necessary hierarchy, conflict theories speak of historically contingent inequality. Where functionalist theory identifies social integration achieved through shared norms and values, conflict theory sees exploitation and oppression maintained through the unequal distribution of power justified by ideologies of a sexist, racist and classist bent.

Scientific status

A second focal point of disagreement among sociologists concerns its status as a science. Regarding itself as the 'science of society', sociology traditionally modelled itself after the natural sciences (biology, chemistry, physics). As a result, sociology adopted a range of assumptions in respect of the status of its analytical object (society), the manner in which this object can be known (epistemology) and the best ways of studying it (methodology). Most popularly known as 'positivism', sociology's traditional approach regarded itself as being based, like the natural sciences, on the accumulation of objective facts about the world which could be gathered in a value-neutral manner and tested by replicable methods to the end of formulating general laws which applied to society as a whole. Over time, however, the dominance of positivism has been challenged by an understanding of the sociological endeavour which rejects the need for sociology to model itself on the natural sciences. While accepting the need of scientific rigour, growing numbers of sociologists argue that the particular nature of society – as both human construct and socially determinative – renders the analytical, epistemological and methodological presuppositions of the positivist paradigm both infeasible and undesirable (Craib and Benton, 2001).

The problematization of established positivistic assumptions has led to an increasing diversity of sociological perspectives in respect of, for example, how society should be analytically conceived, what methods are best suited to studying the social world and why sociologists do what they do. Although rather abstruse at points, theoretical issues such as these have direct consequences for the everyday practices of sociologists on the ground. For example, over recent decades – and no doubt also influenced by the resurgence of conflict theory – growing numbers of sociologists are rejecting traditional assumptions regarding disciplinary neutrality and researcher objectivity. While committed to established disciplinary norms of analytical rigour and critical reflection, certain sociologists hold their task to be not only understanding society as best they can but also helping to make society a better place. Known by a variety of terms and adopting a range of approaches (such as liberation sociology and action research), the sociological endeavour assumes a committed, if not emancipatory, tenor which dismisses value neutrality as both a theoretical myth and avoidance of moral responsibility. As Feagin and Vera remark, 'the point of liberation sociology is not just to research the social world but to change it in the direction of democracy and social justice' (2008, p. 1).

Applied methods

Not unrelated to these developments, the methods used by sociology to engage the social world have likewise diversified. Although the importance to sociology of understanding the motivations and intentions of individual social actors was emphasized by the German social thinker Max Weber (1864–1920), subsequent generations of sociologists failed to develop this insight. Reflecting both functionalist and Marxist preoccupations, many sociologists became overly concerned with analysing macro-structural processes (e.g. urbanization) and institutional dynamics (e.g. integration) to the detriment of engaging the micro-social encounters of individual agents. As a consequence, sociology became heavily reliant upon large-scale, quantitative methods by which the data it needed to understand macro-structural and institutional processes could be gathered. During this time, a minority of social scientists (such as symbolic interactionists and ethnomethodologists) continued to concern themselves with understanding the everyday micro-social interactions through which individuals pass and by which they both sustain their lives and render them meaningful. Given their micro-social focus, these sociologists championed a range of qualitative methods, which they used to engage both the processes of interpersonal encounter and the subjective interpretations thereof by the individuals involved in them.

Within sociology today, qualitative methods such as interviews and discourse analysis enjoy an established place alongside quantitative methods such as questionnaires and statistical analysis. Of course, different types of method lend themselves to acquiring and interpreting different kinds of data and are thereby more or less suited to engaging different sorts of social processes and dynamics. For this reason, many forms of sociological enquiry employ 'mixed methods' approaches which combine both quantitative and qualitative modes of capturing and analysing data. Irrespective of the methods employed, however, fruitful sociological enquiry relies upon an awareness of their respective strengths and weaknesses; not least as they pertain to what kinds of data are sought, where they are found and how they are captured (Bryman, 2004; Robson, 2002).

Conclusion

In combination, differences in the theorization of society, interpretations of its *raison d'être* and the methods employed in its practice make for a highly variegated sociological terrain. At the same time, the continual, rapid, large-scale and increasingly plural nature of social transformation demands of sociology an unstinting willingness to innovate in both its conceptual and practical engagement with modern society. As will be seen throughout what follows, because it addresses the same kinds of challenges, the sociology of religion exhibits the same theoretical fissures, ethical tensions and methodological debates as the overarching disciplinary paradigm in which it sits. No less varied or innovative than its disciplinary siblings, as we shall now see the sociology of religion is just as informative, stimulating and, at times, contentious.

Further reading

Berger, P., 1966, *Invitation to Sociology*, London: Pelican.

Bilton, T., Bonnett, K. and Jones, P., 2002, *Introductory Sociology*, 4th edn, Basingstoke: Palgrave Macmillan.

Cohen, R. and Kennedy, P., 2007, *Global Sociology*, 2nd edn, New York: NYU Press.

Elias, N., 1978, *What is Sociology?*, London: Hutchinson.

Seidman, S., 2004, *Contested Knowledge: Social Theory Today*, 3rd edn, Oxford: Blackwell.

Note

1 Although used in a slightly different sense, the terms 'structured structure' and 'structuring structure' are borrowed from Pierre Bourdieu (Bourdieu and Wacquant 1992, p. 139).

2

Religion in Sociological Perspective

Having sketched the central components of the sociological paradigm, it is now time to introduce how the disciplinary particularities of sociology are played out in respect of its theoretical and practical encounter with religion. The first part of this chapter deals with the seemingly perennial problem of defining religion. Next, issues relating to the contexts in which religion is found and how it is practically engaged are treated. As will become evident, questions relating to the *where* (context) and *how* (method) of the sociological study of religion are directly informed by *what* religion is understood to be (definition).

Defining religion

Like the fabled Trojan horse, definitions of religion carry in themselves more than is visible to the naked eye. Sociologically speaking, there is no such thing as an interest-free definition of religion; at least, not one with enough meat on the bone to be of any academic use (Droogers, 2008, pp. 263–79). As with most things sociological, when treating matters of definition Weber's observation upon the inescapably perspectival nature of the sociological gaze is particularly pertinent (1949, p. 81). As with Marx before him, Weber was acutely aware that ideas and the definitions they comprise do not fall ready-made from the skies. Rather, they are forged with conceptual materials bequeathed by a particular socio-cultural heritage and manufactured in light of specific experiences of a given economic-political context. Definitions have a tendency, then, however implicitly and often despite the attempts of their creators, to reflect the particular worldviews from which they spring. Consequently, definitions carry within themselves a range of theoretical presuppositions, value judgements and practical biases which lead their users to view, interpret and act towards what is being defined in one way rather than another.

Substantive definitions

Writing in a period of progressive global exploration and increasing awareness of socio-cultural diversity, Edward Tylor (1832–1917) offered one of the earliest and, for a time, most influential academic definitions of religion. Understood as a 'minimum definition of Religion', Tylor held it to comprise 'the belief in Spiritual Beings' (1871: I, p. 424). Regarded by Tylor as an essential (necessary) attribute of religion, 'belief in Spiritual Beings' served as a theoretical filter eliminating from religious consideration every form of conceptual and practical disposition, which did not embody some kind of preoccupation with non-natural agencies. To be defined as religious, a collective ritual practice such as harvest thanksgiving or individual belief in life after death must, however tacitly, acknowledge the existence of supernatural beings. At face value, and in view of its alluring simplicity, Tylor's definition is an attractive one.

Appearances, though, can be deceptive. For Tylor's definition excludes from consideration as religious the many historical and contemporary practices and beliefs (such as Theravada Buddhism and modern nature religion), which engage supernatural forces and dynamics lacking subjective attributes of 'being' such as self-awareness and self-determination (Southwold, 1978, pp. 362–79; Shaw and Francis, 2008). Each in its own way, Theravada Buddhism and modern nature religion embodies a religious mode of belief and practice which is not orientated to or by the kinds of 'Spiritual Beings' central to Tylor's definition. In spite of its minimal and purportedly inclusive intent, Tylor's definition nevertheless excludes from consideration certain forms of belief and practice which the overwhelming majority of scholars today include within their definitions of religion. Despite his inclusive aspirations, Tylor's attempt at a universally applicable definition fails by virtue of its unacknowledged Judeo-Christian perspective and limited historical gaze.

Tylor's definition of religion is typically 'substantive' in the way that it goes about saying what religion is. Typically, substantive definitions of religion seek to capture the essential preoccupations or core concerns of the religious worldview. In so doing, substantive definitions of religion tend to downplay, if not entirely overlook, explanations of what religion actually does relative to the socio-cultural context through which it is expressed. As a result, substantive definitions of religion tend to be sociologically thin in that they fail adequately to capture the social influence which religious practices and beliefs exert by means of their concrete expression through individual behaviour and corporate action. It is in this respect that 'functional' definitions of religion make an important contribution to sociological understanding.

Functional definitions

As the term implies, functional definitions of religion strive to express the social role or function which religious belief and practice play within the broader societal context.[1] French sociologist of religion Hervieu-Léger offers the following functional definition of religion:

> [R]eligion is a mode of imposing a social construction on reality, a system of references to which actors spontaneously have recourse in order to conceive the universe in which they live . . . religion is an ideological, practical and symbolic system through which consciousness, both individual and collective, of belonging to a particular chain of belief is constituted, maintained, developed and controlled. (2000, pp. 16, 82)

Hervieu-Léger hereby defines religion as a form of symbolic understanding through and by which humanity makes sense of both its surroundings and experience thereof. In effect, religion enables individuals and communities to function in the world by way of rendering their existence meaningful. For Hervieu-Léger, religion does this by drawing upon a range of theories, principles and practices which are inherited from and authorized by past generations in the form of tradition (here, 'chain of belief').

As with substantive definitions of religion, functional approaches have their limitations. If the strength of functional definitions lies in their ability to communicate the role played by religion relative to its social context, their weakness resides in their inability to identify with any meaningful precision the differences between religion and other non-religious modes of life which fulfil the same functions. If the social role of religion is that of making existence meaningful, for example, in what manner is religion different from the myriad other ways in which people render their world significant? Likewise, if the social role of religion is that of engendering societal cohesion, just what is it about religion which makes it different from other means which fulfil the same function?

By stressing functionality over substance, functional definitions of religion inevitably sacrifice attention to the precise details about religion which enable its differentiation from similar, but non-religious, modes of thinking, feeling, judging and doing. Consequently, functional definitions are unable to furnish sufficient substance to make possible sociological explorations of the precise differences between, for example, regular religious adherence and committed support of a football team. While participation in religious activities might have the same functional consequences as impassioned football support, the simple identification of shared social outcomes is not enough to tease out the precise differences between these two forms of commitment-orientated social behaviour. If substantive definitions of religion can be sociologically myopic, functional definitions are susceptible to analytical vacuity. Lacking the specificity necessary for fruitful critical analysis, functional definitions tell us what religion does without communicating what religion is; and, by extension, what it is not.

Mixed definitions

Setting aside typical distinctions between substantive and functional definitions of religion, the reality is that most social scientists tend to work with
a mixture of the two; albeit a mixture which, in most instances, tilts towards
one typical extreme rather than another. This mixture of emphases is exemplified by what are, perhaps, two of the most quoted sociological definitions
of religion – those of Karl Marx and Émile Durkheim. According to Marx:

> Religious suffering is at the same time an expression of real suffering
> and a protest against real suffering. Religion is the sigh of the oppressed
> creature, the feeling of a heartless world, and the soul of soulless circum-
> stances. It is the opium of the people. (McLellan, 1977, p. 63)

The substantive element in Marx's definition resides in his understanding of
religion as an outward manifestation ('expression') of an inner state of being. Be it the suffering of the proletariat or the satisfaction of the bourgeoisie,
religion expresses the longings and preoccupations of the individual. At the
same time, however, the inner state which religion expresses is, for Marx, a
reflection of external processes which impact upon the self. Consequently,
the externalization undertaken by religion inevitably involves the symbolic
and practical representation of prevailing social forces and dynamics. In so
being, the expressive dynamic of religion assumes a functional quality as its
representation of internalized social forces in the form of religious symbols
and rites serves, in effect, both to pacify the working classes (hence, 'opium')
and reinforce the hand of those already in power. For Marx, religion functions as an inherently conservative force which underwrites existing (conflictual) social relations and prevailing (unequal) structures of power.

As will be seen in the next chapter, Durkheim shares Marx's belief that
religion expresses internal states of being whose ultimate origins lie in external social processes. In his most famous definition of religion, however,
Durkheim chooses to emphasize other things. Religion, he says:

> is a unified system of beliefs and practices relative to sacred things, that
> is to say, things set apart and surrounded by prohibitions – beliefs and
> practices that unite its adherents in a single moral community called a
> church. (2001, p. 46)

The substantive character of Durkheim's definition rests in his identification
of religion as a 'system of beliefs and practices' orientated to 'things' (material and immaterial) held to be 'sacred'. Underlying the first part of this
definition is Durkheim's understanding of religion as a kind of classificatory
system by which different kinds of objects, practices, values and beliefs are
labelled and the most appropriate dispositions towards them identified. As

with Marx, however, the functional nature of Durkheim's understanding of religion eventually comes to the fore. Unlike Marx, though, the function which Durkheim holds religion to undertake is that of reinforcing social cohesion rather than underwriting social division. First and foremost, religion unites. Religion does so by generating among its followers a shared range of dispositions (attachment, obedience, awe) in respect of a given set of beliefs and practices. Taking the word religion at its most literal (from the Latin *re-ligare*, meaning 'to bind'), Durkheim regards religion's fundamental function as that of binding individuals together through its orchestration of their mutual association, common beliefs and shared practices. Importantly for Durkheim, and mediated through the 'single moral community called a church', the mutuality engendered by religion reinforces social cohesion and is thereby conducive to wider societal harmony.

Practitioner perspectives

The challenging nature of studying religion in its sociological contexts is further highlighted when we move beyond consideration of established academic definitions and their conceptual preferences. What about religious practitioners themselves? Surely they're best placed to offer a balanced definition of the word 'religion'? Well, not exactly. Take the case of Spiritism, for example. Known also as Kardecism, after its founder Allan Kardec (1804–69), Spiritism arose in the mid-1800s as Europe underwent large-scale and rapid modernization thanks to the ongoing industrial revolution and emergence of modern capitalism.[2] Reflecting the aspirations of its age, Spiritism styled itself as the modern-day successor to pre-scientific and overly superstitious religions such as Christianity, Judaism and Islam. Spreading from France to other parts of the world (particularly Latin America), it was not long before Spiritism assumed many of the reportorial ingredients which characterize the traditional religions it aspired to supersede.

Today, the overwhelming majority of Spiritists gather in purpose-built locations, at scheduled times of the week, in which designated functionaries lead tightly orchestrated meetings during which prayers are said to supernatural beings, honoured writings are read and edifying lessons taught. In effect, Spiritism exhibits a very large number of the ritual and symbolic traits which are generally regarded as typical of religion – at least, in its traditional format. However, when asked whether Spiritism is a 'religion', Spiritists vehemently resist the application of this term to their practices and beliefs. Continuing to define itself over and against established traditions such as Christianity, and despite overwhelming evidence to the contrary, Spiritism refuses to regard itself as a 'religion'. Although more dissimilar to traditional religious repertoires than Spiritism, the refusal of many new age (such as Transcendental Meditation) and non-mainstream (such as Wicca) groups to own the label 'religion' is further indication of the negative con-notations which this term has for certain practitioners.

Not so, however, for Scientology. The Church of Scientology was founded in the early 1950s by L. Ron Hubbard (1911–86). Heavily influenced by the human potential movement, Hubbard developed Scientology as the insti-tutional channel through which his programme of spiritual enlightenment ('Dianetics') would be delivered to the world. Although recognized in vari-ous parts of the world as a legitimate religious organization, and despite the work of high-profile adepts such as Tom Cruise and John Travolta, Scien-tology has still to achieve unanimous acknowledgement of its claims to be defined as a bona fide religion rather than a 'cult' (see Chapter 7). Unlike Spiritism and Transcendental Meditation, for Scientology the application of the word 'religion' to its beliefs and practices is something very much sought after. Scientology's public response to the ongoing refusal of certain countries (for example Germany) to recognize it as a religion is to argue that the suspicion with which it is treated serves only to hamper its mission and inhibit individual religious freedoms. Unofficially, of course, the continued denial of the label 'religion' renders Scientology ineligible to access the le-gal protections, political privileges and financial benefits which established, mainstream religions have traditionally enjoyed. Scientology's campaign to be accorded the title 'religion' is as much motivated by strategic savvy as it is by evangelistic zeal.

Polythetic definitions

In contrast to Spiritism and certain other non-mainstream movements, Scientology is keen to be labelled a 'religion'. Not necessarily wishing to become involved in the ongoing legal-political machinations in respect of this desire, the majority of sociologists who work in this area nevertheless tend towards the view that Scientology, like Spiritism, exhibits a sufficient range of typical characteristics to justify its academic recognition as 'reli-gion' (Lewis, J., 2009). While both substantive and functional definitions of religion are brought to bear in cases such as Scientology (Beckford, 1980; Frigerio, 1996), social scientists are increasingly using what are termed 'polythetic' or 'multi-factorial' approaches. I have already used this type of approach when arguing above that Spiritism, irrespective of what its adher-ents claim, should be regarded as religion on the grounds that it exhibits a sufficient number of characteristics which are taken to be typical of what we understand a religion to be and do.

Also known as the 'family resemblance' model, the polythetic (literally, 'many attributes or themes') approach to defining religion starts from the premise that no single definition can adequately capture what is, in its actual manifestations, a highly varied phenomenon. As no single concept or theory is able to capture sufficiently the variegated character of religion, polythetic approaches attempt to define religion through an inventory of its most commonly occurring characteristics. Those phenomena adjudged to have a sufficient number of these characteristics (share an adequate number of 'family resemblances') are thereby acknowledged to belong to the category of 'religion'. Alston, for example, includes nine 'religion-making characteristics' in his definition of religion (1967, pp. 140–7), while Southwold lists twelve such 'attributes' (1978, pp. 362–79).

According to Southwold, for example, 'the word "religion" designates cultural systems which have at least some of these attributes':

(1) A central concern with godlike beings and men's relations with them. (2) A dichotomization of elements of the world into sacred and profane, and a central concern with the sacred. (3) An orientation towards salvation from the ordinary conditions of worldly existence. (4) Ritual practices. (5) Beliefs which are neither logically nor empirically demonstrable or highly probable, but must be held on the basis of faiths . . . (6) An ethical code, supported by such beliefs. (7) Supernatural sanctions on infringements of that code. (8) A mythology. (9) A body of scriptures, or similarly exalted oral traditions. (10) A priesthood, or similar specialist religious elite. (11) Association with a moral community, a church (in Durkheim's sense . . .) (12) Association with an ethnic or similar group. (1978, pp. 370–1)

The strength of the polythetic model resides in its ability to offer an inclusive definition of religion which readily reflects the actual variety of religious belief and practice evident across the globe. Provided the list of characteristics/resemblances is not allowed to become too long, the inclusivity offered by this approach need not come at the expense of the analytical precision required of all definitions; that is, they should indicate not only what a thing is but also what it is not.

What polythetic approaches such as those of Alston and Southwold do not do, however, is indicate just how many of the characteristics listed should be identified before any particular set of practices and beliefs can be classified as 'religion'. Presumably this number should not be so low as to suffer from the same weaknesses of singular definitions such as Tylor's, but nor should it be so high as to become too demanding and thereby too exclusive. Nor do Alston and Southwold say if any of these characteristics are more important than any of the others and thereby carry more weight in the definitional stakes. For example, and in reference to Southwold's list, does a particular set of beliefs and practices in possession of characteristics 1, 4 and 10 enjoy a more secure categorization as 'religion' than one exhibiting numbers 3, 5 and 12? Finally, and as with every other attempt to define religion to date, polythetic approaches offer only a superficial ('thin') description of the subject at hand. Although covering more ground by virtue of their inclusive approaches, the lists of Alston and Southwold still leave undefined just what is meant by terms such as 'religious feelings' and 'ritual' – terms which make sense only when fleshed out with detailed ('thick') descriptions of actual processes which occur in particular socio-cultural contexts. While a fact of life rather than a technical failing, the need to define further the constituent parts of lists such as these serves to underline that no matter how seemingly inclusive a definition appears, it still requires an element of interpretation; interpretation which is, by its nature, always a view from a particular socio-cultural point.

Approaching religion

Debates about how religion should be defined are directly related with arguments about how religion should be approached in practice. In addition to influencing where one looks for a particular phenomenon, definitions of that phenomenon (in our case, religion) directly impact upon how it is looked for. Talk of method and where it is to be applied is thereby inextricably bound to the issue of definition (Riis, 2008, pp. 229–44).

Academic approaches

A question related to method in the sociology of religion concerns the relationship between the academic researcher and the religious claims made by those individuals and groups being studied. Writing at the beginning of mainstream sociology's reawakening interest in religion, Berger maintained that sociologists should not concern themselves with 'the ultimate status of religious definitions of reality' (1967, p. 180). Defining his approach as one of 'methodological atheism', Berger argued that questions relating to the truth or falsity of religious claims should be set to one side ('bracketed'). Uncomfortable with the theoretical implications of the term 'atheism', others have chosen instead to talk of 'methodological agnosticism' (Smart, 1973, p. 54). The following quote by Beckford shows methodological atheism/agnosticism in action.

> *Regardless* of whether religious beliefs and experiences actually relate to supernatural, superempirical or noumenal realities, religion is expressed by means of human ideas, symbols, feelings, practices and organizations. These expressions are the products of social interactions, structures and processes and, in turn, they influence social life and cultural meanings to varying degrees. The social scientific study of religion, including social

theory, aims to interpret and explain these products and processes. (2003, p. 2) [emphasis added]

Whether employing the term 'atheistic' or 'agnostic' to describe the methodological bracketing employed, the weight of academic opinion holds that the sociology of religion does not concern itself with seeking to prove or disprove the veracity or falsity of religious worldviews.

As the sociology of religion is an academic discipline, adherents of a religious worldview are challenged to reach a point of critical distance from which they are able to engage religion in a manner conducive to prevailing academic standards and disciplinary expectations. At the same time, the peculiar subject matter of the discipline requires those of an agnostic or atheistic persuasion to reach a point of empathetic understanding from which they are able to engage religion with an awareness of and appreciation for its volitional, affective, practical, intellectual and evaluative particularities. In effect, the challenge to develop the critical empathy required to make the most of the sociological study of religion entails that the perspective of the typical believer, agnostic or atheist is neither more nor less privileged than any other.

The kind of self-critical reflection undertaken in respect of the sociologist's encounter with religion is typical of what is often called 'reflexivity'. Although reflexivity has a number of technical meanings, its most common usage refers to the need for social scientists to reflect upon the influence which their personal experience and academic approach have upon their research. Consequently, the principle of reflexivity combines two elements. First, it includes critical reflection 'upon the ways in which our own values, experiences, interests, beliefs, political commitments, wider aims in life and social identities' shape our research. Second, the principle of reflexivity calls for reflection 'upon the assumptions (about the world, about knowledge) that we have made in the course of the research, and . . . the implications of such assumptions for the research and its findings' (Willig, 2001, p. 10). Sociologically speaking, then, reflexivity encourages those who engage religion to be aware of the particular point from which religion is approached and the respective impact which this given perspective has upon, for example, the definitions used, theories employed, methods applied, analyses undertaken and interpretations preferred.

Religion in social context

Applying the tripartite model outlined in Chapter 1, relevant data pertaining to religion are to be found in the macro-structural, mid-range institutional and micro-social dimensions of society.[3]

Micro-social dimension

When treating the micro-social dimension of religion, sociology turns its gaze upon both individual believers and the interpersonal practices through which individual belief is expressed. Although a philosopher and not a sociologist, Wittgenstein's definition of religious belief provides a useful summary of some key features of religion's individual dimension.

> It strikes me that a religious belief could only be something like a passion-ate commitment to a system of reference. Hence, although it's belief, it's really a way of living, or a way of assessing life. It's passionately seizing hold of this interpretation. (1980, p. 64)

Emphasizing the symbolic aspects of faith, Wittgenstein captures the ir-reducibly subjective and non-vicarious character of religion's individual dimension. He also furnishes a succinct representation of religious belief's volitional, affective, evaluative, signifying and commitment-orientated nature. Although by no means a favoured topic of traditional sociology of religion, contemporary treatment of the individual dimension of belief draws support from established interpretative (also called 'hermeneutical') approaches. Such is the case because the micro-sociological focus of these approaches lends itself to engaging the subjective dynamics of such things as meaning-making, motivation and intent. For example, the individual dimension of belief may be engaged by sociologists wishing to explore the subjective dynamics informing the participation of women or homosex-uals within conservative religious repertoires which both seemingly reject gender equality and apparently give nothing by way of affirmation to gay identity (see Chapter 6). At the same time, the subjective dimension of belief may be explored by asking individuals to explain the significance for them of religious practices and beliefs such as meditation, prayer, reincarnation and salvation (Spickard, 2007, pp. 121–43; Voas, 2007, pp. 144–66).

As Durkheim remarks, 'religion is something eminently social' (2001, p. 11). Consequently, talk of individual religiosity in isolation from the other dimensions which inform it can only ever be regarded as an abstraction by which religion's subjective sphere is artificially isolated ('bracketed') for the purposes of analytical clarity. In actuality, an individual's religious beliefs (along with the values and practices they inform and are informed by) are held, affirmed, challenged or modified relative to ongoing association with other human beings. From the formal interactions of religious ritual to infor-mal encounters with friends and family (religious or otherwise), individual religiosity is informed by and expressed through associational activity. At the same time, associational modes of religious expression do not occur at random. The religious interaction of individuals, objects and events occurs at set times, with specific formats in given places because it is orchestrated by a particular constellation of organizational processes, ideational dynamics and social forces. Compare and contrast, for example, the Shabbat service of a Hasidic synagogue with that of a Liberal Jewish community. In each case, the physical use of sacred space, the oral and literary contents of the liturgical act and the distribution of ritual responsibilities will be different because they reflect varying institutional contexts and divergent theological construals – not least those treating the respective relations both of tradition and modernity and of men and women.

Institutional dimension

Large or small, new or established, mainstream or alternative, every religious group or movement embodies some form of institutional dynamic. Indeed, it is something of a sociological truism that no form of associational activity endures through time and space without assuming some degree of organizational formality. As Moburg notes:

> Every religious organization has some degree of formalism or institutionalization. This is true even of groups that claim to be 'merely a fellowship, not a denomination', and of those so informally and loosely organized that they claim to lack organization altogether . . . This means that, like other institutions, it is subject to the play of social forces in both its formation and its operation. (1984, p. 6)

As an object of sociological scrutiny, the institutional dimension of religion has two important components: the organizational and the ideational.

The organizational dimension of religious institutions pertains to their concrete structures and formalized processes. From goal-setting through finance management to conflict resolution and identity maintenance, formalized organizational processes determine priorities, channel resources and entrench authority. For example, when engaging the organizational dimension of religious institutions, sociologists may focus upon variations in structural dynamics or the different ways in which particular groups and movements mobilize available resources. In the first instance, the different organizational structures in force can be examined to the end of determining the manner in which they facilitate or inhibit institutional adaptability in an increasingly fluid social landscape. For example, whereas established religious institutions enjoy a number of advantages which new religious movements do not, when it comes to institutional adaptability, traditional religions struggle in changing societal environments. This is the case because established organizations find it much harder to evolve and adopt novel structures as quickly and easily as newer groups who do not suffer under the inertial weight of inherited structures which are, by their nature, more resistant to rapid modification. In the second instance, different organizational structures can be compared relative to their efficiency in mobilizing available resources, as might be achieved through the motivation of existing members to make personal sacrifices (e.g. time, money, material things) for the greater good of the institution to which they belong.

At the same time, the institutional processes of religious groups and movements set priorities, allocate resources and confer different kinds of status relative to particular religious construals of the world. These construals constitute the ideational dimension of religion, which comprises an assortment of beliefs, theories and values. In combination, such beliefs, theories and values furnish a religious worldview, which, for example, treats issues such as the nature and activity of the sacred, the origins and purpose of the cosmos and the destiny and responsibilities of humankind. In effect, the ideational dimension constitutes what Kuhn describes as a 'paradigm'; that is, an interconnecting set of presuppositions and values which entail a particular way of viewing and engaging the world (1962, pp. 43–51).

As a paradigm, the ideational dimension impresses itself upon institutional dynamics by influencing matters such as goal-setting, resource mobilization, structural administration and organizational behaviour. The ideational dimension, then, does not simply provide a symbolic description of the world, it actively orchestrates institutional practice within and towards the world. In Clifford Geertz's terminology, the ideational dimension is both a 'model of' the world and a 'model for' the world's engagement (1973, p. 93). Strained relations between the Roman Catholic Church and various national governments and international charities, for example, stem from Catholic institutional policies in respect of artificial contraception, same-sex adoption and sexual discrimination; policies directly informed by theological judgements in respect of sexual activity, expression and status. In effect, the ideational dimension of religious institutions may at times lead them to act in ways which are not, at least for those looking on, in the material best interests of the organization in question.

In tandem with established organizational dynamics, the ideational dimension influences the associational sphere through its practical and symbolic orchestration of interpersonal activities. As indicated above, this orchestration may be reflected through particular uses of sacred space, liturgical contents and ritual divisions of labour. In its turn, the associational dimension informs individual religiosity through, for example, its reinforcement of subjective representations of the sacred, personal moral judgements and private spiritual practices. Allowing for its idiosyncratic nature and irreducibly personal character, individual belief nevertheless involves the subjective appropriation of otherwise collective symbols, shared values and associational practices.

Macro-structural dimension

At its best, sociology explicates individual behaviour and institutional activity by conceptualizing their relationship with prevailing societal dynamics. Consequently, the *raison d'être* of the sociology of religion resides in its understanding the aforementioned dimensions of religion by examining their refraction of and influence upon prevailing social processes. As Maduro notes:

> No religion exists in a vacuum. Every religion, any religion, no matter what we may understand by 'religion', is a situated reality – situated in a specific human context, a concrete and determined geographical space, historical moment, and social milieu. (1982, p. 41)

Sociology thereby engages the *'situated* reality' of religion by identifying, exploring and seeking to explain its relationship with overarching societal structures and processes which both impact upon and are influenced by it.

In the first instance, sociology may concern itself with understanding the refraction of social and biological categories, such as class, race, age and sex, through the membership profiles of particular religious groups and movements. In Brazil, for example, census figures for male–female religious participation in Christianity are more or less equal for Roman Catholicism (49.5 per cent to 50.4 per cent respectively) and average out at approximately 44 per cent male to 56 per cent female for traditional Protestantism and most of neo-Pentecostalism. However, participation within the largest and fastest growing neo-Pentecostal group – the Universal Church of the Kingdom of God – exhibits a distinctly asymmetrical profile with 38 per cent male to 62 per cent female involvement. At the same time, there is also a clear asymmetry among those recorded by the census as 'without religion' (60 per cent male to 40 per cent female) (Campos, 2004, p. 134). In the same vein, new and alternative spiritualities across the industrialized world draw the bulk of their members from the white, urban middle classes and exhibit a greater ratio of female to male participation (Clarke, 2005). What do these figures tell us about society in general and the religious arena in particular – not least its reproduction of or challenge to prevailing class, ethnic-racial and gendering dynamics?

Secondly, for example, the sociology of religion may concern itself with the interaction between religious institutions and prevailing political, economic and legal structures. On the one hand, sociology can engage the ways in which different religious groups are more or less efficient in accessing the mechanisms of political power and thereby gaining financial or juridical privileges through, for example, tax breaks (as charities) or legal protections (via blasphemy laws) and exemptions (equality laws). On the other hand, sociologists might also analyse the manner in which different political, economic and legal structures work to the benefit of some forms of religion (usually mainstream traditional) and to the detriment of others (usually novel religious phenomena). Understanding both the religious interface with existing opportunity structures and the ways in which these structures shape the religious landscape is a central concern of much contemporary sociology of religion.

A third example can be drawn from sociology's attempts to understand the implications of modernity for religious belief and practice. For example, each of the characteristics of modern society mentioned in the previous chapter (e.g. integration, complexity, individualization) generates both challenges to and opportunities for the religious field. For some sociologists, such are the challenges which modernity sets religion that religious decline, if not eventual disappearance, is their rather pessimistic prognosis (Bruce, 2002). For others, however, while the challenges which modernity sets religion may well result in decline in certain (usually traditional) sectors, in other areas modernity is seen to furnish ample opportunity for religious transformation and growth (Martin, 2005). Wherever one stands in respect of growth, decline and/or transformation, the attempt to relate macro-structural processes with micro-social and mid-range institutional activity sits at the heart of sociology's engagement with religion. After all, it is through the interplay of these dynamics that the different dimensions of religion assume in real time and space their multifarious shapes, rhythms, smells and colours.

Methodological considerations

When engaging religion in respect of its various social contexts, sociologists bring to bear a raft of applied methods (Brink, 1995, pp. 461–75). Choosing an applied research method is very much like deciding upon what to have for breakfast. One must first choose what is going to be eaten and then one must decide how it is to be prepared for the plate. If it is to be eggs, for example, are they to come fried, scrambled, poached or hard-boiled? Whatever the choice, in each case a different mode of preparation requires a different set of implements. I use this image to underline how different research methods do not simply acquire data but, like the frying pan, whisk or pot of boiling water, they prepare what is to be consumed in one way rather than another. As with the egg that arrives on the plate, data is cooked relative to the methods used in its acquisition and preparation. There is, in effect, no such thing as raw data. Choice of research method, then, is never simply a question of 'What data needs acquiring?' but also of 'How best to acquire the necessary data in the most appropriate form?'

Different applied methods are more or less suited to different kinds of social terrain. Examination of patterns in movement between different religions, for example, needs to gather data in respect of the amount of switching actually taking place and the profiles (e.g. sex, age, relational status, profession, religious affiliation) of those doing the switching. Once acquired, this data can then be examined for particular trends (such as increased transit by North American Protestants) or compared with data from other social contexts (for example Brazil, where Roman Catholics are more prone to switching) and historical periods (where religious transit was much less likely). Given the nature of the data sought in respect of this issue, large-scale (quantitative) survey methods such as questionnaires lend themselves to the task.

If, however, one wanted to explore the implications of religious transit for the individuals doing the switching or the institutions acquiring or losing members, then other methods may prove more effective in acquiring and engaging the necessary data. Exploration of the personal motives behind switching and the impact of transit upon individual religiosity are best explored through methods geared towards obtaining data of a more intimate (qualitative) nature. In this instance, qualitative methods such as one-to-one interviews are particularly helpful. While interviews may also prove useful to the study of institutional responses to religious switching (as in respect of relaxation or tightening of membership rules), other methods of data acquisition will be required. The researcher may, for example, look for evidence of modified institutional behaviour expressed through changes in official publicity which seek to present a more inclusive or exclusive attitude in respect of would-be religious transients. The method of discourse analysis is one way of exploring changes in the presentational narratives of religious institutions. Alternatively, data evidencing the organizational impact of religious switching might be looked for through an examination of associational practices such as formal ritual activity or informal modes of interaction. First-hand engagement with the associational dimension of religion is a particular strength of the method commonly termed 'participant observation'.

The pursuit, acquisition and interpretation of empirical data gathered through applied methods are directly informed by sociological theory. In the case of religious transit, for example, the concept of 'individualization' may be used to explain the ways in which modern society enables switching. Modern dynamics do this by progressively undermining individual–corporate allegiances (e.g. familial, religious, cultural), which were once thought to be fixed and exclusive (Beck and Beck-Gernsheim, 2002). In the same vein, the concept of 'bricolage' can be employed to explore the subjective implications of religious transit. It does so by engaging individual religiosity as it is fashioned through the subjective appropriation of practices, symbols and values from a variety of different, if not contrasting, contexts (Dawson, A., 2007, pp. 129–57). The institutional implications of religious switching might likewise be explored through the articulation of concepts relating to the public image which organizations project (such as 'collective impression management') and their ability to attract religious consumers through careful packaging of their spiritual goods (Finke, 1997, pp. 45–64).

Choice of applied methods and the concepts used to interpret the data they acquire are themselves subject to the overarching theoretical paradigm within which they sit. As noted in Chapter 1, sociologists conceptualize society, its dimensions and their respective interactions in a wide variety of ways. Add to this aforementioned disagreements in respect of how religion might be defined (and, by extension, where it is to be found and how it is to be engaged), and one can begin to appreciate something of the wonderfully variegated character of the sociology of religion. As with sociology in general, the most fruitful readings of the sociology of religion appreciate the implications of the definitions used, methods applied, hermeneutical concepts employed, and the overarching theoretical presuppositions which inform the *what*, the *how* and the *why*.

Shifting sands

Such has been the rapidity and scale of social change over the course of the modern era that Giddens suggests the image of a 'juggernaut' be used to sum it up. Modernity has become, in effect, 'a runaway engine of enormous power which, collectively as human beings, we can drive to some extent but which also threatens to rush out of our control' (1990, p. 139). By demanding the ongoing revision of social-scientific approaches, the scale and rapidity of modern social change have direct implications for the sociological study of religion. As will be seen in the forthcoming chapters, not only do sociologists continue to contest precisely what is signified by the term 'religion', some are calling for a much more restricted use of the word. Instead, they argue, terms such as 'religiosity', 'mysticism' or 'spiritualities of life' are better placed to conceptualize contemporary modes of religious belief and practice (Heelas, 2008). In the same vein, social scientists disagree as to where religion is now to be found and, therefore, how it is best to be looked for. Holding that religion is progressively assuming an increasingly non-traditional profile, some argue in favour of non-standard means or indirect methods of researching religion (Day, 2009, pp. 86–104). Others, however, continue to argue trenchantly in favour of retaining traditional methods of quantitative research (Bruce, 2009, pp. 7–28). At the same time, disputes escalate in respect of the most appropriate concepts and theories by which contemporary transformations of the religious sphere might best be comprehended. For example, are the spread of religious fundamentalism and perdurance of alternative religiosity to be understood in terms of modernity's re-enchantment or as symptoms of its secularization (Bruce, 2000; Heelas, 1996)? Whether disputing definition, contesting context, arguing over method or disagreeing about theory, by situating religion amidst the warp and woof of ever-changing social processes, the discipline of sociology makes an invaluable contribution to the academic study of religious belief and practice.

Further reading

Bruce, S., 2009, 'The importance of social science in the study of religion', *Fieldwork in Religion* 4.1, pp. 7–28.

Droogers, A., 2008, 'Defining Religion: A Social Science Approach', in P. B. Clarke (ed.), *The Oxford Handbook of the Sociology of Religion*, Oxford: Oxford University Press, pp. 263–79.

Riis, O. P., 2008, 'Methodology in the Sociology of Religion', in P. B. Clarke (ed.), *The Oxford Handbook of the Sociology of Religion*, pp. 229–44.

Spickard, J. V., 2007, 'Micro Qualitative Approaches to the Sociology of Religion: Phenomenologies, Interviews, Narratives, and Ethnographies', in J. A. Beckford and N. J. Demereth III (eds), *The Sage Handbook of the Sociology of Religion*, London: Sage, pp. 121–43.

Voas, D., 2007, 'Surveys of Behaviour, Beliefs and Affiliation: Micro-Quantitative', in J. A. Beckford and N. J. Demereth III (eds), *The Sage Handbook of the Sociology of Religion*, London: Sage, pp. 144–66.

Notes

1 Functional definitions of religion should not be confused with functionalist theories of society (see Chapters 1 and 3).

2 Spiritism/Kardecism is a separate phenomenon from the English speaking movement known as Spiritualism, which traces its roots back to events that took place in Hydesville, USA, in 1848.

3 For alternative conceptualizations of the differing dimensions of religion, see Stark and Glock (1968, pp. 11–21), Smart (1996) and Sharpe (1983, pp. 91–107).

3

The Classical Legacy: Marx, Durkheim and Weber

Introduction

Among the most formative thinkers of the sociological paradigm, Karl Marx, Émile Durkheim and Max Weber are fundamental reference points for the sociology of religion. Of course, the discipline of sociology calls upon far more than the foundational insights of these three men. In doing so, however, what is drawn upon and how it is employed is – to a greater or lesser extent – orchestrated by reference to vocabulary, themes, theories and methods bequeathed to sociology by these individuals. By no means the only features of the sociological landscape, the legacies of Marx, Durkheim and Weber nevertheless remain its most prominent points of reference (Craib, 1997; Giddens, 1971). Consequently, even when in vehement dispute with their respective approaches, social scientists continue to plot a course which takes account of their enduring significance to the sociological terrain.

Each in his own way, Marx, Durkheim and Weber regard religion as both exemplary of prevailing social conditions and an excellent barometer of unfolding societal transformations. As Edles notes:

> The study of religion has been at the heart of sociology since it was first founded as an academic discipline in the late nineteenth century . . . Though they used different terms and definitions, Durkheim and Weber, as well as Marxist-inspired theorists . . . all considered religion a fundamental system of meaning. (2002, pp. 25–6)

Ironically, following leads given by these foundational thinkers in respect of the demise of traditional religion within modern society, subsequent generations of sociologists – with few notable (for example, Talcott Parsons) exceptions – relegated religion to the exotic fringe of sociological thought. It is unsurprising, then, that subsequent to the renaissance of the sociology of religion in the 1970s, Marx, Durkheim and Weber have come to enjoy considerable prominence in contemporary debates pertaining to the status, role and future of religion in modern society. Indeed, I think it fair to say that the prominence given to these thinkers by the sociology of religion far exceeds that afforded by other components of the sociological paradigm.

This chapter concentrates upon providing an appreciation of the respective theoretical frameworks within which Marx, Durkheim and Weber situate their treatments of religion. To best understand these respective treatments, some awareness is needed of their foundational presuppositions and core concepts. To this end, the approach to religion of each of these formative social thinkers is prefaced by a brief overview of their most relevant theoretical concerns. While Marx, Durkheim and Weber each prognosticate upon the likely future of religion within modern urban-industrial society, for the purposes of balance and continuity I reserve these observations for use as the introductory section of our next chapter. Suffice to say here that each of these social theorists foresees the decline – if not eventual disappearance – of religion as an important source of social order and collective meaning.

Karl Marx (1818–83)

Technically speaking, Marx was not a sociologist. His contribution to the sociological tradition, however, is beyond dispute. Marx wrote at a time when the first major reverberations of the industrial revolution were being felt across Europe and North America. For a variety of reasons, Marx's writings were not widely published and became something of a niche concern among radical activists and left-leaning intellectuals. Despite the Bolshevik revolution of 1917, it was not until later in the twentieth century that Marx's writings began to receive widespread interest. Although already gaining popularity among certain sections of the sociological community, it was the cultural revolutions of the 1960s which established Marx as de rigueur reading for all aspiring sociologists. Now an unquestioned part of the sociological canon, Marx's work – or theoretical strands thereof – can be credited with informing many of the presuppositions which underwrite the emancipatory approaches (such as feminist theory and postcolonial studies) so popular today (see Chapter 6).

Born in Germany to middle-class Jewish parents in 1818, Marx received his doctorate in philosophy from the University of Berlin in 1841. Attempting to understand the macro-structural and institutional implications of the widespread and rapid urban-industrialization taking place, Marx employed and/or adapted a range of philosophical, political and economic theories which both articulated and informed his radical social values. Indeed, it was these radical values which resulted in his flight from state persecution in various European countries and his eventual settling in England, where he remained until his death in 1883 (McLellan, 1973).

Up until the late 1840s, Marx engaged in sustained philosophical critique of the political and social implications of particular interpretations of

German idealist traditions. Taking their lead from the German philosopher G. W. Hegel (1770–1831), proponents of idealism regarded ideas as the driving force of historical change. In so doing, idealists believed that socio-cultural and economic-political change could be explained and thereby managed through philosophical understanding of both the dominant ideas of an age and the manner in which these ideas express themselves relative to the epoch in question. As they regarded religion (here, Christianity) as a dominant idea which manifests itself through prevailing societal structures – not least those of the state apparatus – idealists believed that the correct understanding of religion would yield an insightful critique of the socio-cultural processes and economic-political structures through which it is expressed. Social critique, then, is founded on philosophical understanding of otherwise abstract ideas, the essence of which can be captured independently of the concrete historical forms these ideas assume in any given time or place.

It was during his engagement with and eventual break from German idealism that Marx wrote most of his sporadic and otherwise unsystematic comments upon religion. Consequently, the majority of Marx's remarks upon religion are found in his *Contribution to the Critique of Hegel's Philosophy of Right* (1844), *German Ideology* (1845/6) and the co-authored *Communist Manifesto* (1848). After this time Marx turned his attention to understanding the overarching structural conditions and concrete productive processes allied with the industrial revolution and the age of capitalism (for example privately owned business, wage–labour dynamics and the class structure). Exemplified by the multivolume *Capital* (1867–), this period has very little by way of explicit religious critique.[1]

Historical materialism

Once having broken with the German idealists, Marx believed that it was not ideas that drove history forward but rather the relationship ('dialectic') between humankind and its material environment. Driven by the instinct to survive and flourish, humankind reproduces itself – physically, socially, intellectually etc. – by appropriating whatever means its material environment provides. Marx calls this mode of appropriation the 'means of production'. Down the ages, various 'means of production' have been employed (e.g. nomadic herding, hunter-gathering, sedentary agriculturalism), the most recent of which is the industrial-capitalism of modern society. Such is the importance attributed by Marx to the means of production that he held all other forms of societal organization (such as macro-structural, mid-range and micro-social) to originate from it. Marx defined these derivative forms of social organization as 'relations of production'. The means of production of any given society is thereby understood as a foundational base upon which the social superstructure rests and from which it gets its particular historical form. For Marx, then, all social change is driven by transformations in the underlying means of production – the most notable example of which is the agricultural base of medieval feudalism giving way to the industrial base of modern capitalism. The sharp contrasts between medieval rural society and modern urban society are ultimately grounded in the sharp contrasts between their respective means of production.

Situated knowledge

Although most sociologists do not agree with a number of key features of Marx's account of historical development, two of his most important assertions have nevertheless come to form central components of a good many sociological approaches. The first of these is Marx's insistence that all forms of human knowledge be understood in relation to the material contexts within and through which they are produced. Echoing his ongoing battle with idealism, Marx argues that:

> The production of ideas, of conceptions, of consciousness, is at first directly interwoven with the material activity and the material intercourse of men . . . In direct contrast to German philosophy which descends from heaven to earth, here we ascend from earth to heaven . . . Life is not determined by consciousness, but consciousness by life. (McLellan, 1977, p. 164)

Most commonly termed 'constructionism' or 'constructivism', Marx's view that knowledge should be viewed as something produced within and thereby – to a greater or lesser extent – relative to a given social context is for many sociologists a foundational theoretical assumption which applies just as much to religious knowledge as it does to other forms of mental activity (Beckford, 2003; Burr, 2003).

Conflictual society

The second of Marx's formative insights concerns his conflictual view of society. As seen above, Marx believes human history to comprise the successive appearance of different kinds of society whose structures and processes are informed by the particular means of production from which they spring. Marx complements this portrayal of historical development by arguing that the different groups populating society do not enjoy equal access to the dominant means of production upon which their particular society is founded. The three most important things which flow from this assertion are: first, all societies in history have hitherto been unequal; second, society is characterized by different groups vying for access to and control over the prevailing means of production; and third, those groups in control of the means of production wield power and influence in ways which – as unintended consequences – result in society working to their benefit and to the detriment of others. Just as feudal society was characterized by a landed aristocracy whose control of the agricultural means production was transposed into political, social and cultural dominance over other groups (such as serfs and artisans), so capitalist society is characterized by a business-owning (bourgeois) elite whose control of the industrial means of production is transposed into dominance over other classes such as the proletariat and the petty-bourgeoisie.

Although not all sociologists accept Marx's assertion that the 'history of all hitherto existing society is the history of class struggles' (McLellan, 1977, p. 222), many accept the basic contention that society is an unequal arena whose structures and processes serve the interests of some groups and work to the detriment of others. As will be seen in Chapter 6, Marx employs the notion of 'ideology' to explain how dominant groups not only wield and justify their influence but also manage to persuade dominated groups both to accept this influence and to act in ways which are not in their own best interests. Albeit by virtue of being subject to ideological domination, the oppressed are nevertheless complicit in their own subjugation. While Marx identifies a broad range of ideological currents, he regards religion as both a form of ideology par excellence and an ideal medium for the ideological machinations of the dominant elite. Believing religious ideas to originate in the material conditions of existence, Marx views the ideological unmasking of religion as a form of social critique. 'The criticism of heaven is thus transformed into the criticism of earth, the criticism of religion into the criticism of law, and the criticism of theology into the criticism of politics' (McLellan, 1977, p. 64).

Religious critique

In respect of religion's origins, Marx adopts a theory which had been around for some time and to which a number of his German idealist contemporaries (for example Ludwig Feuerbach) subscribed. Here, religion is held to originate through primitive humanity's projection of personal characteristics onto otherwise impersonal natural forces which come eventually to be regarded as divine (that is, 'God') (Feuerbach, 1957). Understood as an attempt to render nature amenable to human persuasion (for example through prayer, sacrifice and thanksgiving), this act of projection is said to result in the eventual denigration of humankind. This is the case, it is argued, because all that is good about humanity is projected onto nature – now divinized and understood as infinite, omnipotent, omnibenevolent etc. – while humankind, in comparison, regards itself as corrupt and sinful. Humanity has thereby purchased leverage upon nature with its own self-abasement; the consequences being 'the more man puts into God, the less he retains in himself' (McLellan, 1977, p. 79). In effect, religion is 'the holy form of human self-alienation' (McLellan, 1977, p. 63).

Originating through the alienating processes of projection, religion is treated by Marx as inherently mystifying. For Marx, the act of 'mystification' involves the misrecognition of a thing as something else (McLellan, 1977, p. 511). Mystification is important because it represents a distortion of relations which allows for people and things – by virtue of their misrecognition – to be treated in ways in which they should not. For example, the opinion that society is both unchanging and hierarchically ordered by God-given nature is an act of misrecognition which both justifies (through 'moral sanction') unequal structures and imbues the downtrodden with an air of resignation and passivity. As a result, religious duty is portrayed as wilful obedience to one's betters for which one receives immaterial consolation through the assurance of eternal blessedness. Criticism of religion, then, involves the unmasking of its mystifying nature and starts with the assertion that 'man makes religion, religion does not make man' (McLellan, 1977, p. 63).

Marx's understanding of religion as ideology is not, however, purely abstract. In contrast to the likes of Feuerbach, Marx claims, he fully appreciates the fact 'that the "religious sentiment" is itself a social product' (McLellan, 1977, p. 157). In his most famous assertion in respect of religion, Marx states that:

> Religious suffering is at the same time an expression of real suffering and a protest against real suffering. Religion is the sigh of the oppressed creature, the feeling of a heartless world, and the soul of soulless circumstances. It is the opium of the people. (McLellan, 1977, p. 64)

Mindful of the horrendous living conditions under which the urban poor were suffering, and despite its mystifying and alienating character, religion is recognized by Marx as at least providing some degree of 'consolation' and 'happiness' – however misplaced – for those at the rough end of the nascent capitalist system. Faced with the realities of social injustice, Marx criticizes established religious institutions for their alliance with the prevailing elite and ongoing refusal to address the real causes of social inequality. Arguing that 'the parson has ever gone hand in hand with the landlord', Marx is scathing of purportedly progressive religious movements such as Christian Socialism, which he maintains 'is but the holy water with which the priest consecrates the heart-burnings of the aristocrat' (McLellan, 1977, p. 239). A beneficiary of its long-standing integration within dominant economic-political systems, the 'Established English Church', Marx says, 'will more readily pardon an attack on 38 of its 39 articles than on 1/39th of its income'.

Indeed, such is its investment in the status quo that 'compared with criticism of existing property relations', the church regards atheism as but a 'minor fault' (McLellan, 1977, p. 417).

Religious mystification and ideological sanction

Marx's critique of religion can be said to be twofold. On the one hand, religion contributes to humankind's inability to perceive itself as an active agent of historical change. By virtue of its mystifying and alienating origins, religion instead identifies humanity as the passive object of supernaturally determined social structures and processes. By no means the only ideological culprit, as a form of ideology par excellence, religion is nevertheless a key part of the problem. On the other hand, religious institutions are integral to upholding prevailing systems of inequality. By virtue of its alliance with and dependence upon the status quo, established religion works hand-in-glove with the ruling elite. While not the only source of 'moral sanction' and 'justification' of dominant modes of societal reproduction, established religion nevertheless provides an important roadblock to social transformation. In combination, the inherent nature of religiosity and the concrete practices of religious institutions make religion both unable and unwilling to contribute to radical social transformation. Furthermore, its alienating character and privileged institutional status leads religion – both unwittingly and intentionally – to agitate against such change ever taking place. On both counts, then, religion is an enemy of those in need of change.

Although engaged by both Durkheim and Weber, Marx's work became something of a niche interest until its later translation and subsequent mainstreaming at the hands of left-leaning academics and successive emancipatory movements which emerged in Europe and the USA in the 1960s. On the one hand, the unsystematic character of Marx's work and its overly deterministic readings of historical development and economic causality have limited its appeal to social theorists. On the other, Marx's egalitarian concerns, reflections upon the unequal nature of society and the relationship between knowledge and social location have proved inspirational to those theoretically and practically committed to understanding and/or engendering social transformation.

Émile Durkheim (1858-1917)

Writing a generation later than Marx, Durkheim's theoretical engagement with society is something more akin to the sociological endeavour as we understand it today. In *The Division of Labour in Society* (1893/1984) and *The Rules of Sociological Method* (1895/1982), Durkheim unites received enquiry with pioneering reflections upon social structure and methodology in ways which continue to be important referents of much contemporary social science. In the same vein, and despite its rudimentary nature, Durkheim's use of statistics in his analysis of the varying suicide rates of different European countries (*On Suicide*, 1897/2006) established patterns of enquiry followed by subsequent generations of sociologists.[2] Although his earlier works treat the social relevance of religious discourse and practice, it was Durkheim's last major work which established him as one of the most formative figures in the history of sociology's engagement with religion. *The Elementary Forms of Religious Life* (1912/2001) continues to be indispensable reading for all would-be sociologists of religion.

Raised as an orthodox Jew, Durkheim's engagement with religion is nevertheless flavoured almost entirely by the typically French preoccupations of the time with social integration (Lukes, 1992). The theoretical backdrop against which Durkheim works can be summed up by the following problematic: Given that the collective reality of society is populated by naturally self-interested individuals, how does it continue to function? Ultimately, Durkheim's response to this question is twofold. First, society functions best when it accommodates individuality through the nurturing of typically human traits such as initiative, creativity and self-expression. While these traits have served humanity well in its long evolutionary ascent, they find their best expressions through the socio-cultural conditions made possible by the historical emergence of society. Second, the optimal functioning of society requires the subordination of individuality to the collective needs of the social whole. Unless individuals are so minded to co-operate, compromise and, at times, make sacrifices, the corporate structures and collective processes through which society is founded simply cannot exist. An irony not lost on Durkheim is that while individuals are at their best when living in society, the successful functioning of society requires the inhibition of unqualified individuality. Consequently, the human condition is such that the individual is best served through her subordination to something greater than herself:

> The individual submits to society and this submission is the condition of his liberation . . . By putting himself under the wing of society, he makes himself also, to a certain extent, dependent upon it. But this is a liberating dependence. (1965, p. 72)

As with the functionalist tradition which he is often credited as founding, Durkheim's response to the above problematic revolves around understanding the optimal functioning of society as achieved through its ability to generate 'social solidarity' through the integration of individuals within socially cohesive structures and processes. Such integration, however, is no easy matter. Given humankind's nature, the subordination of individual self-interest to the collective interests of the social whole comes neither naturally nor easily. As a result, individual submission to social processes must be generated from outside, be constantly reinforced and come with 'a tone of authority' sufficient to engender from individuals something which might 'even tell him to violate his most natural inclinations' (2001, pp. 156–7). It is here that religion has traditionally played its part.

God and society are one

The origins of religion, says Durkheim, are concurrent with those of society. Rejecting alternative versions of religion's origin – such as those of projection favoured by Marx and others relating to dreams – Durkheim argues that religion arises as a discursive and practical expression of human sociality. In making his case, Durkheim uses now contested fieldwork data gathered by others working with aboriginal groups in Australia and elsewhere. Durkheim uses this material because he believed the 'primitive' and 'simple' religiosity practised by aboriginal groups to be the closest thing to religion as it was when it actually emerged.[3] Durkheim also draws on data generated by others working with indigenous groups in North America and Melanesia. Despite their apparent variations, Durkheim concludes, the different kinds of religious symbols and rituals used by these groups actually serve to express the same underlying social dynamics which make human society possible. In effect, religion is 'above all a system of notions by which individuals imagine the society to which they belong and their obscure yet intimate relations with that society' (2001, pp. 170–1).

Believing these indigenous cultures to be living laboratories of social and religious evolution, Durkheim argues that their simple structures and primitive processes show most clearly the ways in which religion emerges as the symbolic and practical representation of collective, societal dynamics. By virtue of their everyday involvement in social interaction, and subject to the overarching dynamics of societal forces, individuals experience life as derived from and dependent upon something not just outside of but also greater than themselves. While we – by virtue of our advanced knowledge – know this something to be 'society', primitive cultures attribute their feelings of derivation and dependence to supernatural forces or entities perceived to give rise to rather than originate from the social world. In such a way, life comes to be seen as a gift from a power greater than ourselves, and humankind regards itself as indebted – and thereby morally obligated – to supernatural forces or entities who claim acknowledgement, merit thanks and may, at times, demand some form of personal abnegation. Society, claims Durkheim:

is quite capable of arousing the sensation of the divine, simply by its influence over the minds of its members. To them, it is like a god to the faithful . . . it has its own nature separate from ours as individuals . . . Society requires us to become its servants, forgetting our own interests, and compels us to endure all sorts of hardships, privations, and sacrifice without which social life would be impossible. Thus we are constantly forced to submit to rules of thought and behaviour that we have neither devised nor desired, and that are sometimes even contrary to our most basic inclinations and instincts. (2001, pp. 154–5)

The propensity for individual service, obligation and submission to society which religion engenders results from its sanctification of social structures and processes as supernaturally derived and thereby underwritten by divine command. Ultimately, it is the moral authority which religion affords the social system – as god-given – which enables it to relativize humankind's natural individuality through claims, demands and sanctions which elicit co-operation, compromise and, where necessary, individual sacrifice. Thankfully, says Durkheim, 'social action works in circuitous and obscure ways, using psychic mechanisms that are too complex for the ordinary observer to perceive their source'. Consequently, the 'social pressure' to conform which actually arises from society is subsequently perceived by individuals as a power and command originating from 'outside ourselves' (2001, pp. 157, 160). In true functionalist fashion, Durkheim asserts that:

the true justification of religious practices is not in their apparent ends but in the invisible influence they work on consciousness, in the way they affect our mental state . . . The moral forces that religious symbols express are real forces to be reckoned with . . . They are as necessary to the proper functioning of our moral life as food is to sustain our physical life. For it is through them that the group affirms and maintains itself. (2001, pp. 266, 284)

Despite appearances, then, the real worth of religion lies in its furnishing society with sufficient moral authority to execute necessary functions such as social integration, value transmission, deviance minimization and structural reproduction.

By way of identifying religion as the discursive and practical expression of social forces acting upon and through human beings, Durkheim shows how the claims made by society upon its individual members strikes them as both 'outside themselves' and with sufficient 'moral authority' to generate a willing submission to the demands it makes upon them. Given the individuality of human beings, however, the extrinsic moral authority which underwrites society's claims has to be constantly renewed and reinforced.

This task again has traditionally fallen to religion. In both its discursive and practical forms, says Durkheim, religion continually reinforces a sense of communal belonging and corporate responsibility which help maintain the 'conscience collective' so essential to society's functioning. Through regular participation in the shared arena of religious ritual, individual attachment to 'collective representations' is strengthened as 'forces that were languishing have been re-awakened in their minds' (2001, p. 256). In perhaps his most quoted statement on religion, Durkheim again underlines the fundamentally unifying nature of religious discourse and practice:

> A religion is a unified system of beliefs and practices relative to sacred things, that is to say, things set apart and surrounded by prohibitions – beliefs and practices that unite its adherents in a single moral community called a church. (2001, p. 46)

Religion as classificatory, regulatory and cohesive

In developing his definition of religion, Durkheim identifies three components which he regards as central to its understanding. First, religion exists as a kind of classificatory system through which different objects are categorized and the most appropriate behaviour towards them stipulated. As the above quote indicates, Durkheim held the central feature of religious classification to be the distinction between things understood as 'sacred' and things regarded as 'profane'. All other forms of categorical representation relate to, if not flow from, this fundamental distinction – be they moral (licit and illicit), spatial (holy and unholy), temporal (special and ordinary), functional (priestly and lay) or relational (believer and unbeliever). Second, religion maintains boundaries through the discursive and practical enforcement of its classificatory distinctions. Underwritten by theological construal and ritual enactment, religion posits a range of acceptable and unacceptable behaviour, thoughts and feelings in respect of different objects which it then encourages, rewards, forbids or punishes.

Third, religion both generates social cohesion and sustains unity. On the one hand, social cohesion arises from religion's postulation of corporate norms and goals which inform a 'collective or common consciousness' (conscience collective) shared by 'the average members of a society' (1984, pp. 38–9). On the other hand, religion sustains unity through its ceremonial generation and ritual reinforcement of particular psychological states which Durkheim defines as forms of 'collective effervescence' (2001, p. 171). Drawing on the emerging science of psychology – not least, in this instance, group psychology – Durkheim argues that communal religious activity has traditionally played a key role in engendering emotional experiences and mental conditions which 'stimulate and sustain or recreate' individual feelings of belonging and commitment to the group at large (2001, p. 11).

The collective effervescence engendered by corporate ritual activity is vitally important because it evokes psychological conditions which render an otherwise self-orientated individual susceptible to the moral, intellectual and practical claims which society makes upon her.

Almost inevitably, given the pioneering nature of his work, Durkheim is criticized for his rudimentary applied sociology; not least in respect of his use of statistics and questionable provenance of some of the fieldwork data upon which he draws. At the same time, his theoretical approach is criticized for both attributing society an overly autonomous status from its human occupants and over-emphasizing social order and continuity to the detriment of societal dynamism and transformation. Despite its limitations, however, Durkheim's work continues as an important reference point for contemporary sociological reflection as it pertains both to religion and matters beyond.

Max Weber (1864-1920)

The most influential figure to date for the sociological study of religion, Max Weber was born in Erfurt, Germany, in 1864. Son a wealthy family with strong political and cultural connections, Weber was raised in a nominally Christian household whose ethos owed more to secular intellectual practice than to religious belief. Although Weber trained in law – for which he received his doctorate in 1889 and professional qualification in 1891 – from the very beginning of his studies he concerned himself also with history and economics, to which he subsequently added a thorough grasp of politics, contemporary public policy, culture and religion (Bendix, 1992). In general sociological terms, *The Methodology of the Social Sciences* (1904/1949), *The Protestant Ethic and the Spirit of Capitalism* (1904–5/1992) and *Economy and Society* (1922/1968a) are Weber's most formative contributions. In respect of the sociology of religion, Weber's interest was piqued by research undertaken for *The Protestant Ethic* and subsequently fleshed out through essays and writings as diverse as 'The Social Psychology of the World Religions' (1913/1991d), 'Religious Rejections of the World and Their Directions' (1914–15/1991b), *The Religion of China* (1915/1968b), *The Religion of India* (1916–17/1967), *Ancient Judaism* (1917–19/1952) and *The Sociology of Religion* (1922/1963), which was originally a section of *Economy and Society* but subsequently published separately.

The overarching theoretical backdrop to Weber's treatment of religion situates religious belief and practice within humankind's historical quest for survival, flourishing, understanding and meaning – all of which occurs through humanity's engagement with its material and social environments. This is the case because Weber holds religion to have been historically central to the human endeavour to meet its physical (e.g. food and shelter), psychological (e.g. meaning) and intellectual (e.g. understanding) needs

(1992, p. 27). Holding that the 'most elementary forms of behavior motivated by religious or magical factors are oriented to *this* world', Weber argues that 'religious or magical behavior or thinking must not be set apart from the range of everyday purposive conduct' which engenders socio-economic reproduction (1963, p. 1). Alongside other forms of socio-cultural and economic-political activity, religion is likewise an inherently reasonable phenomenon in that it too contributes to human survival and flourishing.

In respect of less complex societies and cultures, for which hardships are greater and existence more precarious, Weber argues that religion has contributed to human flourishing as a form of magical manipulation of material things and spiritual forces. Driven by the brute needs of survival, religiosity assumes an explicitly pragmatic character orientated to acquiring or protecting the basic goods essential to servicing life. As societies become more complex and, consequently, existence becomes less harsh and more secure, the all-consuming quest for survival gives way to other preoccupations such as those of individual and social enhancement (e.g. order and morality) and intellectual and aesthetic expression (e.g. learning and art). Now freer from addressing the exigencies of brute survival in this world, religion assumes a progressively transcendent and ethical orientation as the medium through which the religio-moral demands of the gods are impressed upon humankind through increasingly elaborate doctrines reinforced, for example, by promises of heavenly reward or threats of post-mortem sanction.

Unlike Marx and Durkheim, Weber holds a multilinear (literally, 'many lines') view of historical development in which different societies or cultures are acknowledged as developing in a variety of ways through often contrasting phases. At the same time, Weber also believes that a single society or culture can contain within itself a variety of historical forms such that, for example, different kinds of religious expression (such as magical-pragmatism and ethical religion) can exist at the same time and in the same geographical space. Such is the case, Weber maintains, because a particular society or culture may well contain a variety of different forms of socio-economic existence which more or less lend themselves to manifesting different kinds of religio-cultural expression. For example, within the, then, semi-feudal estates of rural Germany, Weber observed among the hard-pressed peasantry the continuing prevalence of magical and superstitious forms of religiosity which lent themselves to addressing the hardships and precariousness of their serf-like existence. However, within the urban-industrializing contexts of Germany's growing cities (forged from the application of modern science and technological reason), different forms of religiosity predominated that were both different from those of the countryside and variegated among themselves relative to their working, middle and upper-class contexts (1963, pp. 80–137; 1992, pp. 35–46).

Self and society

Like Marx before him, Weber sees society as a socially stratified landscape made up of different classes. Unlike Marx, however, Weber offers a much more nuanced understanding of what distinguishes one social stratum from another and thereby moves beyond the narrower definition of Marx which links class rather too straightforwardly to economic standing (1991a, pp. 180–95). Weber also differs from Marx in that he affords intellectual activity a greater freedom from the conditions of material existence which Marx had earlier regarded as wholly determinative of human thought. While agreeing with Marx that it is 'not ideas, but material and ideal interests, [which] directly govern men's conduct', Weber goes on to say:

> Yet very frequently the 'world images' that have been created by 'ideas' have, like switchmen, determined the tracks along which action has been pushed by the dynamic of interest. 'From what' and 'for what' one wished to be redeemed and, let us not forget, 'could be' redeemed, depended upon one's image of the world. (1991d, p. 280)

Using the model of the switchman who changes the points on the railway track to steer the train in different directions, Weber argues that ideal construals of the world – made up of ideas, by which he also means concepts, values and beliefs – have the ability to influence material processes, practical activity and concrete actions in one way rather than another. For Weber, though, ideas in themselves are not able to influence material processes. Rather, ideas wield influence only to the extent that they are adopted and articulated relative to the concrete interests and subjective motivations of actual people living in specific social contexts. Weber regarded his concern with the subjective motivations of socially situated actors as an 'interpretative sociology' or sociology of 'understanding' (*Verstehen*).

Elective affinity

Weber's notion of 'elective affinity' brings together his understanding of the linkage between subjective experience, social stratification and the particular 'world images' which govern the social action of those who hold them (1968a). Like Marx, Weber argues that different social groups tend to articulate different views of the world which best accord with their collective socio-cultural and economic-political experiences. Unlike Marx, however, Weber does not regard these worldviews as simple reflections (epiphenomena) of material conditions on the ground. Rather, Weber sees these worldviews as emerging from the combination of particular kinds of social experience with particular types of ideas, values and beliefs. More than this,

49

however, Weber maintains that different kinds of life experience generate a particular affinity with specific types of ideas. Consequently, as distinct forms of socio-cultural and economic-political experience will be drawn to particular ideas, values and beliefs, the worldviews to which this material-ideal combination gives rise will differ from one social stratum to another. For Weber, then, a socially stratified society entails a mentally stratified landscape.[4]

Uniting the notions of social stratification and elective affinity, Weber pursues numerous lines of enquiry, the three most relevant of which relate to the social contexts of knowledge, the history of ideas and the nature of social change. In relation to the social contexts of knowledge, Weber endeavours to establish the relational affinity between different social strata and particular kinds of ideas, concepts and beliefs. Regarding the history of ideas, Weber sets out to identify the most important types of 'world image' to which particular material-ideal combinations realized through history have given rise. Concerning social change, Weber enquires after the different ways in which specific kinds of worldview inform, promote or hinder particular forms of action and social transformation. As one of the most enduring and influential components of the many worldviews realized through the course of history, Weber regards religion as an ideal focus of his sociological enquiries.

Religion and society

Particularly, but not solely, as it relates to his focus upon religion, Weber is concerned with answering two overlapping questions. First, what factors influenced the emergence of capitalism (and thereby modernity) in Europe and led it to assume its particular shape? Second, what are the differences between Western and Eastern civilizations which resulted in capitalist modernity arising initially in the former and not in the latter? Inevitably overlapping, Weber focuses upon the first of these questions in his most controversial and perhaps misunderstood work, *The Protestant Ethic and the Spirit of Capitalism*, while his writings of 1913–20 attempt to address the second.[5] In each case, Weber regards a proper understanding of the influence of religion – or, better, different types of religion – upon the social contexts engaged as absolutely imperative to answering these questions.

The capitalist mindset

The central thesis of Weber's *Protestant Ethic* arises from the observation that 'business leaders and owners of capital, as well as the higher grades of skilled labour, and even more the higher technically and commercially trained personnel of modern enterprises, are overwhelmingly Protestant' (1992, p. 35). While its roots may well have been more geographically diffuse, that capitalism (as we know it) emerged and subsequently flourished among the Protestant communities of northern Europe and North America is, says Weber, no coincidence. Such was the case because of an identifiable 'connection of the spirit of modern economic life with the rational ethics of ascetic Protestantism' (1992, p. 27). In discussing the linkage between religion and the rise of capitalism, Weber makes two important sets of distinctions, one theological and the other social. Theologically, Weber identifies a particular type of Protestantism which he labels 'ascetic' and situates principally within the Reformation traditions of Calvinism, Puritanism and Pietism. These traditions arose in northern Europe after the 1500s and subsequently furnished the religious mainstay of what eventually became the United States of America. Socially, Weber identifies a particular set of socio-economic strata – mentioned in the above quote – among which the 'spirit of capitalism' first took root and eventually flourished. Employing his notion of elective affinity, Weber argues that the religious ideas of ascetic Protestantism played an important role in the articulation by these social strata of a world image suffused by a modern capitalist mindset.

Central to this modern capitalist mindset was a new attitude towards the world, including a transformed understanding of humanity's role within it and a modified appreciation of the material goods it provides. Among other things, the capitalist worldview manifested itself in a conscientious work ethic coupled with the values of frugality and thrift. By living simpler lifestyles and working harder, those infused by the 'spirit of capitalism' were able not only to amass savings but also invest these funds in other economic ventures: industry, wealth and investment – three of the key pillars of the capitalist enterprise. While he fully accepts that the establishment of the 'spirit of modern economic life' owed much to other developments (such as advances in science, governance and economics), Weber identifies ascetic Protestantism as an influential component of this nascent world image and its preoccupation with 'intense worldly activity' (1992, p. 112). Particularly, Weber recognizes three elements of ascetic Protestantism worthy of note. First, the Reformation notion of 'calling' or 'vocation' involved a distinct valorization of humankind's responsibilities to and role within the world at large which might 'add to the glory of God on earth' (1992, p. 118). Second, the pietistic emphasis upon individual and collective discipline made a virtue of moderation and a vice of excess. Third, the Calvinist doctrine of predestination generated a psychological need to establish one's status as saved ('one of the elect') and thereby to identify signs of election as evidenced through the material fruits of one's 'good works' on earth. In combination, these three components of ascetic Protestantism furnished a moral rationale which both shaped and reinforced the newly emergent capitalist work ethic, the emphasis upon frugality and thrift and the concern with material acquisition and all that it made possible by way of financial investment and entrepreneurial enterprise.

Weber's *The Protestant Ethic* has been criticized from a number of quarters, not least those who place the origins of capitalism historically earlier and in southern Europe, and those who maintain that Weber places too much emphasis upon religion and not enough upon other causal factors. Whatever its limitations, however, *The Protestant Ethic* remains a seminal work in both sociology in general and the sociology of religion in particular. By identifying a number of factors which influenced the emergence of capitalism in Europe and led it to assume its particular shape, *The Protestant Ethic* goes some way to answering the first of the two questions mentioned above. By way of treating the second question about the differences between Western and Eastern civilizations which resulted in capitalist modernity arising initially in the former and not in the latter, Weber broadened the scope of his enquiries to include the Middle East, India and China (1952, 1967, 1968b). As with *The Protestant Ethic*, Weber focuses much of his attention upon the influence of religion upon the kinds of socio-cultural activity and economic-political structures adopted in these regions.

Religions east and west

Building upon work commenced in *The Protestant Ethic*, the most enduring legacy to emerge from these studies is Weber's fourfold categorization of what he regards as the most important 'ideal types' of religious attitude to the world. While identifying other contrasts of note, Weber concludes that a key difference between West and East which helped engender the rise of capitalist modernity in the former and not the latter was the absence of the 'worldly asceticism' (*innerweltliche Askese*) the aforementioned kinds of Protestant Christianity helped encourage initially in Europe and subsequently in the United States. The fourfold typology which informs this conclusion emerges initially from the contrast Weber draws between those religious worldviews which teach salvation as a reality only to be obtained through some form of distance from or indifference to the world, and those religions which offer the possibility of salvation as obtainable through some kind of qualified engagement with or presence in the world. Weber labels the former of these attitudes as 'outside the world/other-worldly' (*ausserweltliche*) and the latter approach as 'inside the world/inner-worldly' (*innerweltliche*). In turn, each of these attitudes to salvation as a possibility in or out of the world can display either an active character, which Weber calls 'ascetic', or one of passive resignation, which he terms 'mystical'. Putting these two sets of distinctions together, Weber produces a fourfold model which offers an idealized representation of four of the most typical religious worldviews through which individuals in different cultures have been orientated in respect of their attitudes to socio-cultural engagement and economic-polit-ical activity. The model may be diagrammatically represented as follows.

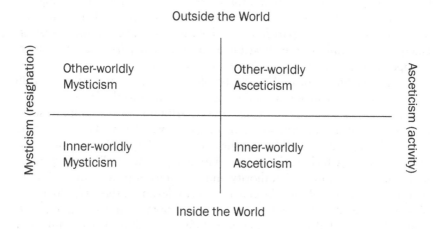

In addition to highlighting key differences in religious worldviews, Weber's model helps answer the two aforementioned key questions: namely, why capitalism emerged in Europe and nowhere else; and why capitalism emerged in a particular part (the north) of Europe and thereby assumed its specific character. As noted above, Weber regards the inner-worldly asceti-cism of certain kinds of Protestantism as a key means of answering each of these questions. Of course, asceticism has been part of traditional religious repertoires both in the West and in the East. In the West, for example, the monastic practices of Catholic Christianity centred upon the active discip-lining of the body through strict ritual regimes and demanding if not, at times, punishing lifestyles. As Weber notes, however, such asceticism was of an other-worldly kind in that its strict corporeal regime was coupled with a denigration of the world informed by the belief that contact with society at large was detrimental to spiritual endeavour. Although other-worldly as-ceticism of this kind is found outside of the West, Weber notes that mystical forms of religiosity have traditionally dominated in the East. In Taoism, for example, this mystical approach assumes an inner-worldly quality. How-ever, although Taoism's inner-worldly character means that the religious quest plays out through participation in the world at large, its mystical em-phasis minimizes this participation to a form of compliant inaction and thereby restricts the assumption of worldly responsibilities. Likewise mystic-al in nature, the religious worldview of Buddhism exhibits, in contrast, an other-worldly character. As with monastic Catholicism, this other-worldly emphasis manifests through a cultured indifference to the world and the material goods it contains. In contrast to these types, however, only ascetic Protestantism combines an inner-worldly preoccupation with an ethos of disciplined activism conducive to the formation of a capitalist work ethic. Criticized by scholars of religion for a stereotypical and homogenizing representation of otherwise variegated religious traditions, Weber's schematic nevertheless plays a key part in his explanation of why capitalist modernity emerged not simply in the West but in a particular part (that is northern Europe) at a specific time (that is post-Reformation).

Despite its limitations, Weber's typology of inner- and other-worldly forms of religiosity makes a significant contribution to the sociology of religion through its attempt to explain the contribution or resistance to social transformation of different kinds of religious worldview. The linkage between religion and social change is further explored by Weber through other ideal typologies which explicate the relationship between different forms of institutional structure and authority and the kinds of transformative action they do or do not facilitate. Among the most relevant of these typologies are those which identify different kinds of religious organization ('church', 'sect', 'cult'), those which distinguish between different kinds of religious functionary ('magician', 'priest', 'prophet') and those which identify different kinds of authority ('traditional', 'rational-legal', 'charismatic'). Although internal relations between these typologies differ according to the specific analytical schema in which they appear, their overarching theoretical unity resides in their representation of particular dispositions in respect of resistance to or facilitation of social change. For example, church structures, priestly activities and rational-legal (that is bureaucratic) modes of authority generally militate against change. However, because they are less invested in the status quo, sectarian movements, prophetic activity and charismatic kinds of authority express a predominantly transformative set of dynamics.

The architectural complexity and far-reaching breadth of Weber's sociological method has led to charges of its being overly abstruse, unwieldy and, at times, inconsistent. At the same time, Weber's treatment of religion has been criticized as unduly generalistic in representation and uncritically one-sided in respect of its actual influence upon the kinds of socio-economic developments he delineates. While pointing out the fallibility of the man and the limitations of his work, criticisms such as these go nowhere near undermining the monumental contribution and ongoing importance of Weber's reflections both to sociology in general and the sociological study of religion in particular.

Conclusion

The works of Marx, Durkheim and Weber continue to exert considerable influence because the limitations of their approaches are far outweighed by the theoretical insights and empirical understandings they enable. Irrespective of intellectual allegiance or empirical preoccupation, it is impossible to engage in sociological reflection without somewhere coming up against or having recourse to concepts, theories and methods pioneered or inspired by these foundational thinkers. As will be seen throughout the chapters that follow, the attempts by these thinkers to understand the processes and implications of the urban-industrializing processes of modernity have spawned insights, models and approaches which occupy centre stage of much contemporary sociology of religion. From social stratification, pluralization and rationalization, to inequality, order and social transformation, the contributions of Marx, Durkheim and Weber continue to inform debate upon the character, function and future of religion within modern urban-industrial society.

Further reading

Craib, I., 1997, *Classical Social Theory: An Introduction to the Thought of Marx, Weber, Durkheim, and Simmel*, Oxford: Oxford University Press.

Durkheim, É., 2001, *The Elementary Forms of Religious Life*, Oxford: Oxford University Press.

Giddens, A., 1971, *Capitalism and Modern Social Theory: An Analysis of the Writings of Marx, Durkheim and Max Weber*, Cambridge: Cambridge University Press.

McLellan, D. (ed.), 1977, *Karl Marx: Selected Writings*, Oxford: Oxford University Press.

Weber, M., 1992, *The Protestant Ethic and the Spirit of Capitalism*, London: Routledge.

——. 1963, *The Sociology of Religion*, Boston: Beacon Press.

Notes

1 As it contains all of Marx's most relevant comments upon religion, I use the texts reproduced in McLellan, 1977.

2 The original date of publication precedes the date of the English translation used here.

3 Like Marx before him, Durkheim works with a unilinear (literally, 'one line') model of historical development which holds that all forms of human existence follow a similar trajectory of socio-cultural and economic-political evolution. Two relevant assumptions follow from this: first, urban-industrial society is regarded as the most advanced form of development to which all other, more or less 'primitive', modes of social existence will eventually evolve; second, 'primitive' cultures such as the aboriginal peoples of Australia are viewed as living fossils which, as earlier versions of now advanced societies such as Europe, furnish immediate insight into the formative processes and stages of social evolution.

4 Despite appearances, the term 'elective affinity' – which Weber borrows from elsewhere – is not meant to convey a sense of self-aware or conscious choosing by individuals and groups between different kinds of ideas. Rather, Weber regards elective affinity as a non-self-conscious process whereby different kinds of social experience orientate individuals and groups towards the unreflexive adoption of one set of ideas rather than another. The relationship between particular social strata and specific worldviews is thereby an unintended consequence of overarching societal processes.

5 The controversy relating to *The Protestant Ethic* arises out of a misreading of the book's central thesis and the particular causal emphasis it places upon Protestant Christianity's role in the rise and establishment of capitalism in the West. In effect, this misreading sees Weber as claiming that 'if it were not for Protestantism, capitalism would never have emerged'. Although, at times, Weber appears to gesture towards this causal relationship, his eventual assertion claims no more than 'were it not for Protestantism (or particular types thereof), capitalism would neither have emerged nor established itself in the way that it did'.

4

Religion Down and Out?
Theories of Secularization

Introduction

The word 'secularization' derives from a Latin term describing the transfer
of material goods or personnel from religious to non-religious (secular)
ownership or status. Used sociologically, the concept of secularization is
generally employed to denote the historical transition from a more to a
less religious social context. Precisely how this transition occurs and what
constitutes a more or less religious society differs from one rendering of
secularization to the next. At the same time, theories of secularization
are by no means universally accepted. As will be seen in Chapter 5, the
argument that the transition from traditional to modern society necessarily involves the decreasing presence and influence of religion is hotly
contested.

Theories of secularization respond to what is interpreted as concrete evidence of the decreasing presence and influence of religion in modern, urban-
industrial society. At a macro-structural level, for example, such evidence
includes the separation of political and religious structures (e.g. state and
church) and the removal of long-standing legal and economic privileges formerly afforded religion. At the mid-range, institutional level, the kind of evidence appealed to involves, for example, the decreasing presence of religious
organizations and their functionaries within both the special (birth, union,
death) and everyday (education, health, work) processes of modern social
life. Micro-socially speaking, evidence supporting secularization draws on,
for example, institutional records and survey data indicating the declining
number of individuals participating in formal religion or self-designating as
religious.

Around since the beginnings of sociology itself, theories of secularization have since formed a staple part of sociological reflections upon the
presence, character and future of religion in modern society. To best capture the nature and development of these theories, what follows comprises
four sections. The first section sketches the classic legacy in respect of
secularization bequeathed by Durkheim and Weber. The second section

treats the theories of two sociologists (Bryan Wilson and Peter Berger) chiefly responsible for articulating the classic secularization legacy in its modern format. Next, the contemporary approaches of Steve Bruce, David Martin and Karel Dobbelaere are delineated. The final section offers a critical overview in respect of the generic strengths and weaknesses of secularization theories.

The classical legacy

As Marx regarded religion as a symptom of human alienation and suffering, the eradication of its underlying causes would likewise do away with their epiphenomenal religious expression. Foreseeing the inevitable establishment of a socialist utopia free from alienation and suffering, Marx predicted the disappearance of religion subsequent to the rise of 'communist society' (McLellan, 1977, pp. 159–91). Little, though, is offered by Marx in respect of the actual social processes through which religion will eventually disappear. Such detail, however, is far from lacking in the very different approaches of Durkheim and Weber.

Émile Durkheim

Having bound the origins and function of religion with the rise and needs of society, Durkheim ties its future to the outcome of the rapid and far-reaching social transformation unleashed by the urban-industrial revolution. Distinguishing between traditional and modern society, Durkheim identifies the former as characterized by, among other things, structural simplicity and socio-cultural uniformity (1984; 2001). Organized by a 'mechanical solidarity' underwritten by collective beliefs and common values, traditional societies are populated by individuals for whom the religious and moral universe is a shared, stable and by-and-large unquestioned reality. Consequently, the vital task of social integration is relatively straightforward in that it is managed through adherence to and participation in a single religion ('church'). In marked contrast, modern society is characterized by macro-structural complexity ('differentiation') and socio-cultural heterogeneity ('pluralism'). As its individual occupants no longer share the same socio-cultural characteristics, society is now organized relative to mutually beneficial interests – a mode of social organization Durkheim labels 'organic solidarity'. Arising from modern society's inherently differentiated and transformative character, its individual occupants are increasingly socio-culturally diverse and thereby no longer share the same religious universe. As a result, the ability of religion to engender social integration through shared beliefs and practices is radically undermined.[1]

Undermining traditional religion

The integrative function of traditional religion within modern society is undermined in two important respects. First, the structurally differentiated nature of modernity results in the emergence of a growing number of societal domains (e.g. economy, politics, law), whose increasingly specialist repertoires have less and less recourse to religious knowledge and spiritual authority. Second, the socio-cultural diversity of modern society impedes unified acceptance of a single set of historical truth claims, doctrinal tenets and ritual repertoires. Consequently, as overall structural integrity and widespread social integration can no longer be nurtured through shared religiosity, other narratives and practices around which societal unity can be fostered have to be adopted. The political and civic space traditionally afforded religion thereby recedes as other more unifying modes of discourse and practice are championed. Furthermore, as the pluralization of society engenders greater socio-cultural diversity, traditional modes of religious allegiance – typified by intolerance of, if not violence towards, the nonbeliever – clearly have to change. Because pluralizing society requires progressive interdependence between those of differing worldviews, religious belonging assumes an increasingly non-militant character. Indeed, over time religion becomes something that is either not talked about in public or treated as the kind of thing about which people should agree to differ if not even be willing to compromise. In combination, these complementary dynamics result in the progressive privatization (as it recedes from the public sphere) and individualization (as it becomes a matter of subjective opinion) of religious belief and practice. As Durkheim remarks:

> if there is one truth that history has incontrovertibly settled, it is that religion extends over an ever diminishing area of social life. Originally, it extended over everything; everything social was religious – the two words were synonymous. Then gradually political, economic and scientific functions broke free from the religious function, becoming separate entities and taking on more and more a markedly temporal character ... In short, not only is the sphere of religion not increasing at the same time as that of the temporal world, nor in the same proportion, but it is continually diminishing. (1984, pp. 119–20)

In view of the 'social life of a new kind' engendered by modernity, traditional religion is increasingly unable to perform the tasks for which society created it. Consequently, traditional religion must give way to other more effective means of generating social integration. Intrigued by the differences between Protestantism (which dominated in more industrialized countries) and Catholicism (then dominant in less developed nations), Durkheim believed that traditional forms of religion were progressively giving way to new forms of religio-moral practice. By virtue of their historical novelty, however, these new religio-moral forms were yet to establish themselves to any great effect: 'In short, the ancient gods grow old or die and others are not yet born' (2001, p. 322). Worried by the apparent lack of an effective replacement for traditional religion, Durkheim feared for the ability of modern society to integrate individuals to the extent needed for its optimal functioning. Highlighting the higher suicide rates of the more industrialized (and Protestant) countries of Europe, Durkheim identified the condition of 'anomie' (normlessness) as indicative of modern society's failure to integrate sufficiently its individual occupants (2006).

The rise of rational morality

In addition to suggesting practical steps to be taken to ensure the development of alternative modes of social integration, Durkheim identified the gradual emergence of what he termed 'rational morality' (1961). Durkheim observed how traditional Catholic religion – founded on historical truth claims and doctrinal tenets – had given way to increasingly rationalized and ethically orientated modes of Protestantism. Durkheim argues that these changes represent adaptations to structural differentiation and social pluralization engendered by the advancing urban-industrialization of the nations within which Protestant Christianity was most popular. As social cohesion could no longer be generated through traditional religious means, Protestant Christianity assumes an increasingly inclusive tenor through its articulation of universal moral principles (e.g. love, justice, equality) to which all reasonable people can and should assent. In effect, religion is increasingly rationalized as traditional appeals to historical truths and doctrinal tenets are replaced by ethical prescriptions underwritten by universal reason.

Given society's dependence upon the successful integration of its individual members, as long as we have society, by definition some means of generating social cohesion must exist. Within pre-modern societies, argues Durkheim, traditional religion has been the most important means of engendering the moral authority necessary to lead individuals to co-operate, compromise and, where necessary, make personal sacrifices for the greater good of the social whole. Given the rapid and widespread transformations provoked by the urban-industrial revolution, however, modern society emerges and is immediately challenged with finding new ways of integrating an increasingly complex and diverse number of structures and individuals. As traditional religion no longer fits the bill, society generates a more inclusive mode of integration in the form of rational morality. Identifying the emergence of rational morality through the rise of Protestant Christianity,

Durkheim regards Protestantism as a transitional phase in the gradual transformation of traditional religion through its progressive privatization, individualization and rationalization. Consequently, Durkheim believed that traditional religion would not only become progressively less visible, it would also become increasingly less recognizable as 'religion' in the traditional sense of the term.

Max Weber

Like others before him, Weber's understanding of historical social processes includes an evolutionary perspective whereby primitive and simple forms of community gradually give way to increasingly complex and differentiated modes of societal organization.[2] Understood as the process of 'rationalization', Weber regards humanity's compulsion to understand, render meaningful and efficiently exploit its environment as central to this move from the simple to the complex. As noted in the previous chapter, Weber holds that religion has been a historically important, if not dominant, element of humankind's intellectual, significatory and practical interactions with its material and social contexts. Religion, then, has been a fundamental component of the rationalizing trajectory through which humanity has passed in the course of its historical development. At the same time, and as an integral part of this process, religiosity has developed alongside other aspects of human existence. This development has been characterized by the transition from the pragmatic concerns of magic through the transcendent orientations of religion to the worldly asceticism of certain Protestant traditions. Part and parcel of the process of rationalization, this development has engendered the incremental 'intellectualization' of the religious quest as evidenced by the emergence of increasingly abstract doctrines and elaborate moral systems such as those of 'ethical-monotheism' (Judaism, Christianity, Islam).

Technocratic reason and disenchantment

Central to Weber's notion of rationalization is the gradual devaluation of forms of knowledge and practice which do not have as their basis appeals to empirically grounded rational principles such as those of calculability and efficiency. Exemplified by the rise of modern science and dominance of technocratic systems, Weber uses the borrowed term 'disenchantment' to label the incremental displacement of non-calculable or inefficient forms of practical knowledge – of which religion is a prime example – by modes of knowing and doing susceptible to measurement and manipulation. Believing that 'the fate of our times is characterized by rationalization and intellectualization' (1991c, p. 149), Weber argues that:

The tension between religion and intellectual knowledge definitely comes to the fore wherever rational, empirical knowledge has consistently worked through to the disenchantment of the world . . . In principle, the empirical as well as the mathematically orientated view of the world develops refutations of every intellectual approach which in any way asks for 'meaning' in inner-worldly occurrences. Every increase in empirical science increasingly pushes religion from the rational into the irrational realm. (1991b, pp. 350–1)

Akin to Durkheim's observations upon the modern fate of traditional religion, Weber foresees its privatization through its gradual 'retreat' from 'public life'. In the same vein, Weber predicts religion's eventual transmutation into 'impersonal forces' imbued by explicitly secular values such as 'the idea of duty' and 'the brotherliness of direct and personal human relations'. Similar to Durkheim's notion of 'rational morality', Weber foresees 'the ghost of dead religious beliefs' ascending 'from their graves' to linger on in the form of secular ethical principles underwritten by the dictates of reason rather than appeal to supernatural authority (1992, p. 182; 1991c, p. 149). Holding religion to be only one of a number of 'ultimate and most sublime values' to be marginalized within the modern worldview, Weber sees the contemporary urban-industrial landscape as constituting 'a departure from an age of full and beautiful humanity'. Imprisoned by the 'iron cage' of 'rational legal acquisition' and subsequently denied established modes of meaning-making which appeal beyond that which is calculable and efficient, contemporary humanity is incrementally impoverished (1992, pp. 179–81). As a result, 'modern man is in general, even with the best will, unable to give religious ideas a significance for culture and national character which they deserve' (1992, p. 183).

Modern recapitulations

Bryan Wilson (1926–2004) and Peter Berger have been instrumental in the revitalization of the sociology of religion in the second half of the twentieth century. In respect of the secularization question, the earlier writings of Wilson (1966) and Berger (1967) pick up pretty much where Durkheim and Weber left off. Although he subsequently refined his understanding of secularization (1982), Wilson's views remained substantively unchanged from those first articulated in the 1960s. Berger, however, moved progressively away from his earliest position and is now regarded as an influential gainsayer of certain key aspects of modern secularization theories (1999, pp. 1–18). Leaving Berger's later position to Chapter 5, this section deals only with his earlier articulations of the secularizing character of modern society.

Bryan Wilson

In one of his earliest treatments of secularization, Wilson defines it as 'the process whereby religious thinking, practice and institutions lose their social significance' (1966, p. 14). In a later work, he identifies the secularization process as comprising such things as:

> the sequestration by political powers of the property and facilities of religious agencies; the shift from religious to secular control of various of the erstwhile activities and functions of religion; the decline in the proportion of their time, energy and resources which men devote to super-empirical concerns; the decay of religious institutions; the supplanting, in matters of behaviour, of religious precepts by demands that accord with strictly technical criteria; and the gradual replacement of a specifically religious consciousness (which might range from dependence on charms, rites, spells, or prayers, to a broadly spiritually inspired ethical concern) by an empirical, rational, instrumental orientation; the abandonment of mythical, poetic, and artistic interpretations of nature and society in favour of matter-of-fact description and, with it, the rigorous separation of evaluative and emotive dispositions from cognitive and positivistic orientations. (1982, p. 149)

Highly reminiscent of Weber, to whom he is greatly indebted, Wilson believes the 'de-mystification of the world' to be an expression of the evolutionary 'process of man's increasing rationality' (1966, pp. 78, 260).

Modern de-mystification

In concrete terms, the de-mystification of the world wrought by secularization involves three interrelated dynamics which arise directly from the urban-industrializing processes of modernity. 'Structural differentiation' is the first of these dynamics and reflects the progressively complex nature of modern society. As with Durkheim above, the structural differentiation of society entails the emergence of increasingly specialized sub-systems such as those treating politics, economy, law, education and health. The second dynamic identified by Wilson relates to the growing importance of modern science and its coupling with industrialized forms of economic activity. In combination, the dynamics of differentiation and scientific instrumentality result in the proliferation of social sub-systems whose internal processes and external integration across society at large are progressively orchestrated by 'rationalistic assumptions' geared to 'economic techniques and procedures'. As a result, the complexification of modern society involves the advance of 'rational pragmatic attitudes' which have increasingly less recourse to mystical modes of practical knowledge such as religion (1966, pp. 58–73).

The third dynamic jointly responsible for the demystification of the world involves Wilson's notion of 'societalization' (1976). Appropriating classical treatments of the modern shift from 'community' to 'society' (notably Tönnies, Durkheim and Weber), Wilson argues that urban-industrial society is an increasingly impersonal environment. Whereas traditional communities are orientated by a shared moral universe reinforced by strong interpersonal relations, modern society is orchestrated by increasingly faceless processes of 'institutionalism' and 'bureaucracy' underwritten by abstract rational principles. Because religion 'has its basis in the local social group and in the solemnization and sacralization of interpersonal relationships', the shift from community to society undermines religion's role as a mode of collective moral authority. Rather, and by virtue of societalization, 'authority' and 'social control' rest now upon 'technical' and 'essentially formal' measures (for example constitutions, contracts and laws) reinforced by 'physical and fiscal' sanctions instead of religious and moral ones (1982, p. 155; 1985, p. 15).[3] No longer implicated within the moral authority systems of communally based interpersonal relations, religion loses both its principal social relevance and chief means of socio-cultural reproduction. Coupled with the advance of rational pragmatism and the growing proportion of the social landscape functioning with complete disregard of the supernatural, the processes of societalization entail religion's demise 'as an agency of social control' (1966, p. 90).

Although his articulation of the secularization process postulates religion's 'diminishing *significance* for the social system', Wilson is at pains to stress that the de-mystification of the world does not entail 'the decline of religious practice and belief *per se*' (1998, p. 66). Rather, he argues that his theory of secularization 'maintains no more than that religion ceases to be significant in the working of the social system . . . What such a definition does *not* imply is that all men have acquired a secularized consciousness' (1982, p. 150). Wilson, then, wishes to distinguish between secularization as the demise of religion as a 'basis for social organization and social action' and secularization as an assertion that modern 'individuals have relinquished all their interest in religion' (1966, p. 256; 1982, p. 150). For Wilson, religion's social decline does not necessarily entail its complete disappearance from human life. Rather, religion continues to exist as an individualized and 'largely private concern' devoid of an overarching, collective significance for the social world as a whole (1966, p. 258).

Peter Berger (the early version!)

In marked contrast to Wilson, Peter Berger's (early) understanding of secularization directly links the social decline of religion ('objective secularization') with the demise of individual religiosity ('subjective secularization').

For Berger, the term secularization not only denotes 'the process by which sectors of society and culture are removed from the domination of religious institutions and symbols', it also implies that:

> As there is a secularization of society and culture, so is there a secularization of consciousness. Put simply, this means that the modern West has produced an increasing number of individuals who look upon the world and their own lives without the benefit of religious interpretations. (1967, pp. 107–8)

Berger's insistence that 'objective secularization' necessarily implies the 'secularization of consciousness' reflects his overarching theoretical linkage of the individual self and the social world at large. Expressed in his joint work with Thomas Luckmann (1966), Berger regards the quest for meaning as a foundational component of human existence. Indeed, such is the importance to humankind of experiencing the world as significant that the absence of meaning directly undermines the human sense of self and thereby provokes a fundamental crisis of being. Rendering the world meaningful is, above all, what makes us human. As with Durkheim and Weber, Berger sees religion as 'the historically most important' means by which humankind has rendered the world meaningful (1967, p. 100). Religion does this through the establishment of a 'sacred cosmos' within which all aspects of existence are rendered 'humanly significant' through their reference to a supernatural order of things (1967, pp. 25–8).

Traditional plausibility

Reflecting the 1960s emphasis upon nurture over nature, Berger regards the arena of culture (as opposed to biology) as the cradle of human signification. To be human is to be open to the world (Berger and Luckmann, 1966, p. 65). Reliant upon the external support of culture rather than internal biological routines, the individual's experience of the world as meaningful is something that must constantly be reinforced and revitalized by other human beings. 'With the possible exception of a few areas of direct personal experience, human beings require social confirmation for their beliefs about reality' (1980, pp. 17–18). For the world to make sense *to me*, it must first be rendered meaningful ('plausible') *by others*:

> For better or for worse, men are social beings . . . Most of what we 'know' we have taken on the authority of others, and it is only as others continue to confirm this 'knowledge' that it continues to be plausible to us. It is such socially shared, socially taken-for-granted 'knowledge' that allows us to move with a measure of confidence through everyday life. Conversely,

the plausibility of 'knowledge' that is not socially shared, that is challenged by our fellow men, is imperilled, not just in our dealings with others, but much more importantly in our own minds. (1969, p. 6)

Herein lies the rub. For while our dependence upon those around us makes us human, this dependence leaves us vulnerable. As a result of its reliance upon something outside of itself, 'subjective identity is a precarious entity' (Berger and Luckmann, 1966, p. 118).

Inspired by the work of Alfred Schutz, Berger maintains that the most effective means of supporting and reinforcing subjective identity are those social processes which engender within individuals a perception of the world as 'taken for granted' (1967, pp. 27–8). In effect, the most stable forms of subjective identity are those which have been socialized into perceiving the world as an 'objective reality' whose existence is so certain and inevitable that it cannot be conceived to exist in any other way. That the world should be thus becomes (through socialization) a matter of simple 'common sense'. Berger uses the terms 'symbolic universe' and 'plausibility structure' to designate the prevailing socio-cultural system through which individual experience of the world is incorporated within 'the same, overarching universe of meaning' (1967, p. 115). As indicated above, Berger recognizes religion as a historically important contributor to the admixture of theories, beliefs and values which have informed successive plausibility structures and the everyday social practices they underwrite.

Modern implausibility

Allying Schutz with Durkheim, Berger argues that plausibility structures work best when they are stable, cohesive and monopolistic. Within the simple and socio-culturally uniform contexts of traditional society, plausibility structures are 'highly reliable' – not least, because social change is slow and alternative worldviews are scarce. On account of its differentiated and socially plural character, however, modern society is 'characterized by unstable, incohesive, unreliable plausibility structures' (1980, p. 19). By disrupting established mechanisms of sociality and introducing a plurality of possible worldviews, the pace of social transformation and the extent of socio-cultural diversity undermine the taken-for-grantedness of once dominant symbolic universes. Having lost their monopolies through the appearance of viable alternatives, dominant plausibility structures are relativized as they become just one among a number of competing representations of the world. Faced with a now vertiginous array of alternative and thereby relative worldviews, the certainty and inevitability of a once taken for granted social reality gives way to an experience of the world as 'relatively unstable and unreliable' (Berger, Berger and Kellner, 1974, p. 73).

Beset with instability and uncertainty, the modern condition is consequently one of 'acute crisis' (1967, p. 124).

Berger's representation of modernity as relativizing worldviews and engendering 'anomy' has direct implications for religion. Most important of all, the pluralization of modern society and the emergence of competing religious and secular representations of the world results in 'a widespread collapse of the plausibility of traditional religious definitions of reality' (1967, p. 127). As with plausibility structures in general, religious worldviews work best in stable, undifferentiated and homogeneous social contexts within which the taken-for-grantedness of a sacred cosmos can most effectively be inculcated. Within modern social contexts, however, traditional religious worldviews have to compete with alternative representations of the cosmos, some of which will also be religious and others of which will be secular. Either way, the fact that different religions are now in competition results in two important developments. First, religious worldviews are progressively relativized as they are called into question – both implicitly and explicitly – by the presence and activity of alternative renderings of the world. Such relativization directly undermines religion's ability to engender the certainty and inevitability essential to humankind's experience of the world. As a result, the ability of religion to win adherents decreases and its social presence inevitably diminishes. Society thereby becomes more secular. Second, the demands of competition force religions to adopt the kinds of processes and dynamics which have proved most successful in secular market contexts (see Chapter 8). Geared to the demands of marketing their wares, religious organizations increasingly assume the character of competitive agencies as they tailor their structures and products according to the economic logic of secular markets. Religion is thereby progressively rationalized as its traditional, supernaturalist character is replaced with an emphasis more attuned to the immanent, here and now needs of the modern consumer. In effect, religion assumes an increasingly secular character.

In addition to the above, Berger identifies the subjectivization of religion as a further secularizing dynamic (see Chapter 5). On the one hand, the demise of religion as a dominant social force disembeds individuals from the traditional socializing processes through which religious worldviews assumed their taken-for-grantedness. To be or not to be religious is now a voluntary matter and is thereby something which is chosen (or rejected) relative to subjective preferences rather than social processes. On the other hand, the modern fragmentation of traditional plausibility structures and resulting loss of inevitability about the social world leads individuals increasingly to look upon themselves as sources of the certainty and stability so essential to existential wellbeing. Subjectivity rather than sociality is the modern author of signification. In tandem with the above secularizing dynamics, the modern turn to the self results in the subjectivization of religion. Here:

religious 'realities' are increasingly 'translated' from a frame of reference of facticities external to the individual consciousness to a frame of reference that locates them within consciousness. Put differently, the *realissimum* to which religion refers is transposed from the cosmos or from history to individual consciousness. Cosmology becomes psychology. History becomes biography. (1967, p. 167)

Echoing Weber's ghosts of religion ascending from their graves as secular morality, Berger sees the subjectivization of religion as resulting in an interiorized, humanistic preoccupation with physical and psychological wellbeing; in effect, religion as therapy.

Contemporary variations on a classical theme

Steve Bruce

Among all of the contemporary theorizations of modern secularizing processes, the most consistently, forcefully and clearly articulated is that of Steve Bruce:

Whether we measure church membership, church attendance, the popularity of religious ceremonies to mark rites of passage, or the more nebulous matter of religious belief, we find that, though each index starts at a different level, and the rate of decline differs for each society, nonetheless, across the industrial world there is a steady and to-date unremitting decline in all religious indices. (2001, p. 250)

Bruce argues that the effects of secularization are explicit at every level of contemporary, urban-industrial society. In macro-structural terms, secularization expresses itself in 'the declining importance of religion for the operation of non-religious roles and institutions such as those of the state and the economy'. Such is witnessed, for example, through the establishment of secular political processes and their articulation of laws and economic dynamics which make little or no allowance for the particularities of religious belief and practice. In mid-range, organizational terms, secularization shows itself through 'a decline in the social standing of religious roles and institutions'. Such is evidenced, for example, in religion's diminishing organizational presence both across society at large (e.g. civil ceremonies, institutional chaplaincies) and in life-course events (e.g. birth, union, death). And at a micro-social level, secularization manifests itself by way of 'a decline in the extent to which people engage in religious practices, display beliefs of a religious kind, and conduct other aspects of their lives in a manner

68

informed by such beliefs' (2002, p. 3). Such is exemplified by decreasing rates of formal religious participation and individuals self-designating as religious. Unlike his mentor Wilson, Bruce is both explicit and unqualified in his assertion that objective secularization – to borrow a distinction from Berger – connotes subjective secularization:

> Although it is possible to conceptualize it in other ways, secularization primarily refers to the beliefs of people. The core of what we mean when we talk of this society being more 'secular' than that is that the lives of fewer people in the former than in the latter are influenced by religious beliefs. (1992, p. 6)

A symptom of modernity, Bruce regards secularization as a gradual but ineluctable process brought on by the cumulative interaction of a number of key modernizing dynamics. The most important of these dynamics Bruce identifies as 'social and structural differentiation, societalization, rationalization, and increasing social and cultural diversity' (2001, p. 258).

Secularizing dynamics

Expressive of the increasingly complex nature of modern society, *structural differentiation* occurs as new and ever more variegated contexts, domains and environments emerge each with their own set of dynamics, technical specialisms and theoretical expertise. Closely related to the diversification of societal structures, *social differentiation* takes place as established (such as middle) classes fragment and new groups (such as administrative and proletarian) emerge. Together, structural and social differentiation create a richly diverse and complex societal terrain comprising a wide variety of different demands, material experiences, knowledge systems and often contrasting worldviews. Overstretched by the differentiated contexts of modernity, Bruce argues, religion's ability to function as an all-embracing system of explanation and meaning is progressively undermined.

Reflected in the growth of the state, individualized urban existence and rise of civil society, the process of *societalization* involves the progressive disembedding of individuals from their traditional contexts of social reproduction (such as family, community and class). Societalization impacts upon religion in two important respects. First, it undermines established patterns of social reproduction through which traditional values, practices and interpretations (exemplified by religion) are maintained and propagated. Second, societalization decreases the likelihood of routine contact with religious institutions as their traditional involvement in everyday life (education, health, charity, rites of passage) is taken over by other institutions (the state, secular charities, civil organizations) or rendered superfluous to requirements (religious ideologies of political power, social hierarchy, sexual divisions of labour).

Championed by Enlightenment thinking and the rise of modern science, and catalysed by the technical demands of structural differentiation, the most relevant aspect of the process of *rationalization* involves the consolidation of non-religious means of explanation and procedural application. From medicine to agriculture and palaeontology to astronomy, the technical and explanatory advances of modern knowledge, Bruce claims, have progressively undermined the need for and persuasiveness of religious interpretations and the supernatural causality upon which they are founded. At best an exotic appendage and at worst a superfluous waste of time, religious explanation is rendered otiose.

Nurtured by the dynamics of social differentiation, *socio-cultural diversity* also results from the physical migration of peoples, goods, ideas and practices made possible by modern technological developments. Modern society is an increasingly diverse environment in which growing numbers of classes, cultures and creeds are faced with both the need to get along and the awareness that their particular worldview is one among many. Augmented by the egalitarian thrust of modern liberalism, Bruce maintains, the dictates of social harmony and the effects of a pluralized worldview engender the relativization of religious conviction and its subsequent relegation from a matter of public concern to a question of individual taste. As a result, religious belief comes to be regarded as just one perspective alongside others and a point of divergence upon which (like so many matters of private taste) one can and should agree to disagree. While social diversity 'drastically curtails the routine low-level social reinforcement of beliefs', it also undermines the traditional structural processes through which belief is transmitted (2006, p. 38). For example, the children of inter-faith marriages (enabled by social diversity) are far less likely to practise their parents' religion than the offspring of same-faith unions (Bruce and Glendinning, 2010, pp. 107–26). Combined with the processes of rationalization, socio-cultural diversity undermines both the traditional certainties of religion and the established mechanisms of their propagation (Bruce, 2002, pp. 5–30).

Multidimensional secularity

The overall thrust of Bruce's understanding of secularization is twofold. First, Bruce argues that the 'socio-logics related to [the] "fundamental features" of modern society' entail the gradual diminution of religion as both a widespread social phenomenon and influential force in the lives of communities and individuals alike (2006, p. 35). Such occurs as religion is progressively dislocated from its traditional embroilment with overarching political, legal, economic and socio-cultural processes. This change in the macro-structural status of religion is accompanied by both mid-range modifications in the status and behaviour of religious institutions and micro-level transformations in the religious practices and beliefs of individuals. This is the less contentious aspect of secularization theory and, allowing for inter-pretative variations, one with which a good number of academics broadly agree. Second, and somewhat more contentiously, Bruce holds that the pro-cesses which have given rise to modern society constitute it as an environ-ment inimical to the reproduction and maintenance of religion at every level. Not only is religion transformed by modernity, it is incrementally under-mined. However, while modern society does not actively conspire to eradi-cate religion, it nevertheless fails to provide conditions conducive to religion's social reproduction. As such, the process of secularization entails for Bruce not simply the decline of religion but its virtual demise. Denuded of relevance and viewed with indifference, religion withers on the vine (2002, p. 235).

David Martin

Although he has written on a broad range of subjects, like Steve Bruce, David Martin's reputation is most closely associated with his work on secu-larization. Unlike Bruce, however, Martin rejects the assertion that structural secularization necessarily implies the eventual disappearance of religion at a subjective or communal level. At a time when others (such as Berger and Wilson) were appropriating classical secularization theories, Martin was raising questions about what he saw as internal theoretical contradictions and secularist evolutionary assumptions in respect of religion's eventual demise (1965, pp. 169–82). While he retains the view that secularization theory 'is not straightforwardly untrue' (2005, p. 123), Martin nevertheless argues that the social processes involved are far more variable than other accounts might suggest.

Theoretical contingency

In keeping with classical accounts, Martin recognizes the structural differen-tiation of modern society as a central dynamic in the 'redistribution of secu-lar and sacred space'. Consequently, 'social activities once carried on inside sacred space and under its umbrella appear in secular space outside that umbrella' (1997, p. 40). Unlike classical accounts and certain modern vari-ations, however, Martin questions whether the secularization of political-economic structures necessarily leads to the secularization of society as a whole, not least its individual members. While an all-encompassing form of secularization may have happened in parts of Europe, might this not be the result of particular contextual conditions rather than a universal law of social evolution in which modernization entails, of necessity, secularization

tout court? Believing the social processes engaged by mainstream secularization theory to be 'dependent on specific circumstances, notably those
which have obtained in Europe', Martin's answer to this question is 'yes'.
Consequently, he argues, because the European experience upon which it is
founded is contingent, traditional secularization theory 'fails to provide the
universal paradigm to which all other societies must in time approximate'
(1990, p. 295).

Although Martin rules out the European model of secularization as universally applicable, as noted above he does not reject the basic assertion that
modernization generally involves some diminution in the social influence
of religion. The nature of this diminution, however, is neither uniform nor
ineluctable but contingent upon a range of variables which Martin has spent
a good part of his academic career explicating (1978; 1990; 2002; 2005).
Martin identifies the two most important factors influencing the status of
religion in modern society as pertaining to the societal context in general
and the 'character of a given religion' in particular (1978, p. 24). In respect
of *the societal context*, Martin highlights the relations between religion and
state, the roles of socio-cultural elites and the religious nature of the social
terrain. Regarding the social context's religious character, Martin distinguishes between societies characterized by a complete religious monopoly
in which a single religion holds unqualified sway, 'mixed patterns' involving
two or more dominant religions, full pluralism in which all religions present
are equal, and secular monopoly. In respect of *particular religious dynamics*, Martin emphasizes internal belief systems and organizational dynamics
(not least how they orientate a particular religion's engagement with the
secular world and other religions) and variable demographic characteristics
such as status (e.g. minority or majority), class (e.g. professional or proletarian) and geographical location (e.g. rural or urban).

Contextual variability

While Martin identifies other factors which impact upon the role and status
of religion in modern society (conflict and foreign domination), he regards
the interaction of social context and religio-cultural dynamics as by far the
most important. As the nature of each of these dynamics and the manner of
their interaction is highly variable, Martin argues that the processes of secularization (where they are shown to exist) must always be regarded as contingent upon particular conditions on the ground. By and large, however,
Martin holds that religion fares best in social contexts characterized by the
differentiation of religion and state and a socio-cultural pluralism which, in
combination, are respectful of difference and facilitative of interfaith competition. Evidenced by Protestant evangelicalism in South America, those
religions best suited to exploit propitious social conditions may well find

success (Martin, 1990; 1996; 2002). As to whether success such as this bucks modernity's secularizing trend or will eventually be lost amidst an inexorable advance of secularization, Martin does not say. The significance of his contribution, however, remains the problematization of secularization theories such that universal assertions of their implications are now somewhat harder to come by.

Karel Dobbelaere

In true sociological fashion, Karel Dobbelaere analyses secularization processes as they manifest across each of the three dimensions of society: the 'societal/macro-level', the 'organizational/meso-level' and the 'individual/micro-level'. In respect of the macro-level, 'societal secularization' manifests itself as:

> a process, by which the overarching and transcendent religious system of old is being reduced in modern functionally differentiated societies to a subsystem alongside other subsystems, losing in this process its overarching claims over the other subsystems. (2002, p. 189)

In line with aforementioned theories, Dobbelaere understands macro-structural secularization as an expression of the complex ('functionally differentiated') nature of modern society. On the one hand, structural secularization arises through the multiplication of social subsystems whose specialist activities become increasingly autonomous from religion and informed by rational economic principles. On the other, structural secularization occurs as a response to socio-cultural diversity and the consequent need for inclusive (and thereby secular) processes best suited to managing a plural social landscape. For Dobbelaere, societal secularization is the outcome of both intentional ('manifest') developments such as the disestablishment of church and state and unintended ('latent') dynamics such as the emergence of specialist subsystems (law, education, medicine).

Secularization at an institutional level occurs through the adaptations made by religious organizations to their practices and beliefs in response to the changed circumstances of a now functionally differentiated society. In addition to catering for increasing social pluralism and the fragmentation of the moral universe it entails, religious institutions must also make allowances for declining state patronage (where it existed), reduced membership numbers, the advance of secular rationalism, and growing individualism. In order to survive, religious institutions must modify their organizational repertoires. Akin to Berger's identification of the shift from the supernatural to the immanent, Dobbelaere uses Thomas Luckmann's (1967) terminology to describe the secularization of organizational repertoires as the movement from a concern with 'great transcendences' to a preoccupation with 'this worldly', mundane affairs (2002, pp. 190–1).

For Dobbelaere, 'individual secularization means that the *religious authorities* have lost control over the beliefs, practices, and moral principles of individual persons' (2009, p. 606). Because the modern individual is now free from the collective obligations and socializing processes through which religious allegiance has traditionally been propagated, religious belonging is voluntarized and 'belief becomes a private decision' (2009, p. 608). As a result, religion assumes an increasingly 'idiosyncratic' and 'heterogeneous' nature as individuals fabricate their own religiosities through 'patchworks', 'bricolages' and 'compositions' orientated by subjective interests rather than communal blueprints (2009, p. 607). Indicative of modern society's differentiated character, micro-level secularization is also manifest through the increasing 'compartmentalization' of subjective religiosity. Such 'secularization of the mind' expresses itself through the failure of individuals to apply their beliefs to the otherwise 'profane subsystems' (for example educational, economic, legal, familial, medical and political) through which they pass in the course of their everyday lives.

Although he maps secularizing processes across the three levels of society, Dobbelaere holds that secularization theory need not suggest the 'extinction' of religion (2002, p. 190). Indeed, he affirms that 'secularization is not only "man-made", it is reversible' (2009, p. 605). Accepting that the chances of 'de-secularization'/'re-sacralization' at a macro-structural level are 'very slim', Dobbelaere nevertheless believes that religion can continue to exist (if not, at times, grow) at organizational and individual levels (2002, pp. 95, 134). As with Martin above, Dobbelaere makes the decline, survival or flourishing of religion conditional upon a contingent and variable configuration of processes. Likewise in line with Martin, Dobbelaere does not say whether any reversal in the processes of secularization is sustainable in the long term or no more than a temporary reprieve.

Conclusion

One of the abiding strengths of secularization theories is that they speak to a general impression that modern society is somehow less religious than societies which have gone before or those which exist today in non-urban-industrialized form. However, both the extent of religion in traditional society and its precise character are harder to quantify than might first be assumed. Thus, when talking about religion in pre-modern and modern society one may not always be comparing like with like. The assertion that modern society is less religious than traditional society is thereby not as straightforward as it might otherwise appear. More than articulating an intuitive sense of difference, however, theories of secularization identify a range of processes and dynamics whose understanding, it is claimed, helps explain this difference. From structural differentiation and social pluralism, through rationalization and societalization, to privatization and subjectivization, a variety of interrelated processes have been identified as causing and/or expressing the secularization of modern society. As noted above, secularization theories by no means offer a homogenized representation of societal modernization. The classical theories of Durkheim and Weber, for example, present variegated interpretations of modernity's secularizing trajectory. Likewise, subsequent theorizations furnish varying accounts of the nature and implications of the transformative processes they engage.

While the 'strong' theories of (early) Berger and Bruce argue that objective secularization entails a concomitant and virtual demise in subjective religiosity, the 'soft' theories of Wilson, Dobbelaere and Martin demur at suggesting the all but complete disappearance of religion. On the one hand, strong theories of secularization may be praised for their grasp of the logical implications of the self–society linkage which is so central to the sociological paradigm. As sociological theory regards self and society as mutually implicated – such that change in one engenders change in the other – talk of structural secularization makes little theoretical sense without the identification of some form of subjective correlate. At the same time, empirical evidence appears to suggest that objective secularization at macro-structural and institutional levels is indeed reflected in declining levels of individual religious participation and subjective religiosity. On the other hand, soft theories of secularization can be appreciated for their attempts to nuance self–society relations in a way which problematizes the simple equation that objective secularization equals subjective secularization.[4] As seen in the next chapter, a number of approaches which argue for the persistence of religion within modern society employ alternative readings of the self–society relationship than those offered by (early) Berger and Bruce. At the same time, these readings appeal to alternative forms of concrete evidence and different interpretations of empirical data which, it is claimed, belie the assertion that macro-structural secularization entails the subsequent disappearance of organized religion and eventual demise of subjective religiosity.

Further reading

Berger, P., 1967, *The Sacred Canopy: Elements of a Sociological Theory of Religion*, New York: Anchor Books.
Bruce, S., 2002, *God is Dead: Secularization in the West*, Oxford: Blackwell.
Dobbelaere, K., 2002, *Secularization: An Analysis at Three Levels*, Brussels: P. I. E.-Peter Lang.
Martin, D. A., 1978, *A General Theory of Secularization*, London: Basil Blackwell.
Wilson, B., 1966, *Religion in Secular Society*, London: Penguin.

Notes

1 Although disagreeing with him in certain fundamental respects, both Durkheim and Weber were influenced by Ferdinand Tönnies' portrayal of the transition from a traditional to a modern social landscape as characterized by the movement from 'community' (*Gemeinschaft*) – founded on shared characteristics and personal relations – to 'society' (*Gesellschaft*), which is orientated by mutually beneficial interests and impersonal forms of association (1887/1955).

2 As noted in the previous chapter, Weber treats social development from a multi- rather than unilinear perspective.

3 Echoing earlier critiques of the industrial revolution by Romanticism, Wilson also regards modern humanity's decreasing first-hand 'involvement with nature' as a form of impersonalization and further contributory factor to our failure to respond to the world 'with a sense of mystery and awe' (1966, p. 78).

4 Social theorists such as Margaret Archer, for example, have long been arguing for more subtle renderings of the self–society relationship which take better account of the particular character of each dimension and the 'independent variations' to which they give rise (1996).

5

Neither Down nor Out?
Ongoing Religiosity in Modern Society

Introduction

> In the last quarter of the twentieth century, the markedly different situa-
> tion in the United States, the growth of Christianity in the southern hemi-
> sphere, the presence of Pentecostalism all over the developing world, the
> affirmation of Islam in global affairs, increasingly heated debates for and
> against proselytism, and so on have prompted scholars of many discip-
> lines to rethink the secularization paradigm as it was inspired by the
> European case and to question the assumptions on which it was built.
> (Berger, Davie and Fokas, 2008, p. 2)

What follows builds upon the previous chapter by exploring a series of
counter arguments to those who postulate an unqualified linkage between
the rise of modern, urban-industrial society and the decline, if not eventual
disappearance, of religion. Understood as counterpoints to notions of disenchantment and secularization, these arguments are often labelled theories
of 're-enchantment' or 'sacralization'. Using the work of (the later) Berger
and José Casanova as working models, the first section delineates arguments in respect of the continued religious vitality exhibited by traditional
forms of religion. The second section offers examples of scholars who look
beyond mainstream institutional religion to make the case for continued religious vibrancy existing in non-traditional religious contexts. The third section outlines a number of approaches which represent what is increasingly
termed the 'sociology of spirituality'. Although new religious movements
clearly fall within these second and third sections, as they have a chapter of
their own (Chapter 7), their treatment is reserved until then. This current
chapter concludes with a critical overview of particular aspects of the argument for re-enchantment/sacralization.

Traditional religious vitality

Once an advocate of the strong version of secularization theory, Peter Berger has moved progressively to a position in which he sees the modern world in a very different light. Acknowledging the mistaken nature of his earlier views that societal differentiation necessarily leads to secularization, Berger now accepts that 'pluralism and the multiplication of choices, the necessity to choose, don't have to lead to secular choices . . . religion is not about to disappear . . . That's not happening. It's not going to happen' (Mathewes, 2006, pp. 153, 157). Having eschewed his previous prognosis in respect of religion's demise in modern society, Berger now argues that:

> the assumption that we live in a secularized world is false. The world today . . . is as furiously religious as it ever was, and in some places more so than ever. This means that a whole body of literature by historians and social scientists loosely labelled 'secularization theory' . . . [in which] Modernization necessarily leads to a decline of religion, both in society and in the minds of individuals . . . has turned out to be wrong. (1999, pp. 2–3)

Berger acknowledges that, most notably in Europe, modernization 'has had some secularizing effects'. Yet he believes that the dynamics of modernity have also 'provoked powerful movements of counter-secularization' through which old and new religious beliefs are 'taking new institutional forms and sometimes leading to great explosions of religious fervor' (1999, p. 3). Importantly, however, only particular types of religiosity are finding success in the modern world.

While religions which have adapted to modern society and thereby conformed to secularizing expectations have declined, Berger notes that 'conservative', 'orthodox' or 'traditionalist' religious movements which have refused such compromises with modernity 'are on the rise almost everywhere' (1999, p. 6). Exemplified by recent Islamic and evangelical Christian 'religious upsurges' (commonly treated 'under the category of "fundamentalism"'), the most successful types of religion comprise a combination of 'great religious passion, a defiance of what others have defined as the *Zeitgeist*, and a return to traditional sources of religious authority'. For Berger, however, the most appealing aspect of fundamentalist forms of religion is their 'claim to give certainty'. Recapitulating his earlier linkage of modernity and the breakdown of traditional plausibility structures (see Chapter 4), Berger argues that the rise of urban-industrial society has undermined 'the taken-for-granted certainties by which people lived through most of history'. As this is an 'uncomfortable', if not 'intolerable' state of affairs for many, 'any movement (not only a religious one) that promises to provide or to renew certainty has a ready market' in which to find success (1999, pp. 7, 11).

Just as Berger identifies religions which have adapted to modernity as being in decline, he also notes that religious movements which unqualifiedly reject modernity likewise find it hard to flourish. Identifying the strategies of outright revolution (for example Iran) or sectarian withdrawal (such as the Amish) as typical rejectionist approaches, Berger argues that 'religious movements with a strongly anti-secular bent' must steer 'a nuanced course between rejection and adaptation' if they are to enjoy long-term success (1999, pp. 11, 5). Such is the case because the pluralizing and powerful forces of modernity undermine both religious monopolies and airtight religious withdrawal. Indeed, it is no coincidence that while they embody a reactionary stance in respect of their counter-secularizing critiques, the most successful religious upsurges of recent times have engaged with and sought the transformation of modern society as a whole. Characterized as 'dripping with reactionary supernaturalism' (1999, p. 4), Berger regards the religious movements behind recent Islamic and evangelical Christian upsurges as evidence that 'the world today . . . is *anything but* the secularized world that had been predicted (whether joyfully or despondently) by so many analysts of modernity' (1999, p. 9). In view of their continuing success, Berger argues, 'there is no reason to think the world of the twenty-first century will be any less religious' than what has gone before (1999, p. 12).

Public religion

In similar vein, José Casanova argues that the late twentieth century witnessed an 'unexpected public interest' in religion provoked by religion's increasing 'deprivatization'. In particular, Casanova identifies four important developments in which 'religion in the 1980s "went public" in a dual sense. It entered the "public sphere" and gained, thereby, "publicity"' (1994, p. 3). These four developments were:

> the Islamic revolution in Iran; the rise of the Solidarity movement in Poland; the role of Catholicism in the [Nicaraguan] Sandinista revolution and in other political conflicts throughout Latin America; and the public reemergence of Protestant fundamentalism as a force in American politics. (1994, p. 3)

What is so important about developments such as these, argues Casanova, is that the adoption of public roles by religious movements undermines traditional secularization theories and their assumptions in respect of religion 'becoming ever more marginal and irrelevant in the modern world'. Understanding its assumption of public roles as 'the "deprivatization" of religion in the modern world', Casanova maintains that:

religious traditions throughout the world are refusing to accept the marginal and privatized role which theories of modernity as well as theories
of secularization had reserved for them . . . One of the results of this ongoing contestation is a dual, interrelated process of repoliticization of the
private religious and moral spheres and renormativization of the public
economic and political spheres. (1994, p. 5)

Casanova holds traditional secularization theories to have three main connotations: the first involves 'the decline of religious beliefs and practices'; the
second comprises 'the privatization of religion'; and the third treats 'the differentiation of the secular spheres (state, economy, science)' from religious
institutions and norms. While the third connotation 'remains relatively un-
contested in the social sciences', the first two appear highly problematic in
view of religion's recent deprivatization (2006, pp. 7, 11).[1]

Although Casanova both acknowledges the reality of structural differentiation and values the modern freedoms guaranteed by the separation of
state and religion, he rejects 'the *myth* of secularization' whereby institutional differentiation is held to entail the wholesale disappearance of religion from the public sphere and its subsequent withdrawal to a privatized
realm of individualized discourse and subjective opinion. By way of countering traditional secularization theories, Casanova offers five case studies
(all involving Christianity) drawn from Spain, Poland, Brazil and the USA.
In combination, these case studies furnish a critique of modern secularist
tendencies which prescribe the complete removal of religion from the public realm as a safeguard of individual liberties and structural neutralities.
Mindful of the need to protect individual freedoms, Casanova nevertheless
argues that 'an indiscriminate position against all forms of public religion
is unfounded . . . there are some forms of deprivatization of religion which
may be justifiable and even desirable from a modern normative perspective'
(1994, pp. 220–1). At the same time, Casanova's case studies provide a
descriptive account of Christianity's increasing presence within 'the modern
public sphere of civil society' as realized through the gradual disentangle-
ment of church and state (in Spain, Poland and Brazil) and 'the public
mobilization of Protestant fundamentalism (in the USA) or the public inter-
ventions of the American Catholic bishops' (1994, p. 222).

The religious intervention in the public sphere explicated by Casanova's
case studies assumes three main forms. The first involves religion's defence
of traditional civic structures and associational ways of life 'against various forms of state or market penetration'. The second comprises religion's
refusal to allow political and economic systems 'to function according to
their own intrinsic functionalist norms without regard to extrinsic traditional moral norms' such as those of the 'common good'. The third entails religion's countering of 'individualist modern liberal theories' through

the articulation of 'intersubjective, interpersonal norms' grounded in the communal experience. For Casanova, these three forms of religious intervention in the public sphere represent a normative critique of particular kinds of modern institutionalization (1994, p. 230). At the same time, they also 'amount to a certain reversal of what appeared to be secular trends' and thereby require us 'to rethink systematically the relationship of religion and modernity' (1994, p. 6). Believing the supposed 'correlation between modernization and secularization' to be 'highly problematic', Casanova concludes that:

> there are good reasons why we should expect religion and morality to remain and even become ever more contentious public issues in democratic politics . . . The penetration of all spheres of life, including the most private, by public policy; the expansion of scientific-technological frontiers giving humanity Demiurgic powers of self-creation and self-destruction; the compression of the whole world into one single common home for all of humanity; and the moral pluralism that seems inherent to multiculturalism – all these transcendent issues will continue to engage religion and provoke religious responses. (2006, p. 22)

As with Berger, Casanova foresees the continued presence of traditional religious forms not simply at the margins but sometimes at the heart of modern public discourse and social processes.

Religious relocation

In addition to those, like Berger and Casanova, who highlight the modern vitality of established religious forms, others have stressed the importance of looking for contemporary religiosity beyond the traditional institutional parameters of mainstream religion. Over the course of recent decades, scholars have thereby sought to engage non-institutional forms of religion through a variety of concepts. Among the most important of these concepts are those of 'civil religion' (Bellah, 2005, pp. 40–55), 'common religion' (Williams, R. 1951), 'diffused religion' (Cipriani, 1984, pp. 29–51), 'everyday religion' (Ammerman, 2007), 'implicit religion' (Bailey, 1997), 'invisible religion' (Luckmann, 1967), 'lived religion' (Hall, D., 1997), 'popular religion' (Lippy, 1994) and 'secular religion' (Hanegraaff, 1999, pp. 145–60). Although each of these approaches, at times, adopts radically different perspectives, they all share the belief that a proper understanding of religion's relationship with modernity is dependent upon an inclusive analysis which looks beyond the familiar expressions and established manifestations of institutional religiosity.

Invisible religion

Perhaps the most formative of such approaches is that of Thomas Luck-mann's *The Invisible Religion* (1967). Mirroring Durkheim's preoccupation with social integration in modern society, Luckmann says that the 'radical transformation' wrought by modernity has resulted in the 'relocation of the individual in the social order' (1967, pp. 11–12). Luckmann identifies this radical transformation as comprising, in large part, the fragmentation of existing 'symbolic universes'. In terms similar to his then collaborator Peter Berger, Luckmann argues that the disappearance of the 'socially fab-ricated' symbolic universe engenders a crisis of meaning for modern hu-manity (1967, p. 101). No longer supported by a coherent and socially shared worldview, modern human beings are forced to rely increasingly upon their own private resources to make sense of both themselves and the world around them. As Luckmann regards humanity's quest for meaning as quintessentially religious, he sees 'the problem of individual existence' provoked by the 'emergence of modern society' as, first and foremost, 'a "religious" problem' (1967, p. 12).

In order to best engage the religious problem of modern society, Luck-mann maintains that the sociology of religion must first rid itself of its the-oretical preoccupation with traditional, institutionalized ('church') forms of religion. Such is the case because the recent transformations wrought by mod-ernity are resulting in the gradual shift of religious meaning-making from the public arena of 'church religion' to the 'private sphere' of the autono-mous individual. Unfortunately, however, Luckmann notes that the 'recent sociology of religion' of which he speaks works with a 'narrow "positivistic" methodology' in which 'the definition of research problems and programs is, typically, determined by the institutional forms of traditional church or-ganization' (1967, pp. 21, 18). For Luckmann, the 'main assumption' of this methodology 'consists in the identification of church and religion'. This identification, he claims, results in the conclusion that while 'religion may be many things . . . it is amenable to scientific analysis only to the extent that it becomes organized and institutionalized'. Consequently, religion is deemed worthy of engagement only to the extent that it manifests as formal ritual ('institutionalized religious conduct') or theological doctrine ('institutional-ized religious ideas') (1967, p. 22). As a side-swipe to contemporary opinion in respect of religious decline, Luckmann continues by arguing that:

> Vestiges of this view have entered the understanding – or misunderstand-
> ing – of secularization . . . In the absence of a well-founded theory, secu-
> larization is typically regarded as a process of religious pathology to be
> measured by the shrinking reach of the churches. Since the institutional
> vacuum is not being filled by a counter-church . . . one readily concludes
> that modern society is nonreligious. (1967, p. 23)

As 'church-oriented' religion is only one particular and historically contingent form of the 'universal anthropological condition of humanity', its
decline within modern society in no way signals the demise of religion *tout
court* (1967, pp. 50, 77).[2] Rather, for Luckmann, secularization represents
no more than the crisis of institutional religion whose 'particular historical
form' should in no way 'serve as a yardstick for assessing religion in contemporary society' (1967, pp. 41, 91).

Only by shifting its methodological gaze beyond the institutionally specialized form of church religion, Luckmann argues, will the sociology of
religion be able to capture the modern shift from collective and socially defined symbolic universes to privately formulated 'individual systems of "ultimate" significance' (1967, p. 91). As 'we are observing the emergence of
a new social form of religion', unless new methodologies and theoretical
approaches are adopted by sociology it risks misunderstanding the character
and implications of this change (1967, pp. 104–5). Arising from modernity's
particular characteristics (e.g. differentiation, pluralism, societalization),
says Luckmann, individuals are progressively freed from social constraints in
respect of what they should believe and how they might render their worlds
meaningful. Relying now on an 'autonomous' sense of self and the 'private'
resources (family and friends) which support it, individuals are increasingly
formulating 'highly subjective' meaning systems directly tailored to a range
of idiosyncratic criteria (such as 'self-expression' and 'self-realization').

Orchestrated by personal predilection and chosen from a growing range
of socio-cultural ingredients, individual meaning systems are characterized
by 'heterogeneity', highly 'flexible' and '*ad hoc*' in nature, and 'relatively
unstable' (1967, pp. 104–5). Orientated to discovering the 'inner self', emotionally expressive and expectant of inner-worldly rewards, the kind of
transcendence celebrated by this 'new social form of religion' differs mark-
edly from that articulated by traditional systems of meaning informed by
institutionalized religion. Elsewhere describing this shift as a 'shrinking of
transcendence' from the 'great' (social) to the 'minimal' (private), Luckmann regards this 'profound change in the "location" of religion' as no less
a form of the 'sacred' (1990, pp. 127–38). Given this change of location,
Luckmann believes it to be incumbent upon the sociology of religion to re-
calibrate its tools and look beyond institutionalized religion to take account
of the sacred wherever it is manifest.

Civil religion

Published the same year as Luckmann's classic text, Robert Bellah's seminal essay on 'Civil Religion in America' likewise offers an analysis of non-
traditional religiosity (1967, pp. 1–21).[3] Bellah adopts the 'Durkheimian
notion that every group has a religious dimension' but recognizes that the

pluralist context of the United States does not lend itself to Durkheim's understanding of established religion (the 'church') as the singular community through which social and structural integration is achieved (2005, pp. 40, 46). Rather, the necessary 'symbols of national solidarity' which serve 'to mobilize support for the attainment of national goals' are furnished by what he defines as 'the civil religion of America' (2005, pp. 50–1). Borrowing heavily from Judeo-Christian traditions, American civil religion is nevertheless non-confessional and 'exists alongside of and rather clearly differentiated from' traditional religious forms. As 'an elaborate and well-institutionalized' source of transcendent principles which underwrite social structures and processes, civil religion is an important source 'of personal motivation for the attainment of national goals'. In view of its 'seriousness and integrity', civil religion 'requires the same care in understanding that any other religion does' (2005, pp. 40, 50).

Drawing on a number of presidential addresses throughout the history of the USA, Bellah maintains that – 'from the earliest years of the republic' – the civil religion of America has developed (à la Durkheim) as 'a collection of beliefs, symbols, and rituals with respect to sacred things and institutionalized in a collectivity' (2005, p. 46). Irrespective of individual beliefs and practices, says Bellah, there are:

> certain common elements of religious orientation that the great majority of Americans share. These have played a crucial role in the development of American institutions and still provide a religious dimension for the whole fabric of American life, including the political sphere. This public religious dimension is expressed in a set of beliefs, symbols, and rituals that I am calling the American civil religion. (2005, p. 42)

American civil religion achieves its unifying goals by selectively appropriating traditional 'archetypes' from pre-existing religious traditions and situating them within a discursive and practical repertoire which is 'genuinely American and genuinely new'. Appealing to traditional notions such as divine sovereignty, sacrifice, rebirth and election, American civil religion nevertheless 'has its own prophets and its own martyrs' (such as Washington and Lincoln), 'its own sacred events and sacred places' (e.g. Thanksgiving and Arlington National Cemetery), and 'its own solemn rituals and symbols' (such as swearing allegiance to the flag and the Statue of Liberty) (2005, pp. 55–6). As 'an understanding of the American experience in the light of ultimate and universal reality', civil religion exists beyond the confines of formal religious institutions and 'has been a point of articulation between the profoundest commitments of the Western religious and philosophical tradition and the common beliefs of ordinary Americans' (2005, pp. 55, 52).

Common religion

Principally addressing the European context, Grace Davie has done much to explore 'the non-institutional dimensions of religiosity' (1994, p. 74). Through a variety of concepts and approaches, Davie engages what she regards as an 'increasing mismatch between statistics relating to religious practice and those which indicate levels of religious belief':

> On the one hand, variables concerned with feelings, experience and the more numinous aspects of religious belief demonstrate considerable persistence in contemporary Britain (as they do throughout Western Europe); on the other, those which measure religious orthodoxy, ritual participation and institutional attachment display an undeniable degree of secularization. (1994, pp. 4–5)

Davie uses the notion of 'common religion' to describe the extra-institutional and 'less orthodox dimensions of individual believing' which she holds to be relatively widespread across Britain and Europe (1994, p. 76). Regarding 'churchgoing minorities' as representing no more than the tip of the religious iceberg, Davie believes it to be incumbent upon sociologists 'to penetrate more deeply in order to understand what is going on beneath the surface' and thereby 'reveal forms of religion that normally lie hidden' (2010, p. 264).

In her earlier work upon religion in Britain since 1945, Davie cites various studies which, she argues, furnish 'evidence that the British are far from being – or becoming – a secular society in any strict sense of the term' (1994, p. 84). Rather than being expressed through regular institutional participation, however, the 'common religion' of the British exhibits a more diffuse character which is best understood as a form of 'believing without belonging'. Citing surveys orientated to engaging belief rather than simple institutional participation, Davie maintains that 'more and more people within British society want to believe but do not want to involve themselves in religious practice' (1994, p. 107). Furthermore, she argues that the influence of 'common religion' is manifest at certain times of life (e.g. rites of passage) or significant events (such as public celebration and tragedy) when individuals and communities make explicit use of institutional religion (1994, pp. 84–91). In the face of such evidence, Davie concludes that:

> Religious life – like so many other features of post-industrial or postmodern society – is not so much disappearing as mutating, for the sacred undoubtedly persists and will continue to do so, but in forms that may be very different from those which have gone before. (1994, p. 198)

In more recent writings, Davie has developed the notion of 'vicarious religion' which she regards as the successor to her concept of 'believing without belonging' (2000; 2006, pp. 23–34; 2010, pp. 261–6). 'By vicarious, I mean *the notion of religion performed by an active minority but on behalf of a much larger number who (implicitly at least) not only understand, but, quite clearly, approve of what the minority is doing*' (2006, p. 24). The concept of 'vicarious religion' is intended to help understand 'the very large number of people (around 50 per cent of the population) who are neither involved in organized religion, nor consciously opposed to it' (2010, p. 261). Although not engaged in formal religious participation, Davie argues that a significant number of the European population in some way regard institutional religion as being practised on their behalf. In effect, large swathes of the European population regard religious institutions as a kind of 'public utility' which, even if they do not personally use it, they accept as having some degree of social value. Davie cites the most notable examples of institutional practice undertaken vicariously (on behalf of others) as ritual provision for rites of passage (such as birth, marriage, death), exhibition of belief (rather than doubt or scepticism), upholding certain standards of behaviour and providing space for debate in respect of matters which might not readily be treated elsewhere (2006, pp. 24–7). While Davie admits that vicarious religion may well have disappeared by the 'mid-twenty-first century', she nevertheless regards its contemporary presence as a form of modern religiosity unaccounted for by existing secularization theories (2010, pp. 263–4).

Spiritualities of life

A long-standing academic of new age religiosity, Paul Heelas (1996) is another who finds fault with totalizing theories of secularization:

> There is at least one major problem with the across-the-board application of secularization theory . . . A great deal of evidence might show that regular church attendance is falling in many countries (including the US), but virtually all indices show that New Age spiritualities of life are growing. (2006, pp. 47, 57)

Working with a 'subjectivization thesis' similar to those of Berger and Luckmann, Heelas argues that modernity's valorization of the autonomous self 'favors those forms of spirituality which resource one's subjectivities and treats them as a fundamental source of significance, and undermines those forms of religion which do not' (2006, p. 57). Consequently, while traditional forms of institutional religion are on the wane, the practices and beliefs of 'inner-life spirituality' are being progressively adopted by 'considerable numbers of the medical profession' (as complementary and alternative treatments), proving 'increasingly attractive' to school teachers (as holistic and multicultural pedagogies), have 'a growing presence within the domain of paid employment' (as a 'self-work ethic') and are 'deemed worthy of government support in the UK and elsewhere' (2008, pp. 5–6).

Building upon research conducted in the north-west of England (Heelas and Woodhead, 2005), Heelas maintains that 'there are almost 200,000 separate holistic milieu activities in Great Britain, provided by some 146,000 spiritual practitioners' and taken up on a weekly basis by 'slightly over 900,000 inhabitants' (2008, p. 187). Having predicted on the back of this earlier research that the alternative religious scene will 'perhaps double its size during the next 40 or 50 years' (Heelas and Woodhead, 2005, p. 149), Heelas further asserts that it 'has a "much better" future than the congregational domain. For whereas the holistic milieu will continue to grow, it is highly likely that the congregational domain as a whole will continue to decline' (2007, p. 78). Indeed, such is his confidence in the 'growth' and 'vitality' of non-mainstream religiosity that Heelas regards it to be 'now quite clear that the debate over numbers has been settled in favour of those who draw attention to the numerical importance of what is in evidence beyond traditional theism' and the religious institutions within which it is practised (2009, p. 761).

Heelas believes the growth and vitality of 'New Age spiritualities of life' to signal a 'spiritual revolution'. In the face of this revolution, 'it very much looks as though a research era is now emerging which will add up to at least an approximation of the great days of Durkheim, Simmel and Weber' (2008, p. 21). By virtue of its broadened scope, this new era of research necessarily goes beyond that of traditional institutional religion to encompass 'the study of spirituality'. Given its broader sweep, Heelas acknowledges that some academics are suggesting 'that the sociology of religion should be renamed the sociology of religion and spirituality', while others advocate a more radical approach in which 'the sociology of spirituality should be a research and teaching enterprise with its own priorities' (2009, p. 758). Irrespective of nomenclature or disciplinary parameters, in light of ongoing transformations of the religious landscape there is no doubt that the sociology of religion has become increasingly sensitized to what is now generically labelled 'spirituality'. We now turn to look at both the contours and implications of this sensitization.

The sociology of spirituality

It is typical of scholars of contemporary spirituality to cite the findings of a range of surveys and studies which, it is argued, furnish evidence of religious vitality in non-institutional contexts. As an appendix to his *Spiritualities of Life*, for example, Heelas mentions eleven surveys and studies which, he claims, offer empirical data indicative of the contemporary robustness of 'inner life "beliefs"' beyond traditional institutional contexts (2008, pp. 233–5). Heelas' first source, for example, argues that during the 1990s, 40 per cent of UK respondents believed in 'God as Spirit or Life force', while 31 per cent believed in 'God as personal' (Gill, Hadaway and Marler, 1998, pp. 507–16). In the same vein, Heelas cites both Heald's (2000) 'Soul of Britain' survey – which records 31 per cent of respondents defining themselves as a 'spiritual person' and 27 per cent as a 'religious person' – and Hood's (2005) finding that 'about 25–30 per cent of individuals in US culture identify themselves as spiritual but not religious'. In addition to other such studies, like many academics of spirituality, Heelas draws on a range of multi-national surveys designed to quantify attitudes, beliefs and values which may be held to signal some degree of spiritual tendency which may not be expressed through institutional participation. Among those cited most regularly by scholars like Heelas are the European Values Study, International Social Survey Programme, Religious and Moral Pluralism project and World Values Survey.

Spiritual but not (necessarily) religious

The possibility of a modern religiosity existing alive and well beyond the traditional confines of institutional religion has given rise to a swath of academic studies seeking to detail and understand both the kinds of belief and practice at play and the types of people involved (Fuller, 2001; Hammond, 1992; McGuire, 2008a; Palmisano, 2010, pp. 221–41; Roof, 1993 and 1999; Wuthnow, 1998 and 2001). Among other things, an important insight to emerge from such studies has been the understanding that a seemingly significant proportion of modern individuals may regard themselves as 'spiritual' while at the same time refusing to self-designate as 'religious'. In their overview of a number of such studies, for example, Marler and Hadaway suggest an average return of approximately 18 per cent of individuals opting to describe themselves as 'spiritual only' – as opposed to the other choices of 'religious and spiritual', 'religious only' and 'neither' (2002, p. 292). Detailing particular findings of the European Religious and Moral Pluralism (RAMP) project, Barker records 12 per cent of respondents who thought that they had a spiritual life but who did not regard themselves as religious. She then goes on to say that:

> [had] the question about spirituality not been asked, more than one in ten (12 per cent) of all these respondents – a quarter (26 per cent) of all those who denied being religious – might have been classified as secular when in fact they considered themselves spiritual. (2008, p. 194)

Indeed, adds Barker, 'when used as an *alternative* to religiosity', the concept of spirituality 'exposes the existence of a statistically and socially significant way of being something other than either "religious" or secular' (2008, p. 196).

According to some sociologists, the discovery of an extra-institutional religiosity has done much to sensitize the discipline to its need of 'new interpretative categories' which might better understand 'a rapidly shifting cultural and religious landscape where spirituality has emerged as an unexpected, pervasive and characterizing phenomenon' (Flanagan, 2007, p. 17). Appropriated from theological circles – in which it served to explicate individual religious regimes and private beliefs – the term 'spirituality' has, for many, come to serve as something of a theoretical catchall for contemporary forms of non-institutional religiosity. Defined over and against institutionalized religion, spirituality comes to represent the 'God within' as opposed to the 'church without' (Barker, 2008, pp. 187–202). For example, in her 'ideal-typical distinction' between traditional religion and spirituality, Barker offers a stylized contrast in which the former is characterized by notions of divine transcendence and separation, belief in creation and end times, dichotomous readings of experience (them and us, good and bad, male and female), revelation and moral absolutes, and notions of sin, salvation and heaven. In contrast, however, 'the spiritually oriented type' is characterized by holistic and integrated accounts of reality, perceptions of time as cyclical, contextual notions of truth and moral relativism, optimistic views of human nature, complementary readings of the world and its environment, and a valued place for personal experience and responsibility (2008, p. 190). In the same vein, Zinnbauer et al. contrast those identified by their survey as 'spiritual not religious' with those considered to be both 'spiritual and religious'. Compared with the latter group, those characterized as 'spiritual not religious' were:

> less likely to evaluate religiousness positively, less likely to engage in traditional forms of worship . . . less likely to hold orthodox or traditional Christian beliefs, more likely to be independent from others, more likely to engage in group experiences related to spiritual growth, more likely to be agnostic, more likely to characterize religiousness and spirituality as different and nonoverlapping concepts, more likely to hold nontraditional 'new age' beliefs, and more likely to have had mystical experiences . . . more likely to hold a pejorative definition of religiousness, labelling it as a means to extrinsic ends such as feeling superior to others and avoiding personal responsibility. (1997, p. 561)

Public spirituality

Although continuing to work within the contemporary spirituality paradigm, a number of scholars have sought to correct what they regard as an overly individualized and privatized characterization (Flory and Miller,

2008; McGuire, 2008a; Stanczak and Miller, 2002). In effect, it is argued, many representations of contemporary spirituality have too readily assumed that it only occurs outside of traditional institutional arenas and has little or no impact upon broader social contexts. In their study of contemporary spirituality, for example, Flory and Miller use the concept of 'embodied spirituality' to describe those seeking 'spiritual experience and fulfilment' in collective contexts 'where meaning is both constructed and directed outward in service to others, both within the religious community and in the community where they are located' (2007, p. 203). Regarding this collectively orientated spirituality as a form of 'expressive communalism', Flory and Miller argue that it:

> is best understood as taking place in an embodied form through visual and physical manifestations of spiritual experience that are practised in and through a particular religious community. That is, spiritual experience takes place within a body of believers and is only meaningful as it is experienced in that context and as lived out through that body. (2007, p. 215)

The fullest appreciation of contemporary spirituality must thereby account for its public and private dimensions not simply as an 'either/or' equation but through its conceptualization as a 'both/and' phenomenon.

In the same vein, Meredith McGuire maintains that whereas 'most people probably assume that "spirituality" refers only to the private aspects of religion', she believes that its proper understanding 'reveals important features of *both the private and the public aspects* of religion in a modern context' (2008b, p. 215). On the one hand, McGuire argues that sociology's traditional 'reliance on overly institutionalized definitions of individual religion has . . . resulted in discounting much' individual religiosity that occurs outside the purview of organized religion. Consequently, McGuire acknowledges that modern sociological usage of the concept of spirituality aids in overcoming 'overly institutional conceptions of individual religion' (2008b, pp. 220–1). On the other hand, McGuire maintains that spirituality – or 'religion-as-lived' – 'has much less of a public-private split than we previously assumed', with many of her own informants emphasizing 'communal support and experiencing the sacred in communal contexts' (2008b, pp. 216, 229). As a result, contemporary understandings of spirituality must account for the considerably diverse ways in which 'ordinary people' enact their spirituality through the relationships, practices and contexts comprising their 'everyday lives' (2008b, pp. 215–16).

By way of further underlining the non-private nature of contemporary spirituality, McGuire highlights a number of direct parallels it shares with demonstrably public, but extra-institutional, forms of pre-modern popular religiosity. In respect of contemporary spirituality, McGuire records some of the features described by her 'middle-class respondents' as including 'holism, autonomy, eclecticism, tolerance, this-worldly activism and pragmatism, appreciation of materiality, and blurring of boundaries between sacred and profane' (2008b, p. 221). She then goes on to show how at least four of these features ('religious eclecticism', 'materiality', 'pragmatic concerns' and 'blurred boundaries between the sacred and profane') constituted key elements of pre-modern popular religiosity which can in no way be understood as private in the modern sense of the term. In view of contemporary spirituality's 'profound interconnectedness and experiential subjectivity', McGuire asserts that:

> We must try to understand more deeply how personal religious experience and expression is linked with collective experience and expression – especially in the late modern context where people participate in multiple and often contradictory communities or impersonal collectivities. (2008b, p. 229)

Such can be done, says McGuire, through the development of a 'sociology of spirituality' which accounts for the individualizing trends of modernity yet is mindful of the continuing relevance of collective and public expressions of contemporary religiosity.

Working outside of the spirituality paradigm, Matthew Wood likewise criticizes the overly individualized approach of certain academic perspectives. By focusing solely upon the 'individual *as an* individual', Wood argues, particular sociological approaches to spirituality have suffered from a 'blind spot' which results in 'a marked lack of attention' both to the 'social interactions' through which religious experience is rendered meaningful and 'the wider contexts of people's lives and biographies' (2010, pp. 277, 275). Wood identifies the source of this blind spot as a *'naive* inductivism', by which he means the tendency of sociologists of spirituality to assume that because informants express their experiences in individualized and privatized fashion, their spirituality must indeed be of an individualistic and private nature. Although valid articulations of subjective experiences, Wood maintains, such individual accounts do not necessarily reflect actual social conditions.

Perceived by informants as individualized and private, in reality these spiritual experiences are implicated in and expressive of a wide range of social relations and practices. By uncritically adopting their informants' perspectives – and thereby failing to take serious account of the social contexts within which spirituality occurs – Wood believes the sociology of spirituality to have abnegated its responsibility to offer 'a properly *sociological* interpretation of the phenomena it addresses' (2010, p. 267). Wood suggests that one solution to this problem lies in sociology's refusal to treat spirituality as an analytically separate category from that of religion. While he accepts that '"religion" and "spirituality" may sometimes and in some contexts relate to distinct discourses and practices', Wood also believes that 'the clear linkage between these [concepts] necessitates a *single* analytical category' (2010, p. 281). Regarding the concept of 'religion' to be a proven and adequate analytical category, Wood argues that the concept of 'spirituality' be treated as a sub-category thereof.

Conclusion

The academic studies and surveys presented above go some way to problematizing an assumed or automatic linkage between the rise of modernity and the decline of religion. In the first instance, they do so by furnishing evidence of the vitality of traditional institutional religion, not least that of a conservative or fundamentalist ilk. In the second, evidence is provided which indicates a vibrant spiritual landscape in existence primarily but not solely outside of traditional institutional ambits. Together, it is argued, this evidence requires fundamental changes to contemporary sociological engagement with religion in at least two respects. First, this evidence demands *theoretical* revision in respect of existing models of secularization which assume a given causal relationship between the rise of urban-industrial society and the eventual demise of religion. Second, this evidence requires *analytical* revision by way of the methodologies and applied tools used in the first-hand study of belief and practice in both its micro-social and organizational contexts.

Statistical significance and definitional latitude

The call for critical revision, however, is by no means all one way. For example, in respect of arguments in favour of the ongoing vitality of traditional institutional religion, two points of contention might be raised. First, the question of statistical significance may be posed. While disagreement reigns over the actual numbers concerned, it remains questionable whether ongoing religious revivals will generate sufficient quantities of people to replace the increasing amounts who continue to move away from traditional institutional religion. Second, it may be no coincidence that traditional religion's greatest successes are occurring in nations undergoing modernization rather than those which have long been embroiled in this process. Be it Brazil, China, the Middle East or Korea and Taiwan, the context of traditional religious vitality appears to be one of rapid and far-reaching socio-cultural upheaval. Once this upheaval dies down and many of the characteristics outlined in Chapter 1 are firmly entrenched, who is to say that the structural dynamics and social processes of established modernity will not engender the same kind of institutional decline as that experienced by the typically modern traditional religious landscape of the northern hemisphere? While the jury remains out, there appear to be no sound theoretical reasons for excluding a scenario such as this. Either way, Berger's assertion that the contemporary world 'is as furiously religious as it ever was' perhaps overstates the overall balance of play.

Regarding non-traditional religiosity such as that designated 'spirituality', a number of issues might be raised. First, like that of conservative religious revivalism, the statistical significance of spirituality is such that it can in no way be expected to make up for the decline in traditional institutional forms of religion. The best-guess scenario of Heelas and Woodhead, for example, is that the 'spiritual revolution' of which they write will amount to no more than three per cent of the population (2005). A second issue, however, further problematizes matters and concerns the analytical approaches employed by spirituality scholars. It may be argued, for example, that the definitional latitude given to spirituality ends up including a whole raft of beliefs and practices which might not otherwise be included by a more analytically precise definition (Bruce and Voas, 2007, pp. 43–61; 2010, pp. 243–59). Furthermore, just because someone labels a belief or practice as 'spiritual' does not make it automatic evidence of the continuing presence of 'religion' or 'religiosity' in the sociological sense of the term. For example, whereas an individual's belief in 'something out there' may well be a fact, in the absence of any empirical evidence that this belief makes the slightest difference in actual behaviour it cannot be considered a 'social fact'. While the individual's belief in 'something out there' may well be of psychological interest, it bears no sociological relevance until it can be demonstrated to have had some manner of impact upon how s/he acts. In the same vein, the labelling as 'spiritual' of activities such as fishing, kayaking, surfing and skiing (Sanford, 2007, pp. 875–95; Shaw and Francis, 2008; Snyder, 2007, pp. 896–922) may constitute no more than an expression of subjective valorization of things as 'special to me'. Such labelling cannot be treated as automatic evidence of the sacralization of otherwise secular pastimes. Taken together, the issues of statistical significance, definitional latitude and uncritical inductivism problematize the evidentiary basis of many practices, beliefs and values which are cited by spirituality scholars as counterpoints to religious decline. Consequently, the replacement of traditional religion by spirituality should not be seen as a zero-sum equation in which like replaces like and we are left more or less where we started. The assertion that 'spirituality has rolled in unexpectedly as a sort of replacement' for traditional religion (Flanagan and Jupp, 2007, p. 251) may, then, be rather far-fetched.

Theorizing spirituality

A third issue of concern in respect of spirituality relates to the representation of the self–society duality so central to sound sociological thinking. As the overwhelming majority of spirituality scholars accept that the macro-structural and mid-range institutional processes of modern society are secular, they must identify a suitably influential and robust range of micro-social dynamics which can sustain individual religiosity in the absence of broader societal support. Put another way, if religiosity is not being engendered or transmitted through social structures and institutions, by what means will future generations become religious and thereby stave off religion's decline and eventual demise? When Davie asserts, for example, that 'the sacred undoubtedly persists and will continue to do so' (1994, p. 198), what sociological grounds does she have to support her claim? As noted above, Davie points to 'believing without belonging' and 'vicarious religion' as evidence of the continuing presence of the sacred in contemporary society. What she does not do, however, is identify the societal processes and social dynamics which will ensure the continued persistence of the sacred in any future society.

The response to this issue most common among spirituality scholars rests upon the assertion of a universal human drive for meaning. Exemplified by Berger, this assertion maintains that:

> The religious impulse, the quest for meaning that transcends the restricted space of empirical existence in this world, has been a perennial feature of humanity . . . It would require something close to a mutation of the species to extinguish this impulse. (1999, p. 13)

Although there are many variations on this theme, its fundamental core revolves around the view that the deepest and most pressing questions of human meaning cannot be satisfactorily answered through reference to material processes and mundane dynamics. As the things of this world do not suffice in furnishing sufficient meaning, adequate signification is found only through reference to things of the world beyond. Dependent upon a transcendent referent for its fullest signification, it is argued, the immanent realm will always seek religious/spiritual resolution of its most fundamental questions. As a result, says Bellah, 'the conclusion grows ever stronger that religion is a part of the species life of man, as central to his self-definition as speech' (1970, p. 223).

Two issues arise from this line of reasoning. On the one hand, if, like Luckmann, we regard all forms of meaning-making as automatically religious, then we come across the same problem of definitional latitude as that mentioned immediately above. Typical of many functional definitions of religion (see Chapter 2), this type of approach lacks analytical specificity and fails to advance sociological understanding of religion in a properly substantive way. On the other hand, if we regard only certain kinds of signification

94

as religious, we are still left with the need to explain why some continue to opt for religious meaning-making while others do not. Put another way, when alternative modes of non-religious (secular) signification are readily available (as they are in modern society), what guarantees the continued recourse to religion? After all, if the social 'structure' is secular, then why not the individual 'self'? For the Catholic social philosopher Charles Taylor, the answer to this question resides in the fact that while some human beings will be content with secular answers to their fundamental questions, by virtue of human nature there will always be others who will reject the 'immanent frame' in favour of some kind of transcendent signification (2007). Religion, then, will always be with us. Whereas the anthropological universalism and psychophysical character of this reasoning is wholly unproblematic for many scholars of spirituality, for other academics it smacks of something beyond the sociological pale. Of course, some will argue by way of riposte, if our understanding of religion can change with the times, so too can our appreciation of what constitutes good sociology.

Further reading

Ammerman, N. T. (ed.), 2007, *Everyday Religion: Observing Modern Religious Lives*, Oxford: Oxford University Press.

Bruce, S. and Voas, D., 2007, 'The Spiritual Revolution: Another false Dawn for the Sacred', in K. Flanagan and P. C. Jupp (eds), *A Sociology of Spirituality*, Aldershot: Ashgate, pp. 43–61.

Flanagan, K. and Jupp, P. C. (eds), 2007, *A Sociology of Spirituality*, Aldershot: Ashgate.

Heelas, P. and Woodhead, L., 2005, *The Spiritual Revolution: Why Religion is Giving Way to Spirituality*, Oxford: Blackwell.

Luckmann, T., 1967, *The Invisible Religion: The Problem of Religion in Modern Society*, New York: Macmillan.

Roof, W. C., 1993, *A Generation of Seekers: The Spiritual Journeys of the Baby Boom Generations*, New York: HarperCollins.

Notes

1 Casanova also holds that while secularization theories 'make sense' of particular European developments, the category of secularization becomes problematic when it is 'generalized as a universal process of societal development' and 'transferred to other world religions and other civilizational areas with very different dynamics' (2006, p. 12).

2 In typical Durkheimian fashion, Luckmann believes that 'the decrease in traditional church religion may be seen as a consequence of the shrinking relevance of the values, institutionalized in church religion, for the integration and legitimation of everyday life in modern society' (1967, p. 39).

3 I cite the 2005 reproduction of the original essay (2005, pp. 40–55).

6

Religion, Ideology and Gender

Given their importance to subsequent discussions, this chapter opens with an overview of the classical frames of Marx, Durkheim and Weber through which the ideological character of religion is engaged. Modern developments in respect of religion and ideology are then outlined, with particular attention to the contribution of Talcott Parsons and a case study of Latin American liberation theology. The final section of the chapter reviews both emic (insider) and social-scientific critiques of religion and gender. Feminist theology is first engaged, and the chapter concludes by discussing the place of women in ritual possession practices and conservative religious traditions.

Classical trajectories

The word 'ideology' was coined in the late eighteenth century and literally means the 'science of ideas'.[1] Although originally conceived as the scientific pursuit of ideas free from prejudice, the term 'ideology' quickly became associated with notions of distortion, misrepresentation and outright error. Used by some as a marker of theoretical conviction and by others as a pejorative label of scorn, ideology remains 'one of the most debated concepts in sociology' (Abercrombie, Hill and Turner, 1984, p. 118). Over the years, the analytical purchase of the concept of ideology has been undermined through its generalization and demonization. In respect of its generalization, ideology is employed by some as a synonym for 'culture' and thereby serves as a general reference to values, beliefs and practices which pattern everyday social interaction. By way of its demonization, ideology is used by others to designate the worldviews of totalitarian regimes such as fascism and communism. As the former understanding of ideology is too inclusive, while the latter is too exclusive, neither construal is particularly helpful to the sociological engagement of religion.

Karl Marx

As seen in Chapter 3, the concept of ideology forms a major part of Marx's critique of religion. Without repeating what is said there, it is worth taking a closer look at the structure of Marx's understanding of ideology. In the first instance, Marx's notion of ideology builds upon the general assertion that all forms of knowledge (such as beliefs, concepts, values and ideas) emerge from material contexts which comprise a range of intersecting economic-political and socio-cultural dynamics. For Marx:

> The production of ideas, of conceptions, of consciousness, is at first directly interwoven with the material activity and the material intercourse of men ... The phantoms formed in the human brain are also, necessarily, sublimates of their material life-process ... Morality, religion, metaphysics, all the rest of ideology and their corresponding forms of consciousness, thus no longer retain the semblance of independence. They have no history, no development; but men, developing their material production and their material intercourse, alter, along with this their real existence, their thinking and the products of their thinking. Life is not determined by consciousness, but consciousness by life. (McLellan, 1977, p. 164)

An element of human experience, knowledge arises within given social contexts which directly influence the form and content of all beliefs, concepts, evaluations and ideas about the world. As a product of situated experience, social knowledge is perspectival and thereby never objectively neutral. More than this, however, knowledge is interest-laden. That is, for Marx, knowledge embodies not only a particular intellectual grasp of the world but also the respective sets of interests of those doing the knowing. Because knowledge embodies a range of material, social and moral concerns, it is always serving a particular set of interests; mine rather than yours, theirs as opposed to ours.

To this general understanding of knowledge as ideological (perspectival and interest-laden), Marx adds a particular notion of ideology which draws directly upon his understanding of society as conflictual. As society is unequal, with some groups more powerful than others, the more powerful groups are better placed to assert their given perspective and thereby ensure the dominance not only of their particular worldview but also their specific set of interests. Material power thereby results in ideological domination:[2]

> The ideas of the ruling class are in every epoch the ruling ideas; i.e., the class which is the ruling material force of society is at the same time its ruling intellectual force. The class which has the means of material production at its disposal, has control at the same time over the means of mental production, so that thereby, generally speaking, the ideas of those who lack the means of mental production are subject to it. (McLellan, 1977, p. 176)

In modern capitalist society, says Marx, the ideologically dominant group is the economically powerful 'bourgeoisie' which uses its wealth to wield not just financial but also political, social and cultural influence.

Ideological domination

Marx's notion of ideological domination may profitably be explored from two angles. On the one hand, we can concentrate on the processes of ideological domination and examine their impact upon society at large. On the other hand, we might focus upon those who are ideologically dominated and thereby engage the subjective implications of ideological domination. In respect of the first approach, three aspects of Marx's understanding of ideological domination merit note. First, ideological domination exerts a *directive* influence in that it steers society in one direction rather than another. In so doing, society assumes a particular form which serves the interests of those doing the steering to the detriment of those being steered. Second, ideological domination involves a *cohesive* dynamic through which otherwise disparate, if not antagonistic, groups are persuaded to adopt practices or co-operate in causes which are not immediately theirs or, indeed, may be contrary to their own best interests. Society thereby assumes a more integrated character and unified appearance than its underlying conflictual nature would otherwise warrant. Third, ideological domination has a *mystifying* dynamic through which exploitative practices and oppressive measures are masked or misrepresented as something other than what they actually are. As a result, the fundamental inequalities and systemic injustices of society go unrecognized and thereby uncorrected.

Regarding the subjective aspects of Marx's understanding of ideological domination, three relevant points merit attention. First, when subject to ideological domination, individuals are prone to misrecognizing what is actually occurring. Such *misrecognition*, however, does not simply comprise the failure to perceive what is actually going on. Rather, and perhaps more importantly, it also involves the adoption of beliefs, values and ideas which run contrary to an individual's basic experiences and fundamental interests. Such is the power of ideological domination that those who are subject to it come to see the world not through their own eyes but through the gaze of those by whom they are ideologically dominated. Second, those subject to ideological domination become *alienated* from the aspirations, desires and preoccupations to which their everyday experiences would otherwise give rise. Coined by Engels – Marx's long-term collaborator – and developed by Lukács and others, the notion of 'false consciousness' conveys Marx's understanding that those subject to ideological domination are somehow unable to construe the world in a manner that truly reflects their own experiences and fundamental interests. Third, the inability of the ideologically dominated to perceive themselves as the victims of an inherently conflictual and unequal society results ultimately in *complicity* with their own subordination. Alienated from themselves and failing to grasp matters as they actually are, those subject to ideological domination not only settle for less than they are due but may also actively collaborate both in their own subjection and the subordination of others like them.

Émile Durkheim

For Durkheim, the term ideology has negative connotations. When treating sociological method, for example, Durkheim defines as 'ideological' particular 'pathological' methodologies which confuse ideal and material forms of causation (1982, pp. 86, 168). Despite the differences in terminology and rejection of Marx's conflictual reading of society, however, Durkheim clearly regards social integration as dependent upon something akin to key aspects of what Marx defines as ideology. As noted in Chapter 3, Durkheim believes society to be dependent upon the successful integration of individuals whose natural inclinations militate against rather than tend towards social cohesion. Consequently, society survives by finding ways to make individuals not only forgetful of their own interests but also willing 'to endure all sorts of hardships, privations, and sacrifice without which social life would be impossible' (2001, p. 154).

Importantly, though, a key element in society obtaining the necessary co-operation, compromise and sacrifice is its ability both to mask its true influence and to engender lasting commitment and willingness on the part of its individual inhabitants. 'Too complex for the ordinary observer to perceive their source', social processes generate feelings of communality and responsibility which help sustain the 'collective consciousness' so important to an integrated and cohesive society (2001, p. 157; 1984, pp. 38–9). While rejecting Marx's conflictual framing of ideology, Durkheim nevertheless treats society as functioning best when it exerts a directive, cohesive and mystifying influence which engenders from its subjects misrecognition, complicity and behaviour which, at times, runs 'contrary to our most basic inclinations and instincts' (2001, p. 155).

Max Weber

Unlike Durkheim, Weber does not use the term ideology in a pejorative sense. In rejecting Marx's deterministic reading of religion as an epiphenomenal 'reflection' of material and class interests, however, Weber refuses to treat religion as no more than a 'stratum's "ideology"' (1991d, p. 271). At the same time, Weber echoes classical Marxist usage when he relates the medieval 'Gregorian reform movement and the struggle for power on the part of the papacy' with 'the ideology of an elite intellectual class that entered into a united front with the rising bourgeoisie against the feudal powers' (1963, p. 133). A key difference in Weber's approach compared with Marx resides in his rejection of ideology as a homogenized, monolithic force to which all dominated groups are subject. For Weber, all groups exert a degree of ideological influence, however small it may be for some. At the same time, Weber regards different kinds of religion as more or less conducive to social

change. Orientated to short-term gains and emotional stimulation, the magical and ritualistic religion of the 'cult', for example, militates against transformative 'social action' (1963, pp. 151–65). Likewise, the 'other-worldly'
forms of religiosity mentioned in Chapter 3. Expressed through his concept
of 'elective affinity', Weber also acknowledges the attraction between particular social strata and specific types of religion (1963, pp. 80–137; 1992,
pp. 35–46). And, as with Marx before him, Weber sees traits of passivity
and fatalism in the religiosity of the rural and urban poor.

Exemplified by his concept of 'elective affinity', Weber regards any group's
worldview – or ideology – as a combination of material interests and particular ideas which, in some way, speak to and from a given set of socio-
cultural experiences. On the one hand, ideology rationalizes a group's social
position by furnishing 'legitimation' of, for example, its status, possessions
and power (or lack thereof). Such might be understood as an 'external'
or relational concept of ideology in that the legitimation offered involves
some degree of acknowledgement, however tacit, that status, possessions
and power are relative phenomena of which some groups have more and
others less. On the other hand, ideological legitimation articulates something of the human quest for meaning. Expressing what Weber terms 'the
inner interests' of human beings, the internal aspect of ideology as legitimation meets the psychological need of justification ('theodicy') in the face of
suffering and the vicissitudes of fortune. Be it suffering or salvation, for
example, the ideological legitimation provided by religion meets important
emotional and rational drives by convincing us that we deserve what we're
getting (1991d, pp. 270–6). As with Durkheim, Weber rejects key aspects of
Marx's understanding of ideology. Nevertheless, and again like Durkheim,
Weber agrees with Marx in seeing individuals as carriers of collective representations which have been internalized through socialization and, as a
result, become taken-for-granted readings of the way the world *really* is.

Modern developments

Historically stronger in Europe, the critique of ideology pioneered by Marx
continued after his death to exert an influence upon those within and sympathetic to Marxist traditions. Although the mainstream Marxist tradition
has done most to perpetuate the modern sociological pertinence of ideology (for example Althusser, Gramsci, Lukács and Poulantzas), others such
as Bourdieu, Foucault and Habermas have effectively demonstrated the continuing relevance of ideology critique to neo- and non-Marxist approaches.
As expected, the Marxist tradition's critique of religion as ideology furnishes
a negative assessment of both individual belief and institutional religion. To
Althusser, institutional religion ('church') represents an important part of
the 'Ideological State Apparatus', while for Gramsci religion plays a key role

in preserving the dominant system of power ('hegemonic bloc') (Althusser, 1971, pp. 127–86; Gramsci, 1971). By no means as explicitly dismissive of religion as mainstream Marxist opinion, the approaches of Bourdieu (1991a, pp. 1–44; 1991b, pp. 107–16, 220–8), Foucault (Kritzman, 1988, pp. 211–54; Carrette, 1999, pp. 106–09, 131–52) and Habermas (2002; 2008) nevertheless reflect similar suspicions in respect of religion's ideological character.

North American functionalism

In the United States – where Marxist renderings of ideology initially exerted little by way of positive influence – the alternative conceptualizations of Durkheim and Weber took a variety of paths. In the work of Talcott Parsons and R. K. Merton, for example, the approaches of Durkheim and (to a lesser extent) Weber were refracted through the lens of 'structural functionalism'. Here, emphasis falls upon the institutional mechanisms and cultural processes through which social integration and systemic order are maintained and societal reproduction ensured. It was because of his preoccupation with the contribution of values and norms to the smooth functioning of society that Parsons concerned himself with the role of religion in relation to social order. Indeed, it was Parsons who first translated Weber's *Protestant Ethic* into English and wrote the Introduction to the English edition of Weber's *Sociology of Religion* (1963b, pp. xix–lxvii). Above all, Parsons is interested by the ways in which society patterns the actions of individuals in a manner which ensures social integration and overall structural cohesion (for example 1937, 1951 and 1964). Although mindful of the role of concrete systems and structures, it was the place of collective norms and shared values which most occupied his analytical attentions. As with Durkheim, Parsons regards religion as a fundamental component of society's integrative function and thereby engaged it (principally in the form of Christianity) throughout his academic career (1960, pp. 295–321; 1963a, pp. 33–70; 1966, pp. 125–46; 1968, pp. 425–47; 1979, pp. 1–48).

In respect of religion, and taking the advanced capitalist context of the United States as an exemplary model, Parsons seeks to demonstrate the mistaken nature of Weber's predictions about the disenchantment of urban-industrial society. While agreeing with much of Weber's analysis in respect of the rise and consolidation of modern society (not least, Christianity's part in it), Parsons argues that the experience of the United States falsifies the disenchantment thesis. American society does this because, among other things, it has developed in a way which staves off the triumph of instrumental rationality and the concomitant demise of religion. Adapting the Durkheimian paradigm, Parsons shows how the evolution of American society has enabled religion to continue to play an important role in the propagation of the shared norms and collective values necessary to social integration and societal wellbeing. The US constitution's separation of church and state, for example, allowed religion to evolve in a way which could take account of modernity's transformational rapidity, structural differentiation, socio-cultural pluralism and individualized character. Evidenced by the emergence of a variegated range of religious 'denominations', a now diversified religious landscape is best placed to cope with the challenges of an increasingly fluid social context characterized by pluriform demands and voluntaristic tenden-cies (1960, pp. 295–321; 1963a, pp. 33–70; 1966, pp. 125–46). Treating de-nominational religion as a form of 'institutionalized individualism', Parsons argues that evolutionary adaptations such as this have staved off religion's demise by allowing it to continue to meet society's needs ('functional pre-requisites'); not least that of integration through its facilitation of the shared norms and collective values essential to the maintenance of social order.

Non-functionalist approaches

Beyond the American functionalist tradition and its macro-structural pre-occupations, the likes of Goffman, Garfinkel, Berger and Luckmann have done much to apply Durkheim and Weber's work to the mid-range and micro-social contexts through which knowledge is produced. Augmenting Durkheim and Weber with post-classical approaches (for example George Herbert Mead and Alfred Schutz), these social theorists analyse the ways in which organizational processes and interpersonal dynamics create and sus-tain collective meaning structures through which individual identity is gen-erated, moulded and transformed. Through approaches such as these, the aforementioned insights of Durkheim and Weber were fashioned as central components of a 'sociology of knowledge' which went some way to avoid-ing the structuralist extremes and deterministic excesses of both functionalist and Marxist traditions. In focusing upon the organizational and micro-social dynamics of meaning-making and identity formation, however, the 'sociology of knowledge' failed adequately to engage the overarching issues of power, inequality and exploitation. In so doing, the sociology of know-ledge showed how individual identity is formed through collective social processes but did not sufficiently account for why some identities (e.g. male, white, heterosexual) fare better than others (e.g. female, black, homosexual). In effect, this approach failed to address Marx's assertion that society works to the benefit of some and the detriment of others.

The emancipatory paradigm

From the 1960s onwards, a range of emancipatory approaches emerged, which united the insights of mainstream sociologies of knowledge, nascent conflict theory and left-leaning readings of institutionalized power and social inequality. Exemplified by feminism, but also engaging issues of sexuality, race and class, the emancipatory paradigm furnished critical analyses of societal institutions (e.g. family, education, medicine, religion) and their (re)production of social inequalities which work to the benefit of some and the detriment of others. On the one hand, emancipatory critiques focused on the concrete processes and practices employed by social institutions and their determination of both individual subjectivities and objective life-chances. On the other hand, critical attention was paid to norms and values embodied within taken-for-granted truths ('a woman's place is in the home'), commonsensical assertions ('homosexuality is unnatural') and prevailing assumptions ('whites are more intelligent than blacks'), which both informed and ultimately legitimated the linkage of unequal life-chances with particular subjectivities. In laying bare the concrete practices and ideal construals through which social institutions manufacture and justify inequality, the emancipatory paradigm brought ideology critique back into mainstream sociology yet did so in a way which transcended the analytical deficiencies and theoretical limitations of its classical Marxist framework.

Somewhat ironically, the implications of the emancipatory paradigm for religion were first explored not by sociologists but by theologians – and, to a lesser extent, philosophers – allied with or sympathetic to faith-based communities. The appropriation of sociological insights by religious groups is, of course, nothing new. Less than two decades after the deaths of Durkheim and Weber, religious communities in both Europe and the USA were taking tentative steps towards appropriating the insights of sociology and using them to better understand their respective institutions and the pastoral and demographic terrains in which they work. In France, for example, initial explorations in 'religious sociology' (*sociologie religieuse*) in the early 1930s led to the establishment in 1948 of the International Conference of Religious Sociology (CISR). This organization subsequently mutated into the non-religiously affiliated International Society for the Sociology of Religion (ISSR) (Dobbelaere, 2000, pp. 433–47). Meanwhile, in the United States, the American Catholic Sociological Society (ACSS) was founded in 1938 and, after broadening its ecumenical base, became the Association for the Sociology of Religion (ASR) in 1970 (Swatos, 1989, pp. 363–75). This having been said, the importance of ideology critique to the emancipatory paradigm does make it somewhat ironical that the earliest developed emancipatory critiques of religion came from within rather than outwith faith-based communities.

The impact within religious circles of the emancipatory sociological paradigm is exemplified by the almost concurrent emergence of 'liberation theology', 'black theology' and 'feminist theology' (Gutiérrez, 1974; Cone, 1970; Daly, 1973). These foundational theologies of liberation have since been complemented by 'gay/queer theology', 'womanist theology', 'Third World theology' and assorted theologies of disability. As with the emancipatory paradigm by which they are informed, liberation theologies combine sociology of knowledge and ideology critique. In Latin America, for example, the theology of liberation has offered a trenchant critique of the Roman Catholic Church's traditional alliance with the state and its ensuing complicity in the exploitation of the poor by successive ruling elites. As well as unmasking the structural mechanisms behind the Church's integration within 'the dominant strata of society', liberation theology engages the cultural implications of Catholicism's incorporation of the prevailing 'characteristics of the dominant class' (Boff, 1986, p. 114).

Liberation theology, for example, applies ideology critique to religious imagery of Jesus and the holy family and claims to unmask the ideological functions of particular forms of iconic representation. Imagery representing the 'Dying Christ of Sorrow and Pain' and 'Lord of Happy Death', it is argued, is part of a broader message to the masses that while the lot of the poor is an unhappy one it is, like the agonies of Jesus, to be endured, if not welcomed, as part of God's broader plan of salvation. While fatalism and passivity are conveyed by images such as these, iconic representations of Jesus and the holy family bedecked in the garb of royalty communicate a different message. As seen in the 'Glorious Christ of Monarchical Grandeur', representations of Jesus wrapped in the trappings of power serve to reinforce not only an association of religious power and wealth but also the belief that those who rule do so with heavenly blessing and appropriate earthly reward. Finally, liberation theologians identify iconic representations of the 'Apolitical Christ'. Here, Jesus is conveyed as an otherworldly figure whose message is one of spiritual enlightenment detached from the socio-economic realities of daily life. More than conveying a sense of religious detachment, however, the 'Apolitical Christ' tacitly condemns as unchristian those who mix religion with politics and thereby stand to threaten the *status quo* (Assmann, 1981, pp. 134–45; Bonino, 1984).

Gendering religion

The word 'gender' is a quintessentially sociological term which serves to distinguish socially constructed forms of subjectivity (such as masculinity and femininity) from the biologically determined status of sex (that is male and female). As a pioneer of gender studies asserts, 'human beings are probably more conditioned by their own gender-differentiated upbringing than they are able, or would care, to admit' (Oakley, 1972, p. 210). While the precise relationship between sex and gender has long been a source of debate, sociology is most interested in how different social and institutional construals of perceived biological states result not only in varied forms of gendered subjectivity but also contrasting kinds of role allocation, expectation and opportunity. As noted in Chapter 1, gender differentiation results in the unequal distribution of resources and life chances – a distributive inequality which favours men over women. The values, beliefs and tacit assumptions which underwrite the gendered (and unequal) distribution of resources comprise an ideological matrix most commonly designated as 'patriarchy'.

Since its inception, gender studies has broadened its critical focus to pay increasing attention to variegated forms of sexuality. Consequently, engagement with lesbian, gay, bisexual and transgendered forms of subjectivity represents an important part of gender studies and is the central focus of an emergent 'sociology of sexuality'. A key component of these approaches is critique of the normative heterosexual paradigm in which 'man + woman = *normal*'. The values, beliefs and tacit assumptions which underwrite this paradigm form the ideological nexus of 'heterosexism'. Academic treatments of religion and sexuality are steadily gaining momentum, with ethnographic and sociological studies standing to the fore (Brown, 2004; Browne, Munt and Yip, 2010; Leyland, 2000; Thumma and Gray, 2005). Central to these and other such works is the attempt to understand how those with minority forms of sexuality render their lives meaningful through religious symbols and practices, many of which are imbued with thoroughgoing heterosexual normativity. Consequently, and among other things, these approaches lay bare the strategies, support networks and interpretations employed by individuals to live with, circumvent and, at times, subvert the heterosexist ideologies of mainstream religious repertoires.

Not least allowing for the emergent status of the religion and sexuality paradigm, the overwhelming bulk of studies treating religion and gender focus upon the interface of women and the respective religious repertoires through which their faith is expressed. As with religion and sexuality, academic treatments of religious constructions of masculinity make a relatively minor, but growing, contribution to understanding the interface of religion and gender. Building upon earlier work informed by the emerging field of 'men's studies' (Boyd, Longwood and Meusse, 1996), engagement with the religious construction of masculinity has steadily grown since the turn of the century (Krondorfer, 2009; Ouzgane, 2006; Wilcox, 2004). In combination, works such as these demonstrate religion's part in shaping and reinforcing societal expectations of manhood as expressed, for example, through the roles of father, husband, leader, provider and protector. Although the overall reckoning of gender differentiation clearly shows men benefitting far more than women, these and other studies offer nuanced appreciations of the sometimes constrictive impact of collective expectations in respect of exemplary masculinity.

Emic/insider critiques of gendered religion

In keeping with evolutionary trends, the interface of religion and sexuality was first meaningfully explored from within rather than outwith communities of faith. For many reasons, religious treatments of religion and sexuality have long been undertaken by communities of faith, with discussions usually centring upon the correct interpretation of and appropriate pastoral response to traditional (e.g. scriptural) sources of authority. Towards the close of the twentieth century, however, an important step-change occurred through the pastoral and theological appropriation of the insights of gender critique and the nascent social-scientific reflections of 'queer studies' (Althaus-Reid, 2003; Loughlin, 2007). Complemented by shifting social attitudes to non-standard forms of sexuality, this sociologization of religious treatments of sexuality is progressively reshaping the discourse and practice of religions worldwide – not least those in late-modern urban-industrial contexts.

It was on the emancipatory wave of feminism that the earliest developed critiques of religion and gender first rode. Part of the emancipatory paradigm mentioned above, the feminist movement which arose in the late 1960s is known as 'second wave feminism' on account of the earlier ('first wave') activities of what would ultimately constitute the campaign for women's suffrage. Arising from the increased educational opportunities for women engendered by modern forms of socio-economic organization, the early feminist movement was not blind to religion's contribution to societal processes of gender differentiation. For example, *The Woman's Bible* (1895–98) produced by Elizabeth Cady Stanton (1815–1902) and the 'revising committee' was provoked by the belief that 'the Bible in its teachings degrades women from Genesis to Revelation' (2002). It was not until the emergence of the emancipatory paradigm, however, that a fully developed critique of religion and gender got under way. Again, the earliest thoroughgoing engagements of religion and gender were undertaken by those allied with or belonging to particular communities of faith.

Then philosophical-theologian Mary Daly, for example, wrote a number of books offering analytical critiques of the male-orientated ('androcentric') character of Christian belief and practice (1968; 1973). Paying particular attention to the underlying assumptions and linguistic structures of Christian authority sources, Daly identified Christianity's implicit divinization of masculinity as a key component in its subordination of womanhood. As she asserts, 'if God in "his" heaven is a father ruling "his" people, then it is in the "nature" of things and according to divine plan and the order of the universe that society be male-dominated' (1973, p. 13). Although philosophically inspired, Daly draws on sociological insights into the social construction of gender and both the masking and legitimation of resulting inequalities by the ideology of patriarchy. Throughout, Daly's analysis rests on insights made possible by the social-scientific critique of a predetermined natural order whose inherent hierarchy serves to justify both a particular division of roles and the fact that some roles fare better than others.

Feminist theologies of liberation such as Daly's earlier work have proved heavily reliant for their theoretical guidance upon second and, subsequently, third wave feminisms. Indeed, both the development of and internal fault lines within mainstream feminist theologies very much reflect the evolutionary trajectory, internal debates and programmatic schema which have shaped feminist social theory since its emergence in the late 1960s. For example, feminist theoretical claims that 'the production of knowledge is a social matter' whose processes are shaped by 'socially advantaged groups' such as men (Harding, 1996, p. 148) form an important jumping-off point for a great many feminist theologians. In her treatment of the early Christian community, for example, Fiorenza argues that 'anyone even slightly familiar with problems raised by the sociology of knowledge or by critical theory will have difficulty' in substantiating a claim to be 'objective, free from bias, nonpartisan and scientific' in a neutral sense (1983, p. xvi). Applying Weber's notion of 'routinization' to analyse the progressive institutionalization of the early Christian community, Fiorenza maintains that the egalitarianism of the early Jesus movement was incrementally subverted by its 'gradual patriarchalization' through which women were progressively debarred from wielding religious authority and institutional power. As a result of its sustained practice of 'androcentric selection', Christianity came to view 'the elimination of women from ecclesial office and their marginalization in a patriarchal church as a historical necessity [and] . . . the patriarchal institutionalization process as the only possible and historically viable sociological form of church' (1983, p. 83). Published in the same year as Fiorenza's seminal work, Ruether's *Sexism and God-Talk* identifies the 'ideological deformation' of Christianity wrought by patriarchy (1983, p. 28). By virtue of patriarchy's all pervasive nature, Ruether argues:

> All the categories of classical theology in its major traditions – Orthodox, Catholic, and Protestant – have been distorted by androcentrism. This not only makes the male normative in a way that reduces women to invisibility, but it also distorts all the dialectical relationships of good/evil, nature/grace, body/soul, God/nature by modeling them on a polarization of male and female. (1983, p. 37)

The internal fault lines of feminist social theory are likewise reflected by the feminist theological community. To name but a few, 'liberal', 'difference', 'womanist', and 'postcolonial' articulations of feminist social theory find their direct equivalents within feminist theological circles. In the same vein, the threefold feminist programme of 'deconstruction', 'reconstruction' and 'construction' (Gunew, 1990, p. 23) plays out theologically through attempts to *unmask* androcentric beliefs and practices, *salvage* what has not been vitiated by patriarchy and *formulate* new religious repertoires celebrating all aspects of womanhood (Parsons, S. F., 2002). Although the mainstay of the earliest religious appropriations of feminist social theory occurred within Christian theological circles, Christianity has by no means monopolized the application of feminist insights to religious belief and practice (Starhawk, 1979; Sharma and Young, 1999).

At the very least, the advent of the feminist emancipatory paradigm furnished religionists with a twofold critique. First, the division of labour through which gender differentiation is operationalized can no longer be claimed to rest on natural (here, biological) differences which predispose one sex to one set of roles and the other to a different set. While biological differences clearly exist, the processes of gender differentiation – along with the values, beliefs and assumptions which underwrite them – are now viewed as socially constructed and, as a result, open to change. Second, the inequalities produced by gender differentiation can no longer be justified as legitimate outcomes of pre-existing natural orientations. Consequently, the ideology of patriarchy loses a key plank of its legitimating force and the inequalities it rationalizes can now be viewed as unwarranted injustices in need of correction. In effect, the hermeneutics of social construction furnished by second wave feminists offers a moral platform for revision of the patriarchal beliefs and practices which infuse both traditional and non-mainstream religious repertoires.

Religion and gender in social-scientific perspective

Spirit possession

The preponderance of women impacted by spirit possession has long been a source of academic interest. Offering what he terms a 'sociology of ecstasy' (2003, p. 15), I. M. Lewis' groundbreaking study of spirit possession (first published in 1971) sought to move beyond existing academic frames in which, for example, the overwhelming presence of women in particular forms of possession practice could not be adequately explained. Before outlining his approach, it is worth noting that Lewis – and a great many others – regard the notion of 'othering' or 'alterity' as a central feature of ritualized spirit possession. Upon being possessed by a spirit or god, it is said, the individual in some way ceases to be herself and, in effect, becomes something *other* than what he normally is. Possession, then, *alters* who and what the possessed individual is understood to be. Becoming something other than oneself is important to the ritual effectiveness of spirit possession for two key reasons: authenticity and impunity. First, what individuals say or do when possessed can be regarded as authentic because they are not the ones doing these things but the spirits or gods acting through them. Second, because the spirit or god is the one who is speaking and doing, the possessed individual should not be blamed for what is said and done during the possession episode. However unpalatable it may be, the messenger should not be punished for the message.

Typical of the functionalist paradigm which informs his analysis, Lewis understands spirit possession relative to the role or 'function' it plays in respect of the overarching processes and structures essential to 'social order'. In so doing, Lewis distinguishes between 'central' and 'peripheral' forms of possession religion. Also termed – à la Durkheim – 'main morality possession religions', Lewis argues that 'central possession religions' perform an essentially conservative function in that they legitimate, and thereby uphold, prevailing social systems (2003, p. 29). Because 'central possession religions' are embroiled with existing power structures, women enjoy no special prominence within them. In contrast to central possession religions, however, 'peripheral' forms of spirit possession are populated overwhelmingly by powerless and marginalized members of society. Given 'that in a great many societies, and perhaps most, women are in fact *treated* as peripheral creatures', it is unsurprising that women preponderate in peripheral possession practices (1986, p. 42).

Although uncoupled from mainstream morality – and thereby unconcerned with upholding the status quo – peripheral possession practices, Lewis argues, nevertheless continue to function in a way which conserves rather than undermines prevailing social systems. Such is the case because spirit possession provides a means through which those subordinate within society can make demands, protest or optimize their position in ways which do not ultimately threaten the overarching structures through which they are subordinated. Drawing on a broad range of case studies, Lewis demonstrates how the repertoire of spirit possession furnishes women with opportunity to render manageable prevailing conditions of insecurity, marginality and subordination. Speaking of the possession of Somali tribeswomen by *sar* spirits, for example, Lewis recounts how the hardships and tensions of their precarious existence are ameliorated by the demands of their possessing spirits for gifts such as 'luxurious clothes, perfume, and exotic dainties from their menfolk'. He goes on to say that:

> These requests are voiced in no uncertain fashion by the spirits speaking through the lips of the afflicted women, and uttered with an authority which their passive receptacles can rarely achieve themselves . . . It is only when such costly demands have been met . . . that the patient can be expected to recover. (2003, p. 67)

By providing an outlet for the otherwise irresolvable frustrations, anxieties and grievances of those without recourse to more efficacious means of satisfaction, peripheral possession practices provide an 'institutionalized means' through which potentially destructive socio-cultural pressures can be channelled (Lewis, I., 1986, p. 30). Despite their manifest unpredictability and anarchic appearance, peripheral possession practices fulfil a latently conservative social function. In respect of women, such functionality occurs through possession practices offering a ritualized safety valve which ultimately circumvents the need for a thoroughgoing reform of existing patriarchal structures of inequality and disempowerment.

By situating spirit possession within the unequal power relations of prevailing social systems, Lewis' *Ecstatic Religion* set the scene for much of what was to follow. The vast majority of what followed, though, moved beyond the conservative, functionalist reading of spirit possession offered by Lewis and is, instead, inspired by a variety of post-1960s emancipatory paradigms such as feminist theory, postcolonial studies and subaltern analyses. In respect of gender differentiation, although the focus on power used by Lewis continues centre stage, contemporary approaches are much more inclined to interpret spirit possession through the lens of strategic resistance, self-conscious subversion and constructive appropriation of liberated space (Boddy, 1989; Keller, 2002; Owen, 1989). The spirit possession repertoire, then, is no longer regarded solely as a systemic preservative of androcentric structures, but one that also furnishes opportunity to oppose, circumvent and undermine prevailing patriarchal processes. In addition to rejecting Lewis' understanding of spirit possession as an inherently conservative phenomenon, some scholars have also been at pains to qualify his linkage of many spirit possession practices with peripheral status and powerlessness. Although not denying the relevance of prevailing systems such as patriarchy, these scholars question the often uncritical identification of particular possession practices as straightforward expressions of marginalization and existential despair. Rather than seeing spirit possession as automatically reflecting or making up for some form of androcentric exclusion, they argue, it might better be regarded as just one among a number of available lifestyles which women adopt as a means of self-exploration, subjective expression or communal celebration (Dawson, A., 2011b, pp. 1–20; Sered, 1994).

Conservative religion

The place of women within conservative forms of religion has also been subject to sustained social-scientific reflection over recent decades. One area of debate concerns why traditional religions – with their patriarchal worldviews and strong support of gender differentiation – still manage to attract women whose social, educational and professional background would normally be expected to inhibit their participation in conservative religious repertoires. In respect of Islam, studies by Ahmed (1992), Brenner (1998), Göle (1996) and Mahmood (2005) have explored this issue in relation to the increasing popularity of particular dress-codes (such as veiling) and conservative piety. Importantly, issues such as this are framed within broader debates in respect of the impact of urban-industrial modernization (e.g. structural differentiation, demographic shift, commoditization) upon Muslim societies and the globalization of Islamic fundamentalism. Whereas earlier studies have viewed the adoption of the veil as a straightforward expression of traditional patriarchal religiosity, these approaches treat veiling as an expression of difference (from older generations or Western forms of secularity), solidarity (with global Islam and other women) and fashion-conscious, but non-Western, forms of modernity. Far from being the straightforward and passive manifestation of traditional religious patriarchy, then, the act of veiling – at least for some women – embodies a reflexive and assertive act of self-expression and collective identity.

In respect of Judaism, both Davidman (1993) and Kaufman (1991) focus upon women who have 'converted' or 'returned' to the Orthodox tradition of the Jewish religion. Each interprets their informants' (re)entry into Orthodox Judaism as manifesting a significant dissonance between their individual quests for meaning and a modern social environment characterized by, among other things, individualism, secularity and indeterminacy. Attracted rather than repelled by the gender-differentiated environment of the Orthodox Jewish family, these women see the religious and domestic world into which they've entered as furnishing much-needed clarity in respect of the responsibilities, complementarity and boundedness attached both to their gender and domestic roles as wife and mother. Rather than feeling hemmed in by the rules and restrictions governing their status as Orthodox Jewish women, the respondents to these studies feel valorized by their newfound domestic responsibilities and reassured by the fixity of the expectations by which their roles (and those of their husbands) are governed.

The enhanced estimation of family life and valorization of the female domestic roles which accompany it are likewise evident in the studies of evangelical and conservative forms of Christianity undertaken by Ammerman (1997), Brasher (1998) and Griffiths (1997). As with the aforementioned works on Orthodox Judaism, these studies show that the androcentric exclusion of women from institutional authority roles is compensated by the establishment of female networks and women-only spaces. Whether through formal women-led prayer groups and Bible studies or informal get-togethers around children and charitable activities, men-free spaces provide women with opportunity to enjoy responsibility, practise leadership and gain confidence in contexts free from male interference. At the same time, and despite patriarchal enjoinders to female submission, it is claimed that the narratives at play within conservative Christianity furnish women with a means of relativizing masculine power through appeals to divine authority and leadership which ultimately trump those of the male head of the earthly household.

Conclusion

Appreciations of diffuse forms of power beyond those enshrined in official institutional roles and treatment of the constructive dynamics of individual agency have allowed exploration of aspects of religion and gender which go beyond established stereotypes of the irredeemably patriarchal, heterosexist and androcentric character of traditional religious repertoires. While not underestimating the enduring strength of patriarchal ideologies, heterosexist preoccupations and androcentric practices at play in contemporary religious contexts, aforementioned studies demonstrate the presence of dynamics and processes which allow for the affirmation and support of varied forms of gendered subjectivity. This appears as true for new religions and alternative spiritualities as it does for conservative forms of traditional religiosity (Goldman, 1999; Palmer, 1994). As gendered spaces of belief and practice – and irrespective of their age or provenance – religious repertoires are subject to the same differentiating forces as the myriad secular social contexts through which patriarchal ideologies, heterosexist concerns and androcentric practices are propagated and resisted, reinforced and subverted.

Further reading

Browne, K., Munt, S. R. and Yip, A. K. T. (eds), 2010, *Queer Spiritual Spaces: Sexuality and Sacred Spaces*, Aldershot: Ashgate.

Griffiths, R. M., 1997, *God's Daughters: Evangelical Women and the Power of Submission*, Berkeley: University of California Press.

Keller, M., 2002, *The Hammer and the Flute: Women, Power and Spirit Possession*, Baltimore: The Johns Hopkins University Press.

Mahmood, S., 2005, *The Politics of Piety: The Islamic Revival and the Feminist Subject*, Princeton: Princeton University Press.

Wilcox, W. B., 2004, *Soft Patriarchs, New Men: How Christianity Shapes Fathers and Husbands*, Chicago: University of Chicago Press.

Notes

1 McLellan (1995), Eagleton (1990) and Williams, H. (1988) offer accessible introductions to ideology, while Abercrombie, Hill and Turner (1980), Hall, S. et al. (1978) and Thompson (1984) provide more detailed treatments.

2 For Marx, the inevitability of material dominance resulting in ideological domination owes more to the unintended consequences of objective societal processes than to the subjective dynamics of intentional strategizing on the part of powerful groups.

7

'In with the New':
New Religiosities in Sociological Perspective

Introduction

Excluding the work of a few pioneers (Wilson, 1967), contemporary socio-logical interest in new religions commenced in the 1970s in response to the apparent exponential growth of novel and alternative forms of religiosity. These new forms of religious expression appeared on the back of the counter-cultural movement which bloomed in the 1960s and included, among other things, claims that a 'New Age' was dawning in which traditional, con-servative ways of life would be replaced by innovative and less restrictive modes of existence (Heelas, 1996). At the same time, the impact of accel-erating globalization was beginning to be felt through the progressive ap-pearance of and exposure to spiritual practices and religious beliefs from other parts of the non-industrialized world. Valorized for their strange and exotic character, previously unheard of beliefs and practices were combined with pre-existing modes of Western religiosity to spawn a raft of innovative and unfamiliar religious repertoires. Piqued by the progressive appearance of novel, if not strange-looking, forms of religion, sociological interest in new religious phenomena soon gathered pace and subsequently blossomed into what is still one of the most popular branches of the sociology of religion.

Of course, interest in the emergence of new religious formations has been at the heart of the sociology of religion since its inception. As seen in earlier chapters, Durkheim and Weber were very much preoccupied with explor-ing transformations in traditional institutional religion through reference to new forms of religio-moral expression better suited to the historically pe-culiar demands of modern society. An important insight bequeathed by the classical paradigm is that new religious phenomena are as likely to emerge through the mutation or combination of elements already in situ as they are from the arrival and impact of beliefs and practices from outside a given socio-cultural context. In respect of the modern era, for example, nineteenth-century transformations of the Christian paradigm gave rise to the Church of Latter-day Saints, the Seventh-Day Adventists and the Jehovah's Witnesses.

Furthermore, although the study of new religious movements (NRMs) focuses upon discrete, independent phenomena which exist separately from mainstream traditions, it should not be forgotten that novel religious formations also emerge and remain within existing institutional parameters. The Roman Catholic Charismatic movement and the traditionalist Catholic organization of *Opus Dei* are cases in point. Known commonly as 'renewal' movements – by virtue of remaining within pre-existing organizational structures – these novel phenomena offer much to sociological understanding that is sometimes overlooked in the mass concentration upon non-traditionally affiliated forms of new religiosity.

On account of their strangeness, new religious movements appear intriguing to some (not least academics) and threatening to others. To this extent, the attention to which they have been subjected is thereby understandable. Such attention has, though, been heightened by a series of controversies involving violence and accusations of brainwashing and illegality. In respect of violence, the most notable examples are those of the killings and suicides associated with the Peoples Temple in Jonestown, Guyana (1978), the Branch Davidians in Waco, Texas (1993), the poison gas attack on the Tokyo subway by members of the Japanese new religion of Aum Shinrikyo (1995), and the respective 'exit' events involving the two UFO religions of the Order of the Solar Temple (1995 and 1997) and Heaven's Gate (1997). Although mostly unfounded, charges of brainwashing and/or ensnaring new converts levelled against, for example, the Unification Church (later, the Family Federation), the International Society for Krishna Consciousness (ISKCON) and the Children of God (later, the Family International) heightened both public interest and academic attention. More recently, high-profile converts, political disquiet and legal action in respect of alleged fraud combine to keep the Church of Scientology in the news. Just as traditional religions have their extremes, so too does the new religious spectrum. By and large, however, new religious movements are no less benign than their mainstream religious equivalents.

The interface of religion and society is such that every social environment at some time experiences the emergence of previously inexistent, and thereby strange-looking, forms of religiosity. That new religions are 'new' is neither particularly novel nor of special academic interest. What is important, however, is what the emergence, consolidation and subsequent growth or decline of new religious phenomena tells us about both society in general and religion in particular. While the phenomenon of religious innovation is not historically unprecedented, as typically modern modes of creativity and experimentation, new religious movements can nevertheless be regarded as quintessential signs of the times. Consequently, while their statistical significance may be somewhat smaller than that of mainstream, traditional religion, what we stand to learn from the study of new religious phenomena significantly outweighs their actual size and number.

Understanding new religions

Such is the diversity and fluidity of the field, it seems that each approach to the study of new religious phenomena employs a correspondingly different set of terminology and defining characteristics and identifies as significant a raft of varying causal processes and substantive issues. Academic nomenclature for new religious phenomena is as varied as the subject matter itself. 'New religious movement', 'alternative spirituality', 'new religion', 'new religious consciousness', 'cult', 'sect', 'new age religiosity', 'mystical religion' and 'neo-esoteric religion' are only the most oft-used terms among an ever-growing range of denominational options. A long-time academic of new religions, Eileen Barker notes that 'one cannot generalise' about novel religious phenomena. Her admonition to tread carefully when treating new forms of religious expression is worth quoting at length:

> The only thing that they have in common is that they have been labelled as an NRM or 'cult'. The movements differ from each other so far as their origins, their beliefs, their practices, their organization, their leadership, their finances, their life-styles and their attitudes to women, children, education, moral questions and the rest of society are concerned. Attempts to produce typologies have been limited and . . . do not really help us to anticipate with much certainty the empirical characteristics that might follow from the defining characteristics of each category . . . The ever-increasing range of alternatives from all corners of the world . . . have made neat, predictive models out of date almost before the ink has dried on their author's paper – or the laser has printed from their author's PC. (1999, p. 20)

Despite the many perils involved in naming and defining new religious phenomena, such is their significance as religious signs of modern times that the theoretical risks involved are far outweighed by the conceptual insights engendered by their academic engagement. At the same time, the second sentence of Barker's quote offers some very helpful guidance concerning some of the most useful categories which may be employed in the formulation of classifications or typologies of new religious movements. Sociologically speaking, though, some categories are better than others.

Classificatory approaches

Employing a simple chronological criterion to define as 'new' any religious group which emerges after a particular point in time, for example, tells us nothing of substance about these groups or in what ways they compare or contrast with other religious phenomena of the same era. In the study of Japanese new religions (such as the Church of World Messianity, Perfect Liberty Kyodan, Seicho-no-Ie and Soka Gakkai), such has been the limitation of chronologically informed definitions that scholars now talk of 'new', 'new, new' and 'new, new, new' religious phenomena (Clarke, 2000). In the same vein, while classifying new religions relative to their origins gives some indication of the different kinds of beliefs and practices at play, it does not in itself reveal much that is sociologically significant. If a simple derivative classification were employed, for example, organizational or demographic similarities between new religiosities of Buddhist (such as Ambedkarite Buddhism), Islamic (such as the Bahá'í faith) or Pagan (such as Druidism) inspiration might too easily be overlooked, while differences within groups of shared origins (such as the Hindu-derived movements of ISKCON and Transcendental Meditation) might also be ignored.

The same goes for thematic classifications which categorize new religions relative to the principal characteristics or chief preoccupations of their religious repertoires. Here, then, extra-terrestrial organizations (such as Heaven's Gate, Order of the Solar Temple, the Raëlians, the Unarians), esoteric religions (such as Anthroposophy, Rosicrucianism, Theosophy) and spirit-based movements (such as Kardecism, Spiritualism, Umbanda) may be distinguished relative to their particular beliefs and practices.[1] In addition to suffering the same analytical limitations as chronological and originary approaches, thematic classifications are further undermined by the typically hybrid character of new religions which results in many of their repertoires exhibiting a broad range of themes, ritual characteristics and theological preoccupations found in other groups. A good number of the aforementioned groups, for example, acknowledge extra-terrestrial existence, contain esoteric material and engage in some form of spirit-orientated activity. Given the analytical limitations of singular classificatory criteria such as those relating to chronology, derivation and repertorial content, some scholars augment their approach with reference to other factors which help flesh out the phenomenon being engaged. Chryssides (1999) and Melton (2004, pp. 16–35), for example, employ a 'positional' or 'relational' understanding of new religious movements which analyses them relative to the dominant – and thereby mainstream – religion(s) of any given social context.

Sociologically speaking, though, the most fruitful kinds of typological classification establish a direct linkage between the specific types in play and the particular modes of social action – both corporate and individual – to which these types are most inclined. By and large, the most influential typologies of new religious phenomena employed by the sociology of religion have been those related to the tripartite framework of 'church, sect and cult' and those formulated under the influence of 'New Religious Movement' theory.

Church, sect and cult

The most enduring classification of new religious phenomena involves their typological comparison with the classic Western form of religious organization known technically as 'church'. The notion of 'church' is used by Durkheim and Weber, with the former characteristically stressing its unifying nature around a 'common conception of the sacred world and its relation to the profane world' which is also expressed through shared ritual practices (2001, pp. 42–3). For Weber, the concept of church is defined principally in opposition to his notion of 'sect', although he also uses the term 'cult' to describe other forms of 'ritualistic' religiosity which lack systematic order and focus chiefly on heightened emotional states and short-term gains for the individual (1963, pp. 151–65). Embroiled with existing political structures (the state), the church caters for all members of society – 'necessarily including both the just and the unjust' – who, because of their socialization, become members as a matter of course. Known also as 'the believer's Church', the 'sect' constitutes a breakaway movement from the dominant church, and is exemplified by 'the Baptist sects', which broke away from the Protestant Reformation churches of, for example, Lutheranism and Calvinism. Initially, of course, by virtue of their break from the prevailing organizational auspices of the Roman Catholic Church, Protestant groups such as Lutheranism and Calvinism formerly constituted sects themselves. Unlike the church, because sects function 'solely as a community of personal believers of the reborn', they are voluntary organizations for which membership is acquired through a conversion experience involving the conscious decision to opt in (through baptism) and thereby opt out of established social norms and practices. Again in contrast to church forms of membership, belonging to a sect involves an 'ascetic pursuit of salvation' which is characterized by a heightened concern with personal striving and subjective experience orchestrated to and by 'the working of the Divine Spirit in the individual'. Unallied with – if not, at times, persecuted by – prevailing state structures, sects reject 'a sinful attachment to the world' and thereby stand in tension to dominant political-economic and socio-cultural paradigms (Weber, 1992, pp. 144–5, 152, 254–5).

Much of what Weber says is made explicit by his pupil and eventual colleague Ernst Troeltsch, who offers 'two different sociological types' by way of '"Church" and "Sect"'. For Troeltsch, the church is 'overwhelmingly conservative' in that it 'accepts the social order' and 'desires to cover the whole life of humanity'. Aspiring to be 'universal' in its reach, the church finds it 'impossible to avoid making a compromise with the state, with the social order, and with economic conditions'. As an 'integral part of the existing social order', the 'Church both stabilizes and determines the social order'. In so doing, the church enjoys access to power and wealth – which, in turn, support well-developed and professionally led institutional structures – but does so at the cost of becoming 'dependent upon the upper classes, and upon their development'. Informed by its universal reach and earthly alliances, the church enjoys the virtually automatic adherence of its members and embodies 'an average morality which is on relatively good terms with the world' and which makes no exacting demands of members in respect of 'personal effort and service'.

In contrast, sects are 'comparatively small groups' whose 'attitude towards the world, the State, and Society may be indifferent, tolerant, or hostile'. By virtue of 'their greater independence of the world', sects may adopt radical, if not oppositional, postures including 'a purely religious attitude towards life which is not affected by cultural influences'. At the same time, a sect does not enjoy the church's access to a readymade constituency of adherents nor does it draw upon the same connections and material resources. Because 'an individual is not born into a sect' but 'enters it on the basis of conscious conversion', a sect is 'a voluntary community'. Directly connected with its voluntary character, a sect employs exclusive criteria of membership, including rigorous, if not 'extremely exacting', claims upon 'individual personal effort' (Troeltsch, 1931, pp. 328–43).

The twofold typology bequeathed by Weber and Troeltsch presents the category of church as the established, mainstream religious tradition of any given society and is intended to apply as much to the European context (such as Roman Catholicism, Anglicanism and Lutheranism) as any other (such as Buddhism, Hinduism and Sunni and Shia Islam). In its turn, the notion of sect applies to new religious movements which originate within but ultimately break away from the prevailing church to exist as an independent organizational entity. Although Weber and Troeltsch focus upon post-Reformation forms of Protestant Christianity, they might just as easily have engaged the Church of Latter-day Saints, the Seventh-Day Adventists and the Jehovah's Witnesses. In the same vein, aforementioned groups such as the Ambedkarites, Bahá'ís and ISKCON would be regarded, respectively, as Buddhist, Islamic and Hindu sects. Prior to discussing the limitations of such an approach, a number of important modifications to the church–sect typology should be noted.

Modern adaptations

The two most important modifications of the church–sect typology arise both from its application to the United States and the desire to account for new religious phenomena which arise not as breakaway movements from established religion but as independent amalgams of otherwise disparate sources. In respect of the United States, in 1929 H. Richard Niebuhr nuanced the twofold typology by the addition of the concept of 'denomination' (1957). As noted above with reference to Lutheranism and Calvinism, Weber and Troeltsch were fully aware that today's sect (breakaway movement) could become tomorrow's church (established religion). Niebuhr adopts this developmental insight and applies it to the secular-pluralist American context in which the notion of established church does not exist. Rather than becoming a church, then, sects develop into denominations. While not enjoying the benefits of state patronage and having to compete in a voluntaristic and pluralist environment, denominations nevertheless have many of the aforementioned organizational, social and moral characteristics of the church-type. As with Fiorenza in Chapter 6, Niebuhr uses Weber's notion of 'routinization' to track the transformation of a newly formed group into an organizational unit whose once person-centred ('charismatic'), zealous and ad hoc features have assumed an institutional tenor characterized by impersonal ('bureaucratic'), rationalized and rigid authority structures.

Such occurs, argues Niebuhr, through a combination of inter-generational development, social mobility, normative integration and the everyday demands of organizational survival and growth. In the first instance, Niebuhr argues that subsequent generations born into a group cannot share the zeal of the sect's founder-members, who will have had to break ties and make personal sacrifices in order to create their movement. Second, the ascetic preoccupation identified by Weber as characteristic of sects results in material prosperity and a social respectability which accompanies it. This, in turn, involves an increased embroilment in the profane world which entails both the management and enjoyment of the goods and status accrued. As a result, the indifferent or hostile posture of sect members is gradually replaced by a less oppositional ethos which both reflects and is invested in prevailing norms, practices and values. Fourth, as with any movement which survives over time and expands through space, organizational mechanisms and institutional structures are needed to ensure, for example, continuity of practice, identity maintenance and authority management. In combination, says Niebuhr, these four factors ensure that a successful sect will soon acquire a number of church-type characteristics which, in the secular-pluralist context of the United States, constitute it as a 'denomination'.

Although each of the four factors identified by Niebuhr is open to differing levels of critique, his nuancing of the church–sect typology was an important step in applying its basic insights to the period of increasingly rapid social transformation occurring after the time of the typology's initial elaboration. The most significant elaboration of this model made after Niebuhr is that of J. Milton Yinger's sixfold typology (1957); itself subsequently modified in a later work (1970). In effect, Yinger splits each of Niebuhr's three types (church, denomination and sect) into two and distinguishes each relative to their inclusivity and experiential preoccupations. The first two types of religious organization are different kinds of church: the 'universal church' and the 'ecclesia'. These 'church' types are distinguished by nothing more than their assumed geographical remit, with the latter existing as a form of national church (such as the Russian Orthodox

Church) and the former enjoying international stature (such as the Roman Catholic Church). The 'denomination' (such as Baptists) and 'established sect' (such as Seventh-Day Adventists) comprise Yinger's third and fourth types and are differentiated relative to their exclusivity and experiential emphases. More exclusive and experiential still are the fifth and sixth types of 'sect' and 'cult'. Whereas the sect (such as Pentecostal Christianity) derives from traditional, mainstream religion, the cult (such as Scientology) arises independently through the conglomeration of variegated sources and otherwise discrete beliefs and practices.

The notion of 'cult' is employed by both Durkheim and Weber but is not used to designate a distinct form of social organization. Although employed later by others, it was not until Yinger that the representation of 'cult' as a form of religious organization independent of 'church' and 'sect' became formally established. Thus, while a sect emerges as a breakaway movement from a church and thereby derives its initial identity from its originary source, a cult emerges as an independent entity. Undoubtedly influenced by some sources more than others, nevertheless the organizational structures, attitude to society, moral ethos and religious repertoire of the cult comprise more a creative amalgam of otherwise disparate elements than a straightforward derivation from a principal source. Consequently, although the Jehovah's Witnesses and the Church of Scientology each represent a new religious movement, the former's derivation from Christianity makes it a sect while the latter's extra-institutional evolution makes it a cult.

In his influential typology of Christian 'sects', Wilson formulates a classification informed by a group's organizational 'response to the world' (1970). Following Weber, Wilson argues that a group's understanding of salvation ('theodicy') directly impacts upon its organizational orientation to society at large. Excluding a small number of groups which defy neat classification, Wilson identifies seven distinct types of neo-Christian sect whose organizational repertoires and engagement with the world reflect particular construals of the ways and means of salvation. 'Conversionist' groups (such as the Salvation Army and Pentecostalism) are evangelistic and experientially focused, stressing the need for personal renewal which is expressed through emotionally charged subjective states. 'Revolutionist' or 'Adventist' movements (such as Christadelphians, Seventh-Day Adventists and Jehovah's Witnesses) espouse a millenarian worldview in which salvific renewal is achieved by the obliteration of the existing world order through often cataclysmic events climaxing with the arrival of the heavenly messiah. 'Introversionist' sects (such as the Amish) concentrate their attentions upon the creation of a spiritually pure environment which is best realized through separation from the world. 'Manipulationist' or 'gnostic' groups (such as Christian Science) employ esoteric repertoires orientated to self-mastery and individual enlightenment through the acquisition of restricted knowledge. By virtue of their individualistic concerns, these groups tend to lack a well-developed communal ethos.

'Thaumaturgical' sects emphasize the miraculous advantages of faith which are expressed, for example, through healing, good fortune and overall well-being. 'Reformist' movements (such as the Quakers) engage the world with a view to ameliorating its worst excesses through charitable activities, which benefit both recipients and executors. Finally, 'utopian' groups are communally orientated and regard their mission as an exemplary one of showing the world what can be achieved through lives of solidarity and collective piety. Although not as inner-worldly as 'reformist' movements, 'utopian' groups are neither as other-worldly as 'introversionist' sects nor as hostile to the profane world as 'revolutionist' organizations.

Typological limitations

Although other types continued to be used, from the late 1950s the threefold typology of 'church, sect and cult' became the staple analytical framework for discussing new religious phenomena. Undermined by sustained criticism and changes in intellectual fashions, however, only the most committed academics continue to employ this analytical frame when treating new religious phenomena (Dawson, L., 1998; 2010, pp. 525–44). In respect of the typology's limitations, three principal points merit attention. First, and although church is an ideal type meant to represent any religious tradition which is institutionally dominant, some scholars object to its overtly Christian-sounding character. Calling Buddhism, Hinduism or Islam a church is, for some, an unwarranted imposition of a term and model developed within and for the Christian context of the Western world. Second, the processes of structural and social differentiation – resulting both in the disestablishment of state and religion and massive socio-cultural pluralization – have rendered the model out of date. Given the analytical centrality of church for an understanding of sect and cult, it is argued, it does not make sense to continue using this tripartite model in contexts where established religion has ceased to be the norm. Third, and while never intended as a pejorative label, the term cult has come to assume a distinctly negative tenor. Clearly, it may be argued that popular misapprehension should not be allowed to impinge unduly upon the 'agnostic' approach of social science (see Chapter 2). However, the academic enterprise is not undertaken in a vacuum, and scholars have an onerous responsibility to ensure where possible that the terms and concepts employed are not unduly offensive to the communities of interest to whom they apply.

NRM theory

The marginalization of the 'church, sect and cult' typology coincided with the adoption of social-movement theory as the principal means of analytically framing new religious phenomena.[2] In actuality, the term 'new religious movement' (NRM) is a direct parallel of the concept of 'new social movement' (NSM). Broadly speaking, a social movement comprises a collective endeavour (of variable size) which exists beyond prevailing institutional structures and is organized around or orchestrated in view of a common interest or goal (Della Porta and Diani, 1999). For our purposes, three central concerns of social-movement theory can be highlighted:

1 What constitutes a social movement and the different kinds of social movement there are.
2 The conditions that give rise to social movements and why some social movements fare better than others.
3 The kinds of people who join social movements, what their motivations are and what modes of collective behaviour and individual participation pertain.

When applied to the study of new religious movements, these concerns have typically been manifested through:

1 The articulation of definitions and types of novel religious phenomena.
2 Consideration of the societal context and organizational repertoires which affect the emergence and success or failure of groups.
3 Engagement with member profiles, participatory patterns and individual trajectories (such as joining, belonging and leaving).

As will be seen below, these distinct sets of analytical concerns often overlap in the treatment of actual new religious movements. For example, a particular kind of NRM may be typologized relative to its organizational interaction with society or dominant modes of membership management.

Worldly orientations

Noting the similarities between Wilson's typology and that developed by Yinger (1970), Roy Wallis proposes a threefold classification encapsulating the 'ways in which a new religious movement may orient itself to the social world into which it emerges'. Defining these three typological orientations as 'world-affirming', 'world-rejecting' and 'world-accommodating', Wallis maintains that:

A new movement may embrace the world, affirming its normatively approved goals and values; it may reject that world, denigrating those things held dear within it; or it may remain as far as possible indifferent to the world in terms of its religious practice, accommodating to it otherwise, and exhibiting only mild acquiescence to, or disapprobation of, the ways of the world. (1984, p. 4)

Within the class of world-rejecting new religions, Wallis includes ISKCON, the Children of God and the Unification Church. These movements share a number of characteristics with Wilson's 'revolutionist' and 'introversionist' types and also have a proselytizing agenda and a strong ethic of self-sacrifice for the community and service to its leader. Lacking 'most of the features traditionally associated with religion', the 'world-affirming type' is individualistic in orientation and regards itself as optimizing the inner powers of human potential. To this extent, it resembles Wilson's 'manipulationist' type. Exemplified by the likes of Transcendental Meditation and Soka Gakkai, world-affirming religion does not oppose society at large but, at the same time, is not principally orientated to its reformation. Instead, the inner perfectibility of the individual is stressed along with the optimization of her ability to benefit more readily from the opportunities, goods and experiences which the everyday world presents. Whereas the world-rejecting type expects the prevailing order to be replaced by a future reality, the world-affirming movement emphasizes the here and now as the means through which individual potential is realized. In contrast to both of these types, the 'world-accommodating' new religion (such as neo-Pentecostalism and the Charismatic Renewal Movement) pays little heed to rejecting or working with the given social order. Similar in emphasis to Wilson's 'conversionist' groups, world-accommodating movements focus upon the spiritual development of the individual which is experienced through heightened subjective states of a deeply intimate and publicly expressive nature.

Although the title of Wallis' book is redolent of Durkheim's classic work on religion, the intentions behind his typology are distinctly Weberian. In keeping with the best typologies of new religious movements, Wallis' overarching aim is to establish a direct linkage between the specific types in play and the particular modes of social action – or lack thereof – to which these types are most inclined (see also Stark and Bainbridge, 1985). As the groups in question are, above all, religiously motivated, their typological classification must take account not only of their concrete organizational arrangements but also the religious worldview – along with its beliefs and practices – which informs both collective and individual action. In Weberian terms, then, the most fruitful typologies of new religions succeed in articulating an 'elective affinity' (see Chapter 3) between different modes of organizational behaviour – both corporate and individual – and the religious worldviews to which they give concrete expression.

Contributory factors

The emergence of new religions comprises far more than the actual appearance of novel religious institutions, movements and groups at any given time or place. On the one hand, macro-structural (e.g. legal and economic) conditions must be such as to furnish an overarching environment conducive to the establishment and survival of non-mainstream religious phenomena. On the other hand, appropriate micro-social (associational and subjective) dynamics must exist which facilitate individuals perceiving new religiosities as viable options *for me*. As the activity of new religions occurs in relation to macro-structural processes and micro-social dynamics, a rounded appreciation of novel religious phenomena furnishes insight not only into their organizational arrangements and religious repertoires but also into the economic-political and socio-cultural conditions which make their existence possible.

Macro-structural conditions

The emergence of new religious movements in the modern epoch is directly related to the all-embracing transformations unleashed by rapid and large-scale urban-industrialization. For example, widespread demographic change and disruption of prevailing modes of socio-cultural reproduction have both uprooted established social patterns and eroded long-standing traditions. In combination with other modern processes – not least individualization – these dynamics increasingly dispose individuals to entertain, if not adopt, practices and beliefs which are either new or had been previously ruled out as beyond the pale. In the same vein, the structural differentiation of state and religion and subsequent erosion of traditional privileges, protections and subsidies enjoyed by 'official' religion have created a leveller playing field on which new forms of religious expression can compete more evenly with their mainstream counterparts. At the same time, the internal forces of structural differentiation (which spawn new social strata and sub-cultures) meld with the external influences of globalization (which bring new peoples, practices and beliefs) to create progressively plural socio-cultural contexts. Overall, modernity has engendered individuals disposed to the new, furnished myriad novelties by way of content and demand and provided environmental conditions wholly conducive to religious innovation.

Institutional contributions

Irrespective of prevailing societal conditions, however, new religious movements must be organizationally equipped to exploit their social environment if they are to ensure survival and secure actual growth. Appropriating insights from social-movement theory, William Bainbridge (1997) and Rodney Stark (1996, pp. 133–46) have done much to explore what they regard as the 'supply side' activities of new religious movements (Stark and Bainbridge, 1985; 1987). Along with their fellow 'religious economists' (see Chapter 8), Bainbridge and Stark take their cue from social-movement theory and focus upon the organizational activity of new religious movements as a key component which determines their success or failure. Such organizational activity is important, it is argued, because new religions enjoy neither the privileges and protections traditionally afforded their mainstream counterparts nor the support of the socio-cultural buoyancy provided by traditional patterns of socialization. So if they are to survive and flourish in the highly competitive environment of late-modern pluralistic society, new religious movements must be highly efficient in optimizing their position. Three aspects of the organizational activity of NRMs are worthy of note.

First, new religions must be very good at mobilizing the usually limited resources they have available. While personnel (members and their experience and contacts) and material goods (finance and property) are the most obvious examples, organizational networks and whatever public goodwill is available are also important resources to be mobilized. New religious resource mobilization might also involve exploitation of the myriad opportunities offered by recent technological advances in communications media. In Brazil, for example, neo-Pentecostal groups have gone so far as to purchase television and radio stations to ensure the efficient propagation of their message. The medium of the internet, however, is by far the most popular form of communicational resource used by new religious movements in Brazil. Aware of the growing importance of the internet among actual adepts and potential constituencies, new religious movements are increasingly willing to invest in the relatively inexpensive costs of site design and maintenance. Given the geographical vastness of Brazil and the attendant problems (time and expense) of travelling across the country, the mobilization of internet resources rewards institutional investment by massively broadening the scope of organizational reach. Indeed, such is the nature of the internet that groups strong in technical expertise but small in numerical size can project a virtual image which greatly belies their modest real-time status. By posting well-presented pages and carefully crafting sites to optimize the capture of internet searches, new religious groups are able to trawl cyberspace in a way which maximizes participant returns relative to initial development costs and the ongoing expenses of site maintenance (Dawson, A., 2007).

Second, new religious movements must be attuned to navigating and exploiting prevailing political opportunity structures. For example, strategic alliances with powerful status groups offer important access to political decision-making processes. Likewise, marrying one's cause (legalization or grant access) to dominant modes of political rhetoric (individual liberties or multiculturalism) further aids the likelihood of organizational success. In addition to reflecting its progressive denominationalization, for example, the renunciation of polygamy by mainstream Mormonism embodies a strategic move designed to facilitate political accord between Latter-day Saints and US federal structures. In recent decades, new religious movements have been quick to exploit the opportunities presented by the shrinkage of central state institutions and the growth of civil society orchestrated by late-capitalist neo-liberal economic policies. Whether as social charities, pedagogical associations or environmental foundations, new religious organizations have adopted juridical identities and institutional structures designed explicitly to enhance their social standing and increase potential funding streams.

Third, new religious movements must work hard at presenting an image of themselves which sits well with society in general and potential members in particular. The manner in and extent to which organizations, like individual human beings, manage their appearance to ensure that the best possible image is projected has been expressed by social-movement theory through concepts such as 'framing' and 'collective impression management'. Concepts such as these help articulate the manner in which new religious movements optimize organizational returns by ensuring the continued 'alignment' of their 'collective' image with their respective social environments. Whether perceived in terms of financial gain, numerical growth, structural expansion or ideological success, maximal organizational return is dependent upon some form of self-conscious management of a projected image capable of adapting to changing circumstances and thereby optimizing prevailing conditions.

Micro-social processes

Some of the earliest treatments exploring why people join new religious movements were undertaken against the backdrop of secularist scientific positivism and established functionalist paradigms. In the first instance, social psychologists and psychiatrists who studied the act of religious conversion – through which a previously non-religious individual assumes an explicitly religious identity – regarded it as fundamentally irrational. Such was the case because it was presupposed that modern, urban-industrial existence and its attendant scientific advance had rendered obsolete religious modes of experience and explanation. Second, the dominance of the functionalist paradigm ensured that the kinds of break from the normative value system entailed by conversion to new religious movements were regarded as 'deviant' forms of behaviour to be explained by some form of dysfunction either on the part of the system (non-integration) or the individual (delinquency). In combination (though functionalist emphases tended to dominate), these approaches influenced much of what followed in that the prevailing perspective upon conversion to new religions tended to regard it as a 'psychopathological' act born of some sort of systemic deprivation or individual deficiency (Stark, 1971, pp. 165–76). There can be little doubt that much of the 'brainwashing' controversies of the 1970s stemmed from psychopathological assumptions about 'vulnerable' (maladjusted) individuals lured into deviant behaviour by 'disreputable' (dysfunctional) elements.

With the break-up of the functionalist paradigm and the resurgence of sociology of religion, the dominance of psychopathological readings of conversion to NRMs was slowly undermined through their progressive modification and eventual rejection in favour of agency-centred perspectives. In respect of their modification, the work of John Lofland has been central in understanding conversion to NRMs as comprising a range of factors which expand upon simple explanations of systemic deprivation or individual maladjustment (Lofland and Stark, 1965, pp. 862–75; Lofland and Skonovd, 1981, pp. 373–85). Known as the 'world-saver' model, Lofland's understanding of conversion sees it as resulting from two related sets of dynamics, one individual, the other contextual. In respect of individual 'predisposing conditions', Lofland identifies: subjective experiences of 'tension' or 'strain' ('*anomie*' in the functionalist tradition) through which the individual is in some way estranged from prevailing norms and practices; subjective tendencies to religious – as opposed to scientific or political – 'problem-solving' as a personal mode of signification and explanation; and an individual bent to 'seekership' expressed through a willingness to look beyond existing organizational arrangements and entertain alternative, non-mainstream approaches. In the absence of conducive contextual circumstances, however, such individual predispositions inevitably come to nought. Such 'situational factors' include: a 'turning point' in which – like the above notion of 'tension' or 'strain' – embodies some form of break (unemployment or migration) with prevailing arrangements; the establishment of 'cult affective bonds' as cordial relationships, friendships and social networks are established with existing members of a new religious organization; the status of 'extra-cult affective bonds' including a weakening of ties with existing social networks or association with others who are also seeking new kinds of relationship; and, finally, some form of 'intensive interaction' with the newly joined group through which nascent bonds are strengthened and new patterns of behaviour and signification established. Subject to criticism and modified over the years, the basic thrust of the 'world-saver' model nevertheless remains an influential component in ongoing discussions about conversion to new religious movements (Dawson, L., 1998, pp. 72–101; Snow and Machalek, 1984, pp. 167–90).

Contemporary treatments of participation in NRMs very much reflect shifting analytical fashions from system-framed to agency-centred approaches. In South America, for example, scholars of new religions note how modern transformations of established individual–collective dynamics have radically modified traditional relationships between religious communities and their respective participants. With emphasis shifting from collective to individual expectation, it is argued, individuals are increasingly interacting with religious movements relative to subjective criteria guided by immediate experience and orientated to personal fulfilment (Dawson,

A., 2007). As late modernity progressively relativizes collective expectation and the individual obligations it entails, the quest for self-fulfilment increasingly constitutes a key dynamic of participation in collective modes of religious expression. Geared increasingly to subjective needs and aspirations, rather than collective expectations and corporate norms, individual participation in religious organizations loses both its life-long and exclusive character.

Discussing the implications of the modern individual's liberation from the 'compulsory ties and loyalties' that once constituted traditional religious belonging, Leila Amaral notes that many new religious participants 'tend to embrace a diversity of discourses, abandoning unitary systems of meaning and combining symbols from different codes and cultural sources irrespective of disjunctions and syncretism' (2000, p. 19). Released from the traditional confines of collective determination, the individual is now freer than ever to pick and choose whatever practical, theoretical or moral resources are best suited to personal predilections and idiosyncrasies. No longer bound to accept ready-made belief systems on a 'take it or leave it' basis, the modern self has become a 'bricoleur' par excellence as she mixes and matches otherwise disparate elements from an increasingly plural sociocultural environment (Magnani, 2000, pp. 12, 88).[3]

In addition to the process of bricolage, contemporary transformations of religious belonging have also resulted in an increased rate of individual transit between religious groups and organizations. Subject to much attention by sociologists of new religion in Brazil, 'religious transit' is characterized by successive switching between and concurrent participation in assorted groups and organizations (Dawson, A., 2005). No longer bound by traditional loyalties and received obligations, the contemporary individual is freed from established patterns of religious belonging that once saw institutional ties and organizational commitments as both life-long and exclusive.[4] In her study of 'mystical-esoteric' participants in and around Brasília, for example, Deis Siqueira notes that the average individual has been involved in 3.2 groups, with this number rising to an average of 5.7 for those between 43 and 49 years of age (2003, p. 109). In the same vein, new religions scholars in other parts of the world note the relatively high turnover of participants which occurs across new religious movements (Bromley, 2006, pp. 42–64).

Instead of regarding conversion to new religions as a form of deviant behaviour or reflecting some kind of systemic dysfunction, contemporary approaches place much of their emphasis upon understanding religious participation as a manifestation of individual agency and subjective expression. At the same time, the increased visibility of NRMs has facilitated both the gradual erosion of their stereotypically sinister profile and their progressive normalization as licit modes of religious expression. In tandem, the typically individualized dynamics of religious transit and the incremental sanitization of NRM profiles conspire to make conversion to new religions both less dramatic and all-embracing. Nevertheless, and along with the recruitment activities and membership profiles of NRMs, individual motives for joining and the behaviour of adepts once they are members remain important focal points of contemporary academic treatments of new religions.[5]

Conclusion

By virtue of their non-mainstream status and counter-cultural ethos, the study of new religious phenomena furnishes insight into the nature of both marginal and minority means of socio-cultural signification and practice. It also engenders an appreciation of societal change through the study of, for example, novel modes of social integration and collective participation, contemporary manifestations of disenchantment and protest, and alternative expressions of lifestyle choice and individual experimentation. Institutional and inter-personal dynamics can also be explored through the study of new religions, along with group formation, the maintenance of collective identity, membership and belonging, leadership styles, the use of violence and the making of authority claims. In addition, the rapid emergence and growth – and sometimes equally rapid decline – of certain NRMs furnishes a bounded opportunity to analyse the concrete impact of the otherwise extended processes and overarching dynamics of modern societal transformation. All in all, the study of new religious phenomena sheds light not only upon the present status and possible future of religion, but also upon the nature and potential directions of the societal forces and dynamics which have spawned them. In effect, new religious phenomena are barometers of religious change in particular and societal transformation in general. It is because new religious movements have an analytical significance well in excess of their actual numerical size that academic attention continues to be trained so intently upon them.

Further reading

Dawson, L. L., 1998, *Comprehending Cults: The Sociology of New Religious Movements*, Toronto: Oxford University Press.

Gallagher, E. V. and Ashcroft, W. M. (eds), 2006, *Introduction to New and Alternative Religious Movements in America*, vol. 1, Westport: Praeger Press.

Lewis, J. R. (ed.), 2004, *The Oxford Handbook of New Religious Movements*, Oxford: Oxford University Press.

Wallis, R., 1984, *The Elementary Forms of the New Religious Life*, London: Routledge & Kegan Paul.

Wilson, B. and Cresswell, J. (eds), 1999, *New Religious Movements: Challenge and Response*, London and New York: Routledge.

Notes

1 The adjective 'esoteric' is derived from the Greek word for 'inner' (*esoteros*), and when applied to religious phenomena it is generally used in contrast to 'exoteric' (outer) knowledge. This contrast founds a distinction between an exclusive corpus of *inner* knowledge and practice available only to initiates and a general body of *outer* knowledge and practice available to all and sundry. Exemplified by the new religion of Scientology, esoteric discourse and practice embodies elements of exclusivity, custodial responsibility, secrecy, initiation and hierarchy.

2 Arising in the 1950s, social-movement theory furnished a number of insights which were drawn upon by scholars who continued to use the church–sect–cult typology. As such, social-movement theory and the threefold typology were and are not mutually exclusive.

3 The French term *bricoleur* refers to someone who does handiwork and repairs by combining bits and pieces left over from prior jobs and was employed by Lévi-Strauss to formulate the concept of 'bricolage' (1966). As appropriated by academics of new religion, bricolage refers to the ongoing construction and reformulation of individual belief systems through the appropriation and combination of elements (practical and conceptual) from a variety of different sources. Although many of these sources may regard themselves as mutually exclusive, the key point is that their subjectively orchestrated combination makes sense to and for the individual concerned.

4 Of course, religious conversion and the switching from one faith allegiance to another are not exclusively late-modern phenomena; nor as African-Brazilians have shown for generations is concurrent participation in more than one sector of the religious field. What is of late-modern provenance, however, is the highly flexible manner and sheer extent of individual transit, particularly between new religious groups, movements and organizations.

5 Allowing for the inevitable variations between groups, NRM members are typically middle class, relatively well educated and overwhelmingly under 45 years of age (Dawson, A., 2007, pp. 7–8; Dawson, L., 1998, pp. 85–90). The extent to which women outnumber men is a matter of some dispute.

8

Religion for Sale: Market Dynamics and Contemporary Religiosity

Introduction

Talk of the 'religious market' or 'spiritual marketplace' has become common over the course of the last decade or so. Not everyone, though, is comfortable with the association between religion and the market. Heelas, for example, rejects the representation of new spiritualities as religious forms of modern consumerism as an overly reductionist analysis which bypasses most of what contemporary spiritual repertoires have to offer. At the same time, he argues, use of market-orientated notions such as consumption and commodity are something of an academic fad. 'Like so many other terms associated with postmodern "thought"', Heelas writes, 'the language of consumption has become a consumer good – one which has been consumed by many within the academy, perhaps taking them over' (2008, p. 181). In marked contrast to Heelas' championing of new life spiritualities, Carrette and King regard the 'increasingly popular discourse of "spirituality"' as indicative of 'what amounts to a silent takeover of "the religious" by contemporary capitalist ideologies':

> From feng shui to holistic medicine, from aromatherapy candles to yoga weekends, from Christian mystics to New Age gurus, spirituality is big business . . . Spirituality as a cultural trope has also been appropriated by corporate bodies and management consultants to promote efficiency, extend markets and maintain a leading edge in a fast-moving information economy. (2005, p. 1)

Believing 'capitalist spirituality' to be underwritten by 'neo-liberal ideals of privatization and corporatization', Carrette and King identify its defining features as: atomization, self-interest, corporatism, utilitarianism, consumerism, quietism, political myopia and thought-control/accommodationism. In combination, these features enable the 'cultural organization of the term "spirituality"' as a 'support for the ideologies of consumerism and corporate capitalism' (2005, p. 170). Whereas Heelas cites the market's adoption of spirituality as a sign of its growing success (2008, p. 6), Carrette and King regard it as part of a broader process in which the religious is subverted by the economic.

In his Weberian-informed analysis of the early-modern period, Campbell is at pains to show how consumer-orientated narratives and socio-cultural practices of consumption are by no means recent historical phenomena (1987). In the same vein, in one of the earliest engagements with the religious marketplace, Moore argues that:

> Commercial aspects of religion are traceable in any century. Markets once flourished in cathedral towns, and the Church shared the profits. Martin Luther complained about the sale of indulgences . . . To say that religion is involved in market trade is not to pose a unique problem of modernity. (1994, p. 7)

Moore immediately goes on to say, however, that 'I am persuaded that transformations of market societies in the nineteenth century . . . did transform the issues, changing the whole texture and meaning of activities labelled "spiritual"'. There is, then, something about the modern context of urban-industrial capitalism which lends itself to the ready application of market-orientated concepts to the contemporary religious field. By way of reinforcing this point, Mara Einstein notes, for example, that in 2003 'research estimates put the [US] market for religious publishing and products at $6.8 billion and growing at a rate of nearly 5 percent annually'. Subdivided into 'books' ($3.5 billion), 'stationary/giftware/merchandise' ($1.4 billion) and 'audio/video/software' ($1.4 billion), Einstein says that the religious market is estimated to 'grow at almost a 5 percent annual rate for at least the next three years, reaching $8.64 billion in sales' (2008, p. 6).

Construals of modern religion as or related to a marketplace tend to revolve around three principal dynamics which arise from the structural and social differentiation of urban-industrial capitalist society. First, enabled by structural secularization and socio-cultural pluralism, the mid-range proliferation of religious groups and movements both increases the number of options available and heightens inter-organizational competition for resources and members. Second, these macro-structural dynamics combine with the processes of individualization to produce increasing numbers of free-floating (disembedded) individuals, who enjoy a historically unrivalled subjective capacity for free choice and objective conditions of optionality. Third, the all-pervasive influence of capitalist market dynamics engender both an increased sophistication on the part of religious organizations in respect of marketing their wares and a consumption-orientated (commodified) subjectivity on the part of actual and potential religious participants. When engaging the relationship of religion and market dynamics, sociologists of religion construe these processes in different ways, relate them in varying fashion and emphasize, downplay or ignore elements to a greater or lesser extent.

Allowing for the variegated character of sociological approaches to the religious marketplace, two paradigms have nevertheless dominated the academic landscape. Formulated during the 1960s resurgence of sociological interest in religion, the complementary – because mutually informed – approaches of Berger and Luckmann have since exerted a tremendous influence upon a broad range of academic engagement with the religious market (see also Chapters 4 and 5). I term this approach the 'marketization paradigm'. Arising in the 1980s, and although it by no means runs contrary to the marketization paradigm of Berger and Luckmann, the 'religious economy' model has become something of a rival approach to conceptualizing the relationship between religion and market forces and dynamics. Given their enduring influence, this chapter is given over to delineating these two dominant paradigms.

The marketization paradigm

Peter Berger

According to Berger, the organizational impact of structural secularization and socio-cultural pluralism is most clearly visible in the 'permanent presence' of competition across the religious landscape. Such is the nature of modern society, however, that religious competition entails rivalry not only among religious groups and movements but also between religious and *non*-religious rivals'. In combination, secularization and pluralism engender a process in which 'religious groups are transformed from monopolies to competitive marketing agencies'. 'As a result' of these dynamics, Berger maintains:

> the religious tradition, which previously could be authoritatively imposed, now has to be *marketed*. It must be 'sold' to a clientele that is no longer constrained to 'buy'. The pluralistic situation is, above all, a market situation. In it, the religious institutions become marketing agencies and the religious traditions become consumer commodities. And at any rate a good deal of religious activity in this situation comes to be dominated by the logic of market economics. (1967, p. 137)

By virtue of religious organizations having to compete for custom in an increasingly open socio-cultural context, two important transformative dynamics ensue. The first of these dynamics is structural in character while the second impacts upon the content of the religious message itself.

Changes in the 'socio-structural aspects of religion' arise from religious organizations having to adopt an increasingly strategic posture in respect of ensuring their continued survival in a competitive context. As Berger notes, 'the marketing of any commodity, material or otherwise, to a modern mass public is an exceedingly complex and expensive operation' (1967, p. 143). Consequently, and however understood, 'the question of "results" becomes important'. The 'rationalization' of religious organizations entailed by their adoption of goal-orientated (technocratic) reason is, for Berger, primarily expressed 'in the phenomenon of bureaucracy'. Responsible for managing 'the rational execution of the group's "mission"' – and irrespective of their theological construal – bureaucratic dynamics impinge upon religious institutions in both their 'internal' and 'external' social relations. Internally, the 'logic' of bureaucracy comes to dominate both the administration and 'day-to-day operations' of religious organizations as they gear themselves to defining, pursuing and attaining the objectives (members, funds, influence) necessary to their survival:

> Externally, the religious institutions deal with other social institutions as well as with each other through the typical forms of bureaucratic interaction. 'Public relations' with their consumer clientele, 'lobbying' with the government, 'fund raising' with both governmental and private agencies, multifaceted involvements with the secular economy (particularly through investment). (1967, p. 140)

In line with his earlier understanding of religious ecumenism as a form of marketized behaviour (1963, pp. 75–90), Berger likewise treats 'ecumenicity' as a mode of 'cartelization' designed to ameliorate the worst effects of inter-religious competition.

As well as impacting upon the institutional arrangements of religious organizations, the implications of the contemporary context 'also extend to the religious contents, that is, to the product of the religious marketing agencies'. 'Probably more potent' than the traditional 'wishes of kings or the vested interests of classes', the modern 'dynamics of consumer preference' wield tremendous influence upon the collective formulation of religious beliefs and practices.

> To repeat, the crucial sociological and social-psychological characteristic of the pluralistic situation is that religion can no longer be imposed but must be marketed. It is impossible, almost *a priori*, to market a commodity to a population of uncoerced consumers without taking their wishes concerning the commodity into consideration . . . The basic necessity of taking on a soliciting stance *vis-à-vis* a public means that consumer controls over the product being marketed are introduced. (1967, p. 145)

Berger highlights a number of effects which arise from 'consumer controls over religious contents'. First, because they are prone to the changing tastes of the market, religious contents are subject to a 'principle of changeability' which both erodes the fixity of established traditions and ties modern religious repertoires to the shifting patterns of contemporary 'fashion'. Second, and 'insofar as the world of the consumers in question' is both 'secularized' and 'privatized', religious products must play down their 'supernatural elements' and emphasize their immanent (such as moral, therapeutic and material) benefits instead. Third and fourth are the processes of 'standardization' and 'marginal differentiation'. The growing similarity (that is 'standardization') between religious repertoires ensues because the purveyors of religious goods strive to optimize returns by adopting the most successful forms of religious production. As the optimal band of performance is relatively restricted in scope, a standardization of religious production takes place as organizations progressively tailor their repertoires to the same, most profitable areas. In the face of neo-Pentecostal success across Latin America, Roman Catholicism's championing of the Charismatic Renewal movement is a case in point. Having standardized their repertoires, however, religious organizations must still find ways to differentiate themselves from those other organizations offering similar (because optimal) products. Should the act of differentiation go too far, though, religious organizations risk placing themselves outside of the optimal range of institutional return. Consequently, and in order to protect organizational interests, what differentiation occurs is always 'marginal' in character. Although marginal differentiation may well involve the adoption of novel elements, Berger also acknowledges that it may frequently involve nothing more than a creative repackaging of 'the same old standardized product' (1967, p. 149).

Thomas Luckmann

Berger's emphasis upon the organizational implications of the modern processes of religious marketization is complemented by Luckmann's treatment of their impact upon the individual. In line with Berger, Luckmann acknowledges the centrality of structural differentiation and socio-cultural pluralism to the ingression of market dynamics within the religious arena. By virtue of these macro-structural processes, the religious organization has become no more than one 'institution among other institutions'. Consequently, religious organizations:

> must compete on what is, basically, an open market. The manufacture, the packaging and the sale of models of 'ultimate' significance are, therefore, determined by consumer preference, and the manufacturer must remain sensitive to the needs and requirements of 'autonomous' individuals'. (1967, p. 104)

Concomitant with the emergence of an open religious market within which religious organizations must compete, the macro-structural processes of modernity have engendered three complementary dynamics. First, they have resulted in the fragmentation of the traditionally homogeneous 'sacred cosmos' into '*assortments* of "ultimate" meanings' with little or no coherence between them. Second, they have disembedded individuals from collective associations so that – 'to an immeasurably higher degree than in a traditional social order' – 'the individual is left to his own devices in choosing goods and services, friends, marriage partners, neighbors, [and] hobbies . . . in a relatively autonomous fashion' (1967, p. 98). Third, they have given rise to an all-pervasive 'consumer orientation' which 'is not limited to economic products but characterizes the relation of the individual to the entire culture'.

In combination, these typically modern dynamics lead the individual 'to confront the culture and the sacred cosmos as a "buyer"' who 'may choose from the assortment of "ultimate" meanings as he sees fit'. More than this, however, such is modernity's estimation of the free-floating consumer that marketized religion bestows 'something like a sacred status' upon individual autonomy. As a consequence, religious expression is characterized by a 'mobility ethos' which is both 'individualistic' and 'manipulative' (instrumentally orientated). Assuming the nature of a 'lifelong quest' for the 'inner man', modern religiosity becomes orchestrated by the goal of 'self-expression and self-realization' (1967, pp. 110–11). In contrast to the 'obligatory themes' of the traditional sacred cosmos, the modern religious 'consumer' moves freely among a 'heterogeneous assortment of possibilities'. Picking and choosing according to subjective tastes and idiosyncratic concerns, the modern individual constructs a 'syncretistic', 'eclectic' and '*ad hoc*' meaning system whose 'thematic heterogeneity' consists 'of a loose and rather unstable hierarchy of "opinions" legitimating the affectively determined priorities of "private" life' (1967, pp. 102–5).

Marketized religion in contemporary perspective

The pioneering insights of Berger and Luckmann continue to exert considerable influence upon contemporary engagements with the religious marketplace. In his treatment of the 'spiritual marketplace', for example, Roof talks of the contemporary religious 'seeker' whose 'quest culture' is 'engendered by confrontation with pluralism, individualism, and modernity', along with its 'therapeutic culture and . . . explicit attention to the self' (1999, p. 39). Directly echoing Luckmann's analysis, Roof argues that the religiosity of contemporary seekers is a 'fluid, less contained form of spirituality' whose 'highly sporadic and volatile' character tends 'not to encourage lasting loyalty to social organizations, privileging instead the individual's own inner world'. In the same vein, because 'religious identities in contemporary society are fluid, multilayered, and to a considerable extent personally achieved', their analysis is 'likely to reveal some degree of eclecticism, or constellation of elements and themes from differing faiths and traditions, put together by individuals exercising their creative agency' (1999, p. 35). In this later study, Roof augments earlier research into seeker spirituality (1993) with in-depth interviews with a variety of seekers whose variegated life experiences lead them to 'quest' through different parts of the religious spectrum. Subsequent to detailing these interviews, Roof asserts that:

> whatever else religion may be, in a mediated and consumption-oriented society it *becomes a cultural* resource broadly available to the masses. Responsibility falls more upon the individual – like that of the *bricoleur* – to cobble together a religious world from available images, symbols, moral codes, and doctrines, thereby exercising considerable agency in defining and shaping what is considered to be religiously meaningful. (1999, p. 75)

Roof subsequently espouses the notion of 'reflexive spirituality' which, he argues, captures the typically self-aware and strategic character of the late-modern spiritual seeker.

Moving on to examine the organizational implications of the spiritual marketplace, Roof identifies the diversification of religious repertoires as a key institutional response to individual religious mobility. Here, Roof makes his point by reproducing another source which details the repertorial diversification of a large, 'seeker-friendly' Christian church in the Midwestern United States. In order to optimize its capture of religious transients, says Roof, the church offers a diverse array of services including, for example:

> a seminar on effective single parenting; twelve-step recovery meetings by category (alcohol, drugs, abuse) and freeway coordinates; a parents-of-adolescents meeting; a class for premarital couples; another for 'home-builders'; something called Bunko Night (Tired of shopping? Low on funds?); a 'woman in the workplace' brunch; a 'fellowshippers' (seniors) meeting; a men's retreat ('Anchoring Deep'); women's Bible studies; a baseball league; a passel of Generation X activities; 'grief support ministries'; worship music, drama, and dance; 'discovering divorce dynamics'; a 'belong class' for new members; and 'life development' ('You will learn to know yourself and begin to see where God has a place of service for you. This is a can't miss class'). (1999, p. 95)

As with the 'reflexive spirituality' of individual seekers, the diversification of organizational repertoires bears equal testimony to the increasingly sophisticated nature of the late-modern religious marketplace.

The sophisticated character of contemporary 'religious marketing' is dealt with at length by Einstein's *Brands of Faith* (2008). Writing as a former marketing executive, Einstein asserts that 'religion is a product, no different from any other commodity sold in the consumer marketplace'. She continues by maintaining that:

> Many forms of religion are being advertised and promoted in a way never seen before. Churches advertise on billboards and in print media. Books sell us all types of religious and spiritual wisdom. Television has become overrun with religious content with no fewer than eight channels presenting sermons and faith-based programming 24 hours a day, not to mention religious content in broadcast prime time and as regular content for nightly newsmagazines. (2008, p. 4)

As with Berger and Luckmann, Einstein cites modernity's creation of a '*real open market for religion*' as fundamental to the growth of religious marketing. She also highlights the importance of 'media saturation' and the 'ubiquitous advertising that goes with it'. In combination, religious choice and information overload mean that 'religion must present itself as a valuable commodity, an activity that is worthwhile in an era of overcrowded schedules'. As a consequence, 'religion needs to be packaged and promoted. It needs to be new and relevant. It needs to break through the clutter' (2008, p. 12). In short, religion needs to establish itself as a 'brand' worthy of consumer attentions.

The Alpha Course

In addition to analysing the processes of brand construction, Einstein looks at a number of successful religious brands, among which she includes the Alpha Course (2008, pp. 107–17). Like Hunt (2004) before her, Einstein recognizes the international success of the Alpha Course as dependent upon a sophisticated and well-funded marketing campaign which drew on the professional services of the global advertising agency of Saatchi and Saatchi. As Hunt notes, by virtue of its marketing savvy, an independent survey at the turn of the century demonstrated that '16 per cent (or 1 in 6) of the UK adult population ... identified Alpha as a Christian course, while 41 per cent knew someone who had graduated through the programme' (2004, p. 1). According to the publishers of the Alpha Course, in 2008 alone, in excess of 33,500 courses were offered across 163 countries in 48 languages by numerous different Christian traditions. By 2009, over 13 million people had attended the course since its inception in the 1970s (see http://uk.alpha.org).

For commentators like Einstein and Hunt, the success of the Alpha Course lies principally in its sophisticated use of marketing techniques which infuse every aspect of course design, manufacture, advertising, and application. The Alpha Course is ten weeks long and is delivered chiefly through a single weekly session which commences with a 'supper', followed by a talk (usually recorded but may also be 'live') and concluding with a general, small-group discussion. The ten weekly sessions are sometimes augmented by an 'away day' event. The simple structure, professionally produced and relatively inexpensive materials, high-tech delivery, product spin-offs and carefully staged informality of course sessions are designed to gel with contemporary consumer tastes. Complementing its presentation, structure and ethos, the Alpha Course has further broadened its appeal by modifying its generic format to account for specific demographic groups. In addition to formats designed for military personnel and prison inmates, the standard course is complemented by 'Youth Alpha', 'Student Alpha', 'Senior Alpha', and 'Alpha in the Workplace'. The Alpha Organization has also diversified to offer additional programmes specifically designed for educational contexts, marital relations, the workplace and ex-offenders. As Hunt concludes, Alpha succeeds because it fits well in 'the contemporary spiritual marketplace'.

> It has a powerful supply-side that has produced a standardized package supported by a £ million industry. It attempts to appeal to the 'consumer-side' and the spiritual seeker – the Alpha 'guest' . . . Alpha is designer Christianity. (2004, p. 250)

For Einstein, Alpha's success resides in its sophisticated 'packaging and promotion' – 'Dinner, a video, and a chat with friends feel like an evening at home, not a Sunday at church' (2008, p. 117).

A New Age marketplace

In his analysis of the New Age spiritual marketplace, Guy Redden observes how the alternative religious scene is marked by a dominance of 'commercial relations' – in which participants pay for 'access to ideas, products, and technologies' – and 'an unprecedented degree of professionalization' on the part of religious providers (2005, pp. 234–6). Such is the centrality of 'commercial exchange', he argues, that distribution of and access to 'non-commodified' elements of the New Age scene are heavily reliant upon some form of market dynamic (see also Ezzy, 2001, pp. 31–44). Although the New Age environment is highly diverse and diffuse, Redden maintains that a degree of structural coherence exists by virtue of a widespread interdependence between religious providers. The New Age marketplace:

> is one in which many different providers co-operate to bring their products to market, sharing elements of organizational infrastructure in a way

that is analogous to how stall-holders co-operate to share the physical space of the fair, along with the financial cost of its overheads. (2005, p. 237)

Redden identifies a host of 'shared fora' or 'intermediary spaces' in which the products of multiple providers are made jointly available in a way which reduces marketing overheads for individual entrepreneurs. At the same time, such shared spaces attract a broad spectrum of potential consumers which, in turn, maximizes the reach of the individual products on show.

The New Age market's reliance upon 'channels of interconnection' engenders a narrative form of standardization which Redden defines as a kind of 'New Age *lingua franca*'. In effect, New Age practitioners espouse a 'value-relativism' which permits diverse, if not contrasting, types of products to be viewed as equally valid modes of alternative spiritual practice.[1] In addition to facilitating in-house co-operation, the holistic paradigm allows for the conspicuous appropriation of otherwise disparate beliefs and practices from a diverse array of sources which are amalgamated within a single, but hybrid, repertoire. Despite appearances, these variegated elements are regarded as complementary aspects of the one, universal reality.[2] As with the diverse offerings of the 'seeker-friendly' church cited above by Roof, New Age hybrid repertoires enjoy a broader appeal than those of a more homogeneous kind. For Redden, the commercial co-operation enabled by 'value-relativism' makes it 'an operating principle of New Age markets in knowledge and practice' (2005, p. 242).

In keeping with Berger's insights, Redden acknowledges that the competitive environment of the New Age market entails that spiritual providers find some way of differentiating themselves from their commercial rivals. Fortunately, however, the variety of New Age clientele and the flexibility of the New Age paradigm combine to allow for a great deal of 'market diversification'. 'The overall result', Redden maintains:

> is the multiplication of personal needs that are catered for, as New Age discourse is continually redirected to address possible opportunities for consumption in the lives of participants. One can find New Age options for all kinds of activity, however intimate or mundane . . . from the core New Age services of mind/body therapies, workshops, and retreats, to wellness accessories and paraphernalia, such as a Zen alarm clock that 'awakens' your consciousness gradually with celestial sounds every morning. (2005, p. 239)

As with the 'quest' mentality identified by Luckmann and Roof, Redden argues that the basic demands of the religious marketplace 'normalise pluralistic seekership by continually presenting participants with multiple alternatives for belief and action'. In both traditional and alternative spiritual circles, however, the dynamics of 'seekership', 'transit' or 'switching' generate particular problems for religious organizations. The institutional implications of contemporary religious transit entail religious organizations experiencing an increasingly high turnover of participants whose relationship with the group is potentially short-term and non-exclusive. The downside of this transient relationship is that religious organizations must work hard to maximize institutional return in the potentially short time that they have with group participants. While not the only means of doing so, the commercialization of organizational repertoires, along with the constant repackaging, remodelling and renewal of what's offered, serves to squeeze the most out of participants during their time with the group. There is an upside to religious transit, however, in that the dynamics of consecutive switching and concurrent participation entail a steady stream of fresh religious transients waiting to be attracted by what is on offer. In addition to working hard to maximize returns from current participants, the aforementioned dynamics of repertorial diversification provide valuable means of broadening appeal to religious seekers in search of novel spheres of spiritual experience.

The religious economy model

The 'religious economy' model was initially developed by North American sociologists and rose to prominence during the neo-liberal consensus when pro-market, conservative politicians (Ronald Reagan and Margaret Thatcher) held office on both sides of the north Atlantic. Pre-eminent among the religious economists are William Bainbridge, Roger Finke, Laurence Iannaccone and Rodney Stark (Finke, 1997, pp. 45–64; Finke and Stark, 1992; Iannaccone, 1997, pp. 25–45; Stark and Bainbridge, 1985 and 1987; Stark and Finke, 2000). As the term suggests, the religious economy model starts from the basic assumption that the religious field is directly analogous to an economy and is thereby open to analysis through the application of concepts and models usually applied to the economic sphere. The understanding of religion gained through the use of economic concepts and models, it is argued, applies equally to the macro-structural, mid-range and micro-social dimensions of society.

Anthropological constants

Two basic anthropological presuppositions underpin the religious economy model. First, humankind is, by nature, predisposed to seeking answers to fundamental questions of meaning ('Where do we come from?', 'Why should I be good?'). Here, the religious economists stand full-square within mainstream sociological tradition in their recognition of human subjectivity as a meaning-making (that is significatory) phenomenon. Second, human beings are naturally inclined to cost–benefit calculation when considering possible courses of action. Here, religious economists step outside of mainstream sociology to draw on traditional (*homo economicus*) and modern (rational-actor theory) understandings of human subjectivity as governed by rational calculation geared to maximizing benefits and minimizing costs. These two basic anthropological presuppositions combine to inform the definition of religion employed by the religious economy model.

Religion exists, it is argued, because human existence poses more questions than everyday experience can resolve. Because fundamental questions of meaning and morality cannot ultimately be resolved through reference to finite human experience, supernatural explanations are mobilized to meet the 'demand' generated by this shortfall (Stark and Bainbridge, 1985, pp. 5–14; Stark and Finke, 2000, pp. 85–91). For religious economists, however, religion's mobilization of the supernatural assumes an explicitly commercial character. Directly analogous to a commercial transaction, religion is understood as a mode of exchange between humankind and supernatural agencies. In effect, religion is conceived as a practical and symbolic framework within which humankind incurs a range of 'costs' (time, effort, goods) in exchange for a given set of 'rewards' (explanations, forgiveness, everlasting life). As in all other walks of life, religion involves giving up one thing in order to gain something else.[3]

Likewise in keeping with everyday human activity, religious practice includes individuals striving to minimize their costs while maximizing the benefits accrued. No different from every other aspect of human life, religion is subject to the rational calculus of maximal return for minimal outlay. Consequently, when seeking to express themselves religiously, individuals will ultimately be attracted to those forms of religion deemed to be the most efficient (cost-effective) means of sating their particular set of religious preoccupations, tastes and desires. Driven both by the need to survive and the desire to flourish, religious organizations seek to maximize their appeal to would-be members by convincing them that they have the best (most cost-effective) product on offer (Iannaccone, 1997, pp. 26–7). There exists, then, a mutually complementary dynamic of individual demand and collective supply. Here, calculating subjects search for the most efficient means of satisfying their religious demand, while strategizing organizations market themselves as the most effective form of religious supply.

Given the aforementioned anthropological constants, religious economists hold that a degree of religious demand will always exist and be expressed as some kind of cost–benefit exchange. Although a universal feature of human existence, religion nevertheless manifests itself in a wide variety of ways relative to prevailing historical and socio-cultural conditions. At any one time, then, there is a potentially variegated spectrum of religious tastes and preferences and a possibly diverse array of collective religious expression. More importantly, however, the religious economy model argues that both the degree of religious variation and the amount of religious activity exhibited by any one society are ultimately determined not by subjective demand but by mid-range and macro-structural dynamics which determine the manner and extent of religious supply. If supply-side conditions are good, religious demand is well met and expressed both through varied repertoires and heightened activity. If supply-side conditions are poor, religious demand is insufficiently catered for and the religious landscape restricted in variety and size.

Concrete applications

By way of concrete application, three examples will suffice to aid appreciation of the religious economy model's contribution to academic understanding of contemporary religious belief and practice.

Institutional endeavours

First, the religious economy model stresses the importance of organizational activity to the creation and maintenance of a vibrant religious environment. As noted in Chapter 7, religious economists draw on social-movement theory to argue the importance of organizational activity as a key determinant of religious vitality. In modern, plural society religious organizations do not enjoy the privileges and protections traditionally afforded established religion by state-enforced monopolistic practices. Consequently, if they are to survive and flourish in a highly competitive modern environment, religious organizations must be extremely efficient in extracting the most from themselves and their respective social contexts. For example, religious organizations must be good at mobilizing what personal, material and associational resources they have to hand. They should also be alive to identifying and exploiting existing political and civic opportunity structures through savvy exploitation of, for example, potential funding streams and prevailing popular discourses. Furthermore, religious organizations must be adept at formulating and projecting a public image which plays well with contemporary trends and expectations. Without vibrant organizational activity, religious supply is seriously undermined.

Environmental dynamics

Second, the religious economy model offers a countervailing analysis to that of established secularization theories (Stark, 1999, pp. 249–73). According to the religious economy model, for the dynamic of religious supply and demand to be optimal – and religion thereby to flourish – the appropriate mid-range and macro-structural conditions must be in place. Whereas human nature dictates that some level of individual religious demand and some degree of collective religious supply will always exist, if over-arching conditions conducive to their efficient interaction are not in place, this dynamic is seriously undermined to the point of enervating both demand and supply. With an eye to the 'secular' societies of Western Europe, proponents of the religious economy model argue that traditional religious monopolies comprise the most inimical conditions for the optimization of religious supply and demand. This is the case because religious monopolies impose a uniform religious model and thereby stifle open competition. In so doing, religious monopolies undermine both supply (organizational innovation) and demand (pluriform tastes and preferences). Citing the United States as the paragon of a deregulated religious market, the dynamics of religious supply and demand are said to work best in societal conditions characterized by open competition free from state interference (Finke and Stark, 1992, p. 18; Stark, 1999, pp. 249–73).

By delimiting the scope of free competition, state interference (statutory regulation and financial subsidy) restricts the extent to which religious organizations are allowed, prepared or need to experiment, innovate and change in pursuit of institutional survival and expansion. As in Europe, for example, unnecessary legal-political intervention in the religious sphere has traditionally constrained organizational vitality which, in turn, constricted the supply of religious goods. In so doing, the restriction of a free religious market also dampened demand as religious suppliers were less able or inclined to offer religious products likely to stimulate or broaden prevailing tastes and preferences. Exemplified by the European experience, constricted supply inevitably suppresses demand. The secularity of contemporary Europe, then, arises not from its modern, urban-industrial status but results from a depressed religious economy bequeathed by a history of long-standing and widespread religious monopolization.

In contrast to Europe, the United States is said to demonstrate that the freer a religious market is from unnecessary interference, the greater the degree of religious competition. At the same time, the greater the degree of religious competition, the more organizational innovation there is and, as a result, higher levels and quality of religious supply ensue. As a consequence of heightened levels and quality of religious supply, it is argued, demand is further stimulated and thereby broadened in scope. Furthermore, the stimulation and broadening of demand leads to greater levels of organizational innovation as new forms of supply compete to meet emergent kinds of demand. No less modern than Europe, the fertile religious landscape of the United States is said to belie the assertions of secularization theory that urban-industrial society is inherently inimical to the maintenance and reproduction of religious belief and practice. For religious economists, it is not modernity as such, but its particular socio-cultural configuration that determines the vibrancy or otherwise of the religious landscape.

These two key insights of the religious economy model have been taken up and applied by scholars in various parts of the world. In South America, for example, the relatively recent demise of Roman Catholicism's traditional monopoly is credited with opening up a free religious market within which previously suppressed or newly emergent religions are now coming to the fore (Chestnut, 2003; Guerra, 2003). According to Chestnut:

> at the start of the twenty-first century, there is growing realization that beyond the rise or fall of any one particular religious organization, the greatest transformation of the Latin American religious landscape in the past half-century, if not the past half-millennium, is the transition from a monopolistic religious economy to a free-market one. Of such significance is the development of religious pluralism that the fate of any faith-based organization during the past five decades cannot be understood without understanding its position in this new unregulated spiritual economy. (2003, p. 147)[4]

Chestnut and Guerra agree that the opening of the Brazilian religious market facilitated by the demise of Catholicism's traditional monopoly has best been exploited by neo-Pentecostal organizations such as the Universal Church of the Kingdom of God. The organizational structures of neo-Pentecostal denominations, it is argued, have enabled them to adapt quickly to a deregulated religious economy and thereby outperform their nearest competitors. Organizationally flexible and strategically astute, neo-Pentecostals have stolen a march on other religious suppliers whose institutional structures are both cumbersome and highly inefficient. Facilitated by the combination of structural manoeuvrability, marketing savvy and enthusiastic 'sales personnel', neo-Pentecostal organizations are able to market an increasingly popular product in a way which stimulates further demand. Such has been the success of neo-Pentecostal approaches that other mainstream religious organizations (such as Roman Catholic, Spiritist and Afro-Brazilian) have increasingly appropriated them. Not only has this employment of the most effective structures and methods resulted in the progressive 'standardization' of mainstream organizational behaviour, it has also engendered 'the adoption of an increasingly rational and commercial vision of religious activity' (Guerra, 2003, p. 153).[5] In the process of modifying organizational behaviour and individual expectation, the processes of marketization reconfigure the nature of religion itself.

Transactional relations

Third, the religious economy model contributes a particular transactional understanding of the interface between the organizational supply of religion and individual religious consumption. Laurence Iannaccone, for example, explores a number of dynamics which relate to the ongoing success of conservative forms of religion (1992, pp. 271–91; 1997, pp. 25–45; 2002, pp. 203–23). On the one hand, Iannaccone is interested in why individuals join conservative religious groups which, by their nature, make far greater demands on their members than more liberal forms of religion. Given that the 'costs' of membership of liberal religious organizations appear less than that of their conservative counterparts, why are the more demanding forms of traditionalist Christianity enjoying greater success? On the other hand, Iannaccone is interested in how religious organizations deal with calculating human beings who, by their nature, are constantly striving to maximize individual rewards while minimizing personal costs. Traditionally framed as the 'free rider problem', organizations are continually challenged by the need to deal with individuals who enjoy the benefits of organizational participation but make little or no contribution to the collective endeavours of the group in question. In seeking something for nothing, the free rider is a drain on collective resources and a cause of organizational inefficiency.

Iannaccone's response to the free-rider issue is to argue that conservative religious groups minimize its impact by virtue of the relatively high demands they make upon their members. Unlike their liberal counterparts, traditionalist organizations make a series of demands upon their members which involve individuals incurring a range of costs (labour, money, diminution of 'worldly' ties) which go above and beyond those that the average free rider is willing to shoulder. As conservative religious groups are adept at reinforcing their membership demands through the imposition of sanctions, the costs of free riding are likely to outweigh those of the benefits accrued. In addition to putting off the 'half-hearted', however, should not the relatively high costs demanded by conservative religious groups also discourage membership take-up? As the success of traditionalist religions is increasingly evident, says Iannaccone, this is clearly not the case.

It is not the case, he argues, for two principal reasons. First, and as with most commercial transactions, religious goods which cost more to obtain are perceived by their recipients as having greater value than goods which cost less; the higher the cost, the greater its subjective appreciation. By making greater demands upon their members, conservative religious groups are also perceived to offer more valuable religious rewards. So, while it may 'cost' more to belong to a conservative religious group, the rewards obtained are perceived as duly commensurate to the efforts expended. Second, as membership of traditionalist groups often involves a diminution in 'worldly' activities, members become increasingly reliant upon organizational provision of social goods formerly acquired through non-religious channels (hobby clubs, leisure associations, friendship networks). As organizational provision is relatively scarce (compared with what is available 'in the world'), privileged (available only to members) and costly to obtain, it is valorized by recipients as a benefit gained rather than an inferior substitute for what has been sacrificed. In combination, the reduction of free riding and enhanced membership appreciation of corporate repertoires result in both an increased ability to mobilize personal resources and an enhanced organizational efficiency which places conservative groups at a distinct advantage over their less-demanding (and thereby less efficient) competitors.

Conclusion

Talk of the commodification of contemporary society is well-established within mainstream sociological reflection. Zigmunt Bauman, for example, argues that whereas 'consumption' has always been an important driver for modern capitalist society, recent historical developments – not least the neo-liberal paradigm – have considerably radicalized inherent consumerist processes. Within our contemporary 'society of consumers', he argues, 'consumerism' dominates as:

> the *principal propelling and operating* force of society, a force that co-ordinates systemic reproduction, social integration, social stratification and the formation of individuals, as well as playing a major role in the processes of individual and group self-identification and in the selection and pursuit of individual life policies . . . The 'society of consumers', in other words, stands for the kind of society that promotes, encourages or enforces the choice of a consumerist lifestyle . . . everyone needs to be, ought to be, must be a consumer-by-vocation. (2007, pp. 28, 53 and 55)

Within the society of consumers, human nature is defined by the ability to choose. *Homo sapiens* becomes *homo eligens/optionis* (Bauman, 2005, p. 33; Beck and Beck Gernsheim, 2002, p. 5).

Given the weight of mainstream sociological attention to modern consumer society, the use by sociologists of religion of market-orientated critiques and economically informed analyses of religion is fully understandable. By appropriating and bringing to bear such approaches, the marketization paradigm and the religious economy model furnish an understanding of contemporary religious dynamics which is both empirically informed and theoretically insightful. What these approaches do not do, however, is capture the totality of religious dynamics as they unfold within contemporary consumer society. Yes, commodification is an all pervasive process which has fundamentally impacted upon modern society in both its secular and religious domains (Dawson, A., 2011a). To understand every aspect of contemporary life as nothing but a manifestation of consumerist existence is, however, an act of analytical reductionism which stands to miss much of the bigger sociological picture.

The charge of analytical reductionism applies far more to the religious economy model than it does to those working within the marketization paradigm. By and large, those engaging marketized religion do so with an eye to the broader picture in which a range of other, at times countervailing, dynamics contribute to shaping the contemporary religious landscape. In contrast, the religious economy model is an all-embracing theoretical stance which treats all kinds and every aspect of religious activity as a form of commercial exchange. As Bruce's sustained critique of the religious economy model maintains, religious belief and practice encompass far more by way of intent, experience and understanding than the commercial dynamic of rationalistic calculus allows for (Bruce, 1999). Consequently, and as Beckford concludes, the 'exclusive focus on rationality' employed by religious economists 'is rarely capable of providing well-rounded explanation' of religion in both its individual and collective forms (2003, p. 170).

Further reading

Berger, P., 1967, *The Sacred Canopy: Elements of a Sociological Theory of Religion*, New York: Anchor Books.

Luckmann, T., 1967, *The Invisible Religion: The Problem of Religion in Modern Society*, New York: Macmillan.

Roof, W. C., 1999, *Spiritual Marketplace: Baby Boomers and the Remaking of American Religion*, Princeton: Princeton University Press.

Young, L. A. (ed.), 1997, *Rational Choice Theory and Religion: Summary and Assessment*, London: Routledge.

Stark, R. and Finke, R., 2000, *Acts of Faith: Explaining the Human Side of Religion*, Berkeley: University of California Press.

Notes

1 Other studies of New Age religiosity have understood this 'value-relativism' to be ultimately grounded in a holistic worldview which treats different beliefs and practices as but varying kinds of the same universal truth (Dawson, A., 2007; Heelas, 1996).

2 An analysis of the 'Course in New Gnosis' produced by the new religion of the Gnostic Church of Brazil, for example, identifies citations from or references to the Bhagavad-Gita, Rig Veda, Upanishads, Tibetan Book of the Dead, Hebrew Bible, Christian Gospels, Gnostic writings, Hermetic literature, esoteric materials, New Age elements, and miscellaneous Aztec, Maya and Incan sources (Dawson, A., 2007, p. 106).

3 As the 'rewards' furnished by religion are somewhat different from the ordinary benefits of everyday life, religious economists originally defined them as 'compensators'; here, a thing accepted in lieu of something else (Stark and Bainbridge, 1987, pp. 36–42). As the word has negative connotations, however, it was later dropped

in favour of the more neutral term 'otherworldly rewards' (Stark and Finke, 2000, p. 88).

4 If, indeed, there is one, the religious economy arising from the demise of the traditional Catholic monopoly is neither as 'free' nor as 'unregulated' as Chesnut appears to suggest. The prevailing religious economy is not 'free' because a range of historical and socio-cultural factors continues to exist which advantages some religious organizations more than others. At the same time, legal-political frameworks (consumer rights, juridical definitions of 'religion' and 'charity', state–civil society relations) continue to ensure the presence of regulatory constraints upon the Latin American religious field.

5 Exemplified by neo-Pentecostal employment of the popular media formats of television and radio, the 'mediatization' of the Brazilian religious landscape progressively involves Roman Catholic, Spiritist, traditional Protestant and Afro-Brazilian use of televisual, radiophonic, print and virtual platforms (Burity, 2003, pp. 77–9; Galindo, 2004, pp. 24–52).

9

Religious Fundamentalisms: Religion Ancient and Modern?

Introduction

As noted in Chapter 5, Berger makes much of the late twentieth-century re-surgence of religion as proof of the falsity of secularization theory. Importantly, Berger also notes how those movements principally responsible for this religious resurgence embody 'conservative', 'orthodox' or 'traditionalist' concerns which are commonly treated 'under the category of "fundamentalism"' (1999, p. 6).[1] In his engagement of Christianity, Philip Jenkins maintains that not only have the largest indices of growth occurred in the developing world ('global South') but that this growth overwhelmingly comprises conservative forms of Christianity and Islam (2007). While conservative forms of Christianity have grown in Africa, China and Latin America, for example, traditionalist Islamic movements have enjoyed success across the Middle East, north and central Africa and south-east Asia. At the same time, conservative forms of Judaism have exerted increasing political influence in Israel, while nationalist Hindu, Sikh and Buddhist religious revivalism has impacted upon precariously balanced geopolitical settlements in the Asian sub-continent (Almond, Appleby and Sivan, 2003; Antoun, 2008).

In respect of its religious connotations, the term 'fundamentalism' derives from the early twentieth-century context of the United States. As part of a broader religious revival which gave rise to Christian Pentecostalism, a series of pamphlets were produced (1910–15) under the over-arching title of *The Fundamentals: A Testimony of Truth*. Although a range of Christian belief and practice was treated, the 'fundamentals' espoused amounted to biblical inerrancy, a six-day creation, the authenticity of miracles, the Virgin birth, the crucifixion and bodily resurrection of Jesus, the atonement of humankind's sinful condition and the future (imminent or otherwise) return of Jesus Christ to judge the living and the dead. The label 'fundamentalist' was first coined in 1920 to refer to those 'ready to do battle for the Fundamentals' (Ruthven, 2004, pp. 1–34). According to Lawrence, the term 'fundamentalism' was applied to certain kinds of Islam as early as the late 1940s (1989, p. 272). It was not until after the 1979 Shi'ite revolution in Iran, however, that the term was widely applied both to particular forms of the Muslim faith and other religious traditions of a radical or controversial bent.

Like the word 'cult', the term 'fundamentalism' has a pejorative tone which leads some scholars to avoid its use. At the same time, others believe that it should be applied only to particular manifestations of the Christian tradition from which it sprang. The fact that 'the label "fundamentalism" conceals important differences between radically conservative religious world-views' (Beckford, 2003, p. 128) further problematizes its use as an analytical category. As the conclusion to the first volume of the *Fundamentalism Project* maintains, treatments of fundamentalism should not fail to acknowledge that:

> those people and groups now known as 'fundamentalists' emerge from different regions of the world, cite different holy books, or have different interpretations of the same holy book, or follow no holy book at all but a venerable tradition instead. Some movements have resorted to violent means, while others assemble and proselytize within the limits of the law. (Marty and Applebey, 1991, p. 815)

The variety of religious fundamentalisms in existence is further underscored by studies of Christian and Islamic movements whose individual membership profiles are characterized by 'social heterogeneity' and significant demographic diversity (Arjomand, 1995, pp. 179–98; Lawrence, 1989; Riesebrodt, 1990). Variety, then, features not just across different fundamentalisms but also within one and the same movement. While they warrant caution in respect of its employment, these issues do not, though, fatally undermine the usefulness of fundamentalism as an analytical concept. As witnessed by the Chicago-based *Fundamentalism Project* of the 1990s, due care and attention to the use of fundamentalism as an analytical category furnishes insight not only into a range of similarities across different groups and movements but also specific differences in the particular religious and concrete socio-cultural forms through which it is manifested.

What follows opens by treating fundamentalism as an 'ideal type' which is defined by the attribution of a range of characteristics which both indicate how religious fundamentalism is to be understood and differentiate it from similar, but non-fundamentalist, forms of conservative religion. Again using an ideal typology, the next section examines different modes of fundamentalist action in the world, the most common theme of which is orientated to the use of political means for religious ends. The chapter concludes by treating a number of issues relating to sociological understandings of religious fundamentalism.

Defining fundamentalism

Given the empirical variety of socio-cultural manifestations to which it refers, the term 'fundamentalism' acts as an 'ideal type' which serves to bring a degree of analytical clarity to an otherwise complex and variegated terrain (Antoun, 2008; Caplan, 1987; Kaplan, 1992). Established by Weber as a key tool of sociological analysis, ideal typing relies both upon the bracketing out or elision of some characteristics and the 'one-sided accentuation' of others (Weber, 1949, p. 89). By virtue of this process, ideal types never completely match the empirical terrain from which they are abstracted. What they lack in empirical detail, however, ideal types make up for in the analytical clarity they enable. Classic ideal types used by Weber refer to modes of religious organization ('church' and 'sect'), authority ('traditional' and 'charismatic') and functionary ('magician' and 'prophet') (see Chapter 3). By providing a simplified model of otherwise complex phenomena, an ideal type allows for the identification of key processes, relationships and features which are not immediately apparent or readily comprehensible. Alongside all of the other ideal types employed by sociologists of religion, the term fundamentalism comprises a variety of characteristics which serve as definitional criteria by which particular concrete features are classed as belonging or not belonging to this specific type of religious phenomenon.

A reactionary phenomenon

Almond, Sivan and Appleby, for example, employ the concept of fundamentalism to refer to 'specific religious phenomena that have emerged in the twentieth century . . . in the wake of the success of modernization and secularization'. Emerging particularly in the latter part of the twentieth century, fundamentalist movements are primarily to be understood as 'historical counterattacks', which are mounted by 'threatened religious traditions, seeking to hold ground against this spreading secular "contamination" and even to regain ground by taking advantage of the weaknesses of modernization' (1995c, p. 403). Bruce and Sharot likewise regard religious fundamentalism as a reactionary phenomenon. For Bruce, 'the term "fundamentalist" is better kept for movements that respond to problems created by modernization'. Among those features of modernity to which fundamentalism reacts, Bruce identifies the liberal ideal of equality ('that all individuals should be accorded the same liberties irrespective of their faith'), the structural differentiation and social diversity wrought by urban-industrialization ('that you may choose your spouse on the grounds of religion but not your workmates. Or that you may sing God's praises in church but not in school or at work'), the advance of postmodern relativism (in which 'truth is impossible' and 'my views are as good as yours'), and the collusion of mainstream religion which has 'either actively promoted the new order or acquiesced in it' (2000, pp. 33–5). In the same vein, Sharot identifies secularity, sexual permissiveness, individualism, social pluralism and moral relativism as key structural and cultural developments to which religious fundamentalism reacts (1992, pp. 24–45).

In her studies of the 'new fundamentalism' which emerged among US Protestant Christians in the 1960s, Ammerman identifies a number of specific developments which, she argues, served collectively to galvanize a reactionary movement subsequently giving rise to the New Christian Right and its sundry components (such as the 'Moral Majority' of Jerry Falwell, the 'Christian Coalition' of Pat Robertson and the 'Christian Voice' of Robert Grant) (1987, pp. 188–211; 1991, pp. 1–65). Providing the socio-cultural backcloth to the emergence of the new fundamentalism were post-war America's accelerating urban-industrialization, increasing relaxation of its immigration policies, ongoing equality agenda in respect of race and gender, and progressive liberalism in matters of personal freedoms and public morality. In tandem with such rapid and far-reaching social change, federal and state agencies introduced a raft of legal changes which conservative Christians perceived as impinging directly upon the role and status of religion as they knew it. For example, attempts to equalize women's rights were seen to undermine biblical warrants to female submission. Likewise, juridical expectations in respect of the domestic sphere (parental disciplining of children) were felt to interfere unduly upon the God-given duties of familial authority structures. Government taxation of religious institutions and the accompanying administrative need to define 'religion' were perceived as a further incursion within the religious domain – an incursion doubly resented for the recognition of non-Christian religions as legal equivalents. The extension of legal and civil protections to lifestyles and practices (homosexuality and abortion) deemed to be immoral were likewise perceived as attacks upon the Christian faith, as were restrictions upon religious or explicitly Christian rituals (prayer) in public institutions and the furtherance of educational curricula which included humanist values and secular science (evolution).

Although in each case the particulars are inevitably different, like Ammerman's engagement with the new fundamentalism of the Christian right, treatments of Islamic, Jewish and other forms of religious fundamentalism have at their core a range of legal-political, socio-economic and religio-cultural changes over and against which these respective movements are understood to be reacting (Frykenberg, 1993, pp. 233–55; Liebman, 1993, pp. 68–87; Voll, 1991, pp. 345–402). Unlike Christian fundamentalism in the USA, however, many non-Western forms of religious fundamentalism are understood as reactions not just to the 'internal' transformations wrought by modern urban-industrialization but also to the advance of otherwise 'external' forces collectively perceived as creeping 'Westernization'. Exemplified by the Shi'ite revolution in Iran, fundamentalism arose not simply as a response to the disruption of traditional practices and established meaning-structures engendered by rapid urban-industrialization. It also emerged as an orchestrated reaction – understood as a campaign against *jahiliyya* ('ignorance of divine guidance') – to the perceived imposition of Western, secular-liberal values embodied by the dominant regime of the Shah (Lawrence, 1989; Riesebrodt, 1990).

Other key traits

The reactionary character of religious fundamentalism, along with the practical and discursive dynamics to which it gives rise, are concisely distilled in the following passage. According to Marty and Appleby, religious fundamentalism:

> manifests itself as a strategy, or set of strategies, by which beleaguered believers attempt to preserve their distinctive identity as a people or group. Feeling this identity at risk in the contemporary era, they fortify it by selective retrieval of doctrines, beliefs, and practices from a sacred past. These 'retrieved' fundamentals are refined, modified, and sanctioned in a spirit of shrewd pragmatism: they are to serve as a bulwark against the encroachment of outsiders who threaten to draw the believers into a syncretistic, a religious, or irreligious cultural milieu. Moreover, these fundamentals are accompanied in the new religious portfolio by unprecedented claims and doctrinal innovations. By the strength of these innovations and the new supporting doctrines, the retrieved and updated fundamentals are meant to regain the same charismatic intensity today by which they originally forged communal identity from the formative revelatory religious experiences. (1991, p. 835)

This passage serves Marty and Appleby as a partial summation of a range of characteristics which they regard as central to a 'pure' (ideal typical) definition of fundamentalism abstracted from the empirical treatments of actual fundamentalist movements which precede their concluding chapter (1991).

Among the most important characteristics of fundamentalism cited by Marty and Appleby are: an emergence at 'times of crisis, actual or perceived'; 'religious idealism', in which divine guidance ('revelation') is obtained through sanctified, authoritative sources (scripture, tradition, inspiration) providing access to an 'ontological' reality ('truth') from which concrete programmes of resistance and renewal are extrapolated; an 'eschatological' reading of time which interprets current events within a broader historical framework whose path and victorious ending have been predetermined by divine will; a rhetorical and practical 'extremism' which is both intentionally 'scandalous' in respect of what is opposed and helps separate the spiritually pure from the unholy; the setting of boundaries differentiating the true believer from the 'enemy' which 'name, dramatize, and even mythologize' those beyond the fold; 'missionary zeal'; charismatic and authoritarian male rule; a pragmatically driven appropriation of modern features; the selective use of tradition; and the desire to replace existing structures with a comprehensively new and religiously inspired system (1991, pp. 817–26).[2] In line with the discussion in Chapter 2 about definitions of religion and the use of polythetic ('family resemblance') approaches, a group or movement may still be classified as fundamentalist even though it does not instantiate every single feature of this list.

Ideological and organizational characteristics of fundamentalism

First formulated upon the completion of the opening volume of the *Fundamentalism Project*, by the time of the final volume some four years later, the above list had been refined into an ordered series of definitional characteristics. Now classified under 'ideological characteristics' and 'organizational characteristics', the list of family resemblances offered served both as a means of distinguishing fundamentalist from non-fundamentalist movements and – by way of rating these characteristics as 'low', 'high' or 'absent' – as a measure of the degree of fundamentalism exhibited by any one movement (Almond, Sivan and Appleby, 1995c, pp. 399–424).

Ideological traits

In keeping with aforementioned emphases, 'reactivity to the marginalization of religion' appears first in the list of ideological characteristics. According to the authors, reactivity 'constitutes the very essence of fundamentalist movements. They are by definition militant, mobilized, defensive reactions to modernity' (1995c, p. 409). The second ideological characteristic is that of 'selectivity'. Ideological selectivity applies to fundamentalists' engagement with their claimed traditions and with the modern context within and against which they function. As the authors maintain:

> While fundamentalists claim to be upholding orthodoxy (right belief) or orthopraxis (right behavior), and to be defending and conserving religious traditions and traditional ways of life from erosion, they do so by crafting new methods, formulating new ideologies, and adopting the latest processes and organizational structures. (1995c, p. 402)

For Sharot, religious fundamentalists believe in an 'authentic tradition' which 'provides a model to be reconstructed or emulated' in the current epoch (1992, p. 25). In actuality, however, the 'authentic tradition' mobilized by fundamentalists comprises a selective appropriation and revisionary construal of received authority sources. It is for this reason that Sharot prefers the term 'neo-traditional' to designate what others more commonly term fundamentalism.

Hermeneutically speaking, fundamentalists claim to recover a sacred tradition from which certain fundamentals are extracted and subsequently applied to the 'corrupt' and 'degraded' context of the present. As a purportedly simple process of recovery, extraction and application, the interpretative process articulated by fundamentalists may be represented thus: *Tradition* → *Fundamentals* → *Contemporary Context*. In reality, though, what actually occurs is a more nuanced process whereby the sacred tradition supposedly recovered is actively construed, and thereby reconstituted, from a particular standpoint directly informed by the modern problematic to which the fundamentalist appropriation of tradition is reacting. As a contextually orchestrated reading of tradition, the hermeneutical process as it actually occurs may be depicted as: *Modern problematic* → *Tradition* → *Fundamentals* → *Contemporary Context*. Along with the fundamentals derived from it, what fundamentalists claim as tradition is actually a situated construal of revered authority sources, which, by its nature, involves their selective appropriation, constructive reworking and, more often than not, the creative addition of non-traditional features orientated to addressing the contemporary context of the movements concerned. As Eisenstadt remarks, 'fundamentalist movements, despite their seemingly traditional flavor . . . can – perhaps paradoxically – best be understood against the background of the developments of modernity and within the framework of this development' (1999, p. 39). The *fatwa* issued in 1989 by Ayatollah Ruhollah Khomeini against Salman Rushdie – the author of *The Satanic Verses* – is a case in point. According to Islamic tradition, the *fatwa* issued by Khomeini should apply only within the geographical bounds of the Muslim world and be incumbent solely upon members of the Shi'ite community who accept the Ayatollah as their spiritual ruler. However, by appealing to 'all intrepid Muslims' to effect the *fatwa* 'wherever they may be', Ayatollah Khomeini refashioned the traditional remit of the *fatwa* in a way which reflected his fundamentalist reading of *Dar al-Islam* (House of Islam) and accounted for the modern Islamic diaspora and the globalized world in which they live.

In respect of fundamentalism's selective approach to modernity, Mendelsohn argues that:

> One of the striking aspects of fundamentalist movements . . . is the open willingness of their members, in many instances, to adopt the instrumentalities and technologies of modernity in order to 'reclaim' a society that they believe has been (mis)shaped by the manner in which these modern means have been used by secularists. (1993, p. 23)

Noting that fundamentalists reject modern cultural developments such as secularity, permissiveness and relativism, Sharot identifies a pragmatic disposition which, he argues, renders fundamentalists amenable to appropriating features of modernity perceived as useful to their cause (1992, p. 44). While railing against TV programmes, radio shows and internet platforms as outlets for secular values and irreligious practices, for example, fundamentalist practitioners will purchase, invest in or employ the very same media to optimize the delivery of their message and the execution of their agenda.[3] 'Neither uncritically modern nor thoroughly traditional', religious fundamentalists are 'careful adaptors to modernity even as they attempt to reinterpret significant elements of the traditional' (Mendelsohn, 1993, p. 23). Orientated by tradition, yet responsive to the demands of the present, as Marty and Appleby conclude, 'contemporary fundamentalism is at once both derivative and vitally original' (1991, p. 835).

After reactivity and selectivity, three other ideological characteristics typical of fundamentalist movements are listed by Almond, Sivan and Appleby. They are: 'moral Manicheanism',[4] in which the world is dualistically divided into those who are 'pure and redeemed' and those outwith the movement who are 'contaminated, sinful, doomed'; 'absolutism and inerrancy', in which authoritative traditions are understood as 'true and accurate in all particulars' and modern interpretative methods rejected; and 'millennialism and messianism', in which history is believed to end in a victorious culmination of the divine plan and the accompanying vindication of those who remain committed to the fundamentals (1995c, pp. 406–7).

Organizational characteristics

Complementing these ideological traits are four organizational characteristics typical of fundamentalist movements. Characterized by an 'elect, chosen membership', fundamentalist movements comprise a 'chosen, divinely called membership, described variously as "the faithful," "the remnant," the "last outpost," the "Covenant keepers," those who "bear witness," who "walk with the Lord," and the like'. Second, fundamentalist movements draw 'sharp boundaries', which articulate a clear separation 'between the saved and the sinful'. Such is the honoured status of election and definitive separation between saved and sinful that fundamentalist ire 'is directed more strongly against drifters from one's own tradition . . . than against competing religions, atheists, and agnostics' (1995c, p. 412). Third, fundamentalist movements employ 'authoritarian' modes of organization typically expressed through a 'charismatic, leader-follower relationship in which the follower imputes extraordinary qualities, heavenly grace, special access to the deity, [and] deep and complete understanding of sacred texts' to those in authority. Finally, particular types of 'behavioral requirements' serve both to identify fellow fundamentalists and distinguish group members from those outside the movement. Such behavioural requirements might include 'distinctive music', 'rules for dress', dietary regimes, lifestyle choice, and relationship practices (1995c, pp. 407–8).

Fundamentalist movements

Bringing these ideological and organizational characteristics together, Almond, Sivan and Appleby identify ten groups which, by virtue of these definitional criteria, they consider to be full-blown fundamentalist movements. Of the six Christian case studies examined at length by the Fundamentalist Project, the authors identify both the kind of US Protestantism examined above by Ammerman and the Italian Catholic movement of *Comunione e Liberazione* as possessing 'the defining characteristics of fundamentalism'.[5] *Comunione e Liberazione* (Communion and Liberation) is a predominantly lay Catholic movement founded in the 1960s as a response both to the growing liberalization of Italian society and the perceived betrayal of traditional Catholic values by church-sponsored youth movements such as Catholic Action. Active in rightwing politics, *Comunione e Liberazione* continues to campaign within and outwith Catholic circles in defence of traditionalist principles and against the advance of secular, liberal laws (such as abortion, divorce and sexual equality). The accession of long-time ally Cardinal Joseph Ratzinger (now Benedict XVI) to the papal throne is widely held to have strengthened the movement's hand over competing conservative Catholic movements such as *Opus Dei*.

Of the Islamic movements examined in depth, the Sunni jama'at of Egypt, Syria and Tunisia, the Shi'ite movement principally in Iran, Hamas in Palestine' and the Jamaat-i-Islami of Pakistan are recognized as full-blown fundamentalisms.[6] Less so with Hamas, these Islamic fundamentalist movements arose as direct responses to post-colonial secular nationalist projects (and the liberal institutions accompanying them) of the mid-twentieth century and the practical and symbolic disruptions engendered by urban-industrialization. Articulating a return to traditionalist Islamic values (variously understood), these movements pursue the internal reform of the Muslim community which is undertaken against the backdrop of an overarching struggle against the external incursions of Western culture. In respect of Jewish fundamentalism, the Haredim, Habad and Gush Emunim are so classified, while the Kach movement – which scores consistently 'low' in the organizational ratings – is not. Differing in many respects (such as origins, geography and politics), the Haredim, Habad and Gush Emunim share a strong concern for boundary maintenance which is reinforced through the formation of enclaves and the strict adherence to a range of behavioural requirements such as those mentioned above. Finally, the 'Sikh radicals' of south Asia are identified as a full-blown fundamentalist movement, while other south Asian nationalist movements such as the Hindu RSS (National Volunteer Organization) and Sinhala Buddhists are excluded (1995c, pp. 414–23).[7]

Religious nationalism

In respect of religious nationalism – such as that expressed by the Hindu RSS, Sikh radicals and Sinhala Buddhist groups like the JHU (National Heritage Party) – Gardell says that it 'postulates that nations are divine creations with specific God-given purposes and features'. In his treatment of the Nation of Islam and its leader Louis Farrakhan, Gardell argues that religious nationalism generally holds the 'nation':

> to stand in a unique relationship with the Creator(s), from which both specific obligations and exclusive rights are derived. Nations are thus ascribed certain roles in the grand design known as the history of mankind, the outcome of which frequently is revealed and included as central to the national identity. One's own nation is often regarded as the predestined leader of the nations of the earth. (1996, pp. 8–9)

Following on from the mid-twentieth-century demise of the traditional colonial order, the end of the Cold War contributed to unleashing previously suppressed tensions relating to racial, ethnic and religious identities. Commenting upon the increased incidence of religious nationalism across the world, Juergensmeyer argues that:

> what appeared to be an anomaly when the Islamic revolution in Iran challenged the supremacy of Western culture and its secular politics in 1979 has become a major theme in international politics . . . In Sri Lanka, India, Iran, Egypt, Algeria, Afghanistan, Mongolia, Central Asia, Eastern Europe, and other places where independent nations are experimenting with nationalism of a religious nature, they are doing far more than resuscitating archaic ideas of religious rule. They are creating something new: a synthesis between religion and the secular state, a merger between the cultural identity and legitimacy of old religiously sanctioned monarchies and the democratic spirit and organizational unity of modern industrial society. (1993, pp. 1, 201–2)

While Almond, Sivan and Appleby include Sikh radical movements as a form of religious fundamentalism (excluding aforementioned nationalist movements because of their 'low' characteristic ratings), Bruce refuses to acknowledge such groups as bona fide examples of religious fundamentalism. Bruce does so because he regards movements such as these to be more concerned with ethnic identity politics than religious revitalization and to be 'only tangentially a reaction to secularization' (2000, p. 97). As Bruce acknowledges elsewhere, though, the dynamics of 'cultural defence' and 'cultural transition' which are so often central to religious national- ism may engender some degree of religious vitality. Although disagreeing with his reading of modernity and secularization, Bruce shares Martin's opinion that the identity politics connected with socio-cultural erosion and perceived threat may encourage religious vitality through the mobilization of traditional symbols and practices in the cause of cultural defence and strategic resistance (Bruce, 1996; Martin, 1978).

Fundamentalism in action

According to Marty and Appleby, religious fundamentalism's reinvigora- tion of traditional authorities furnishes it with an 'exclusive and absolute basis for a recreated political and social order':

> By selecting elements from tradition and modernity, fundamentalists seek to remake the world in the service of a dual commitment to the unfolding eschatological drama (by returning all things in submission to the div- ine) and to self-preservation (by neutralizing the threatening 'Other') . . . Boundaries are set, the enemy identified, converts sought, and institutions created and sustained in pursuit of a comprehensive reconstruction of society. (1991, p. 835)

The 'comprehensive reconstruction of society' sought by fundamentalists is, however, pursued through a variety of strategies which reflect, among other things, the respective traditions of which their movement is a part, the move- ment's particular expression of aforementioned characteristics and the pre- vailing social context(s) within which the movement exists. As with Islamic fundamentalist campaigns for wholesale 'Islamification', for example, the comprehensive reconstruction sought by some movements is intended to em- brace society in its entirety. For others, such as the Jewish Habad (Lubavitch Hasidim) of Israel, however, the comprehensive reconstruction sought per- tains solely to the social networks internal to the movement itself.

As Garvey maintains, 'fundamentalist movements invariably reject' a 'cer- tain way of thinking about law and politics that is characteristic of modern industrial nations'. Such is the case because fundamentalists see the world as moved by a divine will and thereby ordered relative to a sacred plan. Given their conviction 'that God is active in the world', fundamentalists judge modernity to be acting 'at cross-purposes to the divine will by fencing reli- gion into a private arena'. Reading historical events through reclaimed fun- damentals distilled from revitalized tradition, fundamentalist movements perceive the divine will as a moral imperative to act within and upon the world through prevailing structures of power. For Garvey, fundamentalist movements generally adopt one of three possible stances in respect of political power structures. The first he labels 'exit', which may consist of *either* a physical dislocation to a new geopolitical context (such as the independent states sought by aforementioned religious nationalisms) *or* the formation of 'enclaves' which exist as sectarian spheres within the broader societal context (such as those formed by the ultra-orthodox Hasidim).[8] Garvey terms the second political strategy 'union'. Here, fundamentalist movements seek a revision of overarching power structures in a manner which reflects their worldview, yet would still allow space for other religious groups to practise their faith within the newly reformed societal context. Overall, though, the state would function with a view to forwarding a particular set of religious fundamentals to which not all members of society could or should assent. North American Christian fundamentalism – for which liberal values of toleration and individual liberty hold a modicum of sway – is perhaps a case in point (Bruce, 2000, p. 99). The third political strategy identified by Garvey is called 'coercion'. Unlike the 'union' agenda, wholesale reformation of prevailing power structures would include the exclusion and accompanying suppression of belief systems, which dissent from the religious fundamentals now orchestrating the state. The wholly intolerant approaches of extremist Islamic Shi'ite groups in the Middle East best exemplifies the coercive agenda (Garvey, 1993, pp. 13–27).

Worldly orientations

Writing towards the close of the Chicago-based Fundamentalist Project, Almond, Sivan and Appleby identify 'four patterns of fundamentalist interaction with the world' which, they maintain, constitute 'four ways of abolishing the enemy' or, at the very least, the threat posed by the enemy's existence. These patterns are: 'world conqueror', 'world transformer', 'world creator' and 'world renouncer' (1995a, pp. 445–82; 1995b, pp. 425–44). As ideal-typical representations of possible strategies available to any movement at any time, different modes of relating to the world may be adopted by the same movement at different points in its history. Founded in late-1920s Egypt, for example, the Muslim Brotherhood commenced life as the more moderate 'world transformer' type before adopting the 'world conqueror' mode subsequent to its mid-twentieth-century radicalization.

The 'primary strategy' of the *world conqueror* movement is the absolute control of societal structures which are perceived as having 'given life to the enemy'. Having taken control of society's power structures, 'the world conqueror is in a position to define and dominate outsiders, eliminating them, or placing them in cultural or political or geographic exile, or converting them forcibly to the cause' (1995b, p. 428). On the one hand, the world conqueror strategy is directly informed by the movement's theological self-understanding. For example, a worldview (such as realized eschatology) in which the divine plan can be partially effected through the concrete historical processes of political power lends itself to the world conqueror strategy. On the other hand, the world conqueror approach is most likely to be adopted in social contexts in which the successful takeover of societal structures is perceived as a realizable possibility. In typical fundamentalist style, pragmatic calculation complements theological certitude. Among the movements which have adopted or employ a world conqueror stance, the authors list Iranian revolutionary Shi'ism, the later life of the Sunni Muslim Brotherhood, post-1980s Hamas in Palestine, Northern Irish Protestant Loyalism, US New Fundamentalism and the Jewish ultra-orthodox Gush Emunim (1995a, pp. 447–61).

In contexts where full control of societal structures is less feasible in the short term, the longer-term strategy of the *world transformer* may be adopted. Retaining the same goals as the world conqueror mode but utilizing different means, the world transformer engages societal power structures with a view to undermining all forms of opposition to its fundamentalist worldview. Working upon rather than directly against prevailing structures, the world transformer 'adopts a variety of accommodating strategies' which seek to enervate structural resistance to a point of rendering dominant institutions susceptible to eventual assault:

> Ideologically, the movement may selectively relax its boundaries to include some shades of gray, and adjust organizational requirements to this strategy. Legal advocacy, political lobbying, cultural welfare, and missionary work may be emphasized as heavily as militant activism. Civil society rather than the battlefield is the primary arena for fundamentalist interaction with the enemy. (1995b, p. 428)

Among those movements listed as world transformer types are: pre-1925 US Christian fundamentalism; *Comunione e Liberazione* in Italy; the Hindu nationalism of the RSS, VHP and BJP parties; pre-1984 (Golden Temple conflict) Sikh militancy; Egyptian Sunni movements between the 1920s and 40s; and pre-1980s Hamas (1995a, pp. 461–71).

In contrast with the two previous types of interaction with society at large, *world creator* and *world renouncer* movements eschew pursuit of a wholesale takeover of prevailing structures of power. Instead, they 'both devote considerable energies to the building up of the enclave, the demarcation of boundaries, the securing of the niche' (1995b, p. 429). While still possibly an actual historical event, the final vindication of the fundamentalist worldview may be effected through divine agency rather than concrete militancy and political agitation on the part of the movement itself. The contrast between world creator and transformer strategies resides both in the theological construal and actual extent of contact with the outside world. For the world creator movement, contact with society at large is extremely minimal, while the enclave formed by the fundamentalist community is understood 'as a clear alternative to the fallen world' and thereby in direct competition with it. Consequently, any action in the world (such as missionary endeavour) is orientated to the immediate good of the movement (such as growth) rather than the benefit of society as a whole (such as social transformation). The establishment of a community network encompassing all aspects of individual and social existence is absolutely central to the world creator movement as it seeks to render most forms of interaction with the world both symbolically insignificant and practically redundant.

A 'relatively rare mode of fundamentalism', the world renouncer strategy eschews both societal transformation and alternative social formation. Accepting the need for a greater degree of social interaction than that articulated by the world creator approach, the world renouncer movement concentrates on the formation of educational, domestic and ritual contexts conducive to orientating individual behaviour both within and outwith the community of the righteous (1995b, p. 429). In respect of empirical expressions of these two types, examples of world creator movements include the Habad (Lubavitch Hasidim) of Israel, south Indian Christian groups and 1890s–1930s Sri Lankan Buddhist communities. The scarcer world renouncer type includes, for example, Haredi Israeli Jews and the Society of Saint Pius X founded by the French Catholic traditionalist archbishop, Marcel-François Lefebvre (1995a, pp. 472–81).

Conclusion

Be it religious fundamentalism or the kinds of alternative spiritualities treated in Chapter 7, there is a tendency among certain mainstream sociologists to treat some forms of modern religiosity as exemplary manifestations of an inability to cope with the contemporary challenges of our age. For Giddens, 'there is nothing mysterious about the appearance of fundamentalism in the late-modern world'. Constituting 'an assertion of formulaic truth without regard to consequences', fundamentalism is best understood, says Giddens, as a response to the 'prevalence of radical doubt' and the 'disquieting scenarios of risk' which characterize the late-modern condition (1994, p. 100; 1991, p. 207). In the same vein, non-mainstream and alternative forms of new spirituality are written off by others as variations of late-modern 'subjectivity fetishism' (Bauman, 2007, p. 14) whose 'flight into magic, myth

[and] metaphysics' (Beck and Beck-Gernsheim, 2002, p. 7) is a pathological symptom of contemporary individualism. These authors do not employ the functionalist worldview and its framing of adherence to non-mainstream religiosity as a dysfunctional expression of deviance and maladjustment (see Chapter 8). Nevertheless, the pejorative tenor of their remarks certainly gives the impression that they regard religious fundamentalism as, at best, a form of denial and at its worst a direct threat to civilized society. Rather than formulating a constructive response to the challenges and opportunities of late modernity, the argument goes, religious fundamentalism instead seeks refuge within the infeasible certainties and unwarranted absolutisms of a romanticized past and its mythologized traditions. At its most benign, such escapism fails to make a worthwhile contribution to the political and civic programmes necessary to the betterment of late-modern society. At its most harmful, fundamentalism's oppositional mindset both undermines and imperils the projects, structures and processes at the heart of our contemporary social world (Beck, 2010).

Setting to one side the validity or otherwise of arguments such as these, it is fair to say that their normative agenda goes some way to informing a rather negative – if not one-sided – assessment of religious fundamentalism. While aforementioned treatments of fundamentalism do not necessarily exclude such negative assessments, their broader analytical concerns nevertheless furnish a more rounded appreciation of this particular religious phenomenon. Even if religious fundamentalism can justifiably be characterized as escapist and oppositional, there is little doubt that it is a lot more besides. Indeed, while some bemoan the relative detachment of the sociology of religion from its overarching disciplinary paradigm, it is perhaps the latter's ignorance of what the sociology of religion brings to the academic table that results in an often enervated representation of modern religious phenomena of a fundamentalist or non-mainstream bent.

The allied dismissal of religious fundamentalism and alternative spiritualities by late-modern theorists is somewhat ironic given their traditionally separate treatment within the sociology of religion. As evident from preceding discussions, the overwhelming bulk of sociological treatments of religious fundamentalism engage movements and groups from established religious traditions. At the same time, treatments of new religious phenomena which exhibit a good many of the fundamentalist characteristics delineated above make little or no reference to the term 'fundamentalism' in their analyses (Lewis, J. and Peterson, 2005). In a significant number of ways, for example, the new religion of Scientology shares as much with the new Christian fundamentalism of the United States as does the ultra-orthodox Jewish movement of Gush Emunim. Yet the latter is readily classified alongside new Christian fundamentalism while the former would not normally enter the same analytical frame. Furthermore, a good many of the aforementioned definitional criteria (such as reactivity, moral Manichaeism, millennialism, elect/chosen identity, sharp boundaries, authoritarianism and exacting behavioural requirements) apply as much to certain kinds of NRM as they do to the traditional fundamentalist movements treated above. In the same vein, certain of the above mentioned modes of societal interaction employed by traditional fundamentalist movements (such as world transformer, world creator and world renouncer) correspond with a number of the worldly orientations adopted by NRMs outlined in Chapter 7. In view of the overlap of empirical characteristics and the potential gains for both fields of study, the lack of analytical cross-fertilization between studies of new religiosity and religious fundamentalism is both artificial and unhealthy.

Writing of the new Christian fundamentalists of the USA, Ammerman argues that it 'is not yet clear' whether fundamentalism 'will remain a visible and active force in the larger culture'. She suggests, though, that 'the political structures in place and the experience accumulated would seem to predict a continued role for fundamentalists as participants in political life' (1991, p. 55). Bruce, however, is somewhat less circumspect in respect of Christian fundamentalism's impact in the United States:

> Apart from repeating the catalogue of failure in court cases and elections, all we can do is look at the big picture. Since Falwell launched the Moral Majority, the number of women in the labour force has continued to increase, as have the rates for divorce, abortion and illegitimate births. Homosexuality is increasingly accepted as a legitimate expression of sexuality. And prayer is still banned from schools. (2000, p. 81)

As the almost daily news bulletins continue to show, the influence of religious fundamentalism is elsewhere rather more impactful. Arguing that 'fundamentalism will subsist well into the twenty-first century', Almond, Appleby and Sivan believe it likely that 'it will thrive mostly in opposition as a dissenting minority'. 'In some settings', however, fundamentalist movements 'may assume power directly or by infiltration':

> If the prospects for the growth of politically effective fundamentalisms seem dim, their persistence is telling. The undeniable impact of fundamentalists on church, state, family, and secular society has compelled virtually every religious community to confront the issue of adaptation and survival and to formulate for itself a viable answer to the question posed by the fundamentalist phenomenon. (2003, pp. 242–3)

Irrespective of its actual size, such is the character and potential impact of religious fundamentalism that its continued relevance to the sociological study of religion appears virtually assured.

Further reading

Almond, G. A., Appleby, R. S. and Sivan, E., 2003, *Strong Religion: The Rise of Fundamentalisms Around the World*, Chicago: University of Chicago Press.
Antoun, R. T., 2008, *Understanding Fundamentalism: Christian, Islamic, and Jewish Movements*, 2nd edn, New York: Rowman & Littlefield.
Bruce, S., 2000, *Fundamentalism*, Cambridge: Polity Press.
Lawrence, B. B., 1989, *Defenders of God: The Fundamentalist Revolt against the Modern Age*, San Francisco: Harper & Row.
Marty, M. E. and Appleby, R. S., 1991, 'Conclusion: An Interim Report on a Hypothetical Family', in M. E. Marty and R. S. Appleby (eds), *Fundamentalisms Observed. The Fundamentalism Project*, vol. 1, Chicago: University of Chicago Press, pp. 814–42.

Notes

1 Whereas all forms of traditional religious fundamentalism are, by definition, conservative and traditionalist, not all forms of conservative and traditionalist religion (such as Latin American Pentecostalism) are fundamentalist (Martin, 2002, p. 1).

2 Antoun offers a similar list comprising: 'activism', in which agitation against and confrontation with prevailing institutions and dominant structures is central; 'controlled acculturation', whereby aspects from other cultural systems are adopted in a way which does not impinge upon the dominant traditionalist value system; 'millennialism', in which a future victory over the enemy is held to be already assured; 'scripturalism', in which sanctified, inerrant texts are read as blueprints and warrants which guide and justify present-day activities; 'selective modernization', whereby particular aspects of modern life are appropriated while others are rejected; 'totalism', in which every aspect of human existence – individual and collective – comes directly under the purview of religion; and 'traditioning', in which a received tradition provides a central reference point for contemporary belief and practice (2008).

3 As with NRMs, and in addition to the use of violence, the employment of modern technologies allows fundamentalist movements to project an image and create an impact which, at times, far exceeds their actual numerical size or organizational strength.

4 The term 'Manicheanism' is more commonly rendered 'Manichaeism' and refers to the movement founded upon the teachings of the Persian prophet Mani (c 216–76 CE), who taught that two divine powers (one good, the other evil) battle for cosmic supremacy.

5 The other four Christian movements exhibiting a range of fundamentalist characteristics but which are ultimately excluded as full-blown examples of religious fundamentalism are 'Catholic traditionalist', 'Guatemalan Protestant', 'Ulster Protestant', and 'South Indian'. While exhibiting 'high' rates in respect of a number of ideological characteristics (excluding millennialism), these movements tend to score 'low' under the 'organizational ratings of religious movements'.

6 The Tablighi Jamaat movement of south Asia is excluded on the grounds of scoring consistently 'low' on both ideological and organizational ratings.

7 Antoun (2008) and Almond, Appleby and Sivan (2003) furnish relatively recent treatments of many of these movements.

8 Antoun suggests that 'separation' may be executed as a radical strategy in which contact with an impure world is severely restricted through the formation of enclaves (Garvey, 1993, pp. 13–27) or in moderate form as a mode of *being in* the world but *not of* the world. Within the latter approach, fundamentalists must develop sophisticated strategies for interacting with society at large in a way which accepts the necessity of interaction but nevertheless strives to minimize the risk of contamination arising from it (2008).

10

Globalization, Religion and Modernity

Introduction

According to the American sociologist of religion James Spickard, 'though no one doubts that we live in a global era, the term "globalization" has many different meanings'. 'In the hands of various writers', maintains Spickard, globalization:

> has been used to refer, among other things, to increased global economic integration, the increased reach of global political institutions, increased international trade, increasing standardization in the production of popular culture, and increasingly far-reaching international communications networks. All of these processes affect many aspects of life. A persistent, though still under-investigated, question among scholars of religion is just how globalization in each of these areas affects the religious sphere. (2004, p. 47)

The 'under-investigated' nature of the relationship between globalization and religion is likewise remarked upon by James Beckford. For Beckford, 'careful consideration of religion, from the viewpoint of globalization, is rare'. Furthermore, 'integration of the findings of empirical research about religion into high-level theorizing about globalization is rarer still' (2003, pp. 104–5).

Writing only a half-decade later, Csordas offers a contrasting perspective in which 'the relationship between religion and globalization has rapidly become a central concern for the social sciences and religious studies'. Such is the case, argues Csordas, because of the combination of five factors which have resulted in 'a virtual explosion of interest in religion and global culture'. First, such has been 'the sheer momentum of studies on globalization and transnationalism' that the 'religious dimension' of these developments proved ultimately 'impossible to avoid'. Second, further studies in this area were encouraged by the publication of the first book-length treatment of religion and globalization in the mid-1990s (Beyer, 1994). Third, the emergence of 'Pentecostalism as a global social movement' entailed the increasing expansion of academic interest beyond established Western contexts.

(I would also add here the spread of religious fundamentalism.) Fourth, the development of diaspora studies in response to the escalating migration patterns of the second half of the twentieth century called for a more inclusive transnational perspective. Fifth, the increasing internationalization of religious pilgrimage and tourism likewise demanded a globalized academic understanding of emergent dynamics and processes (2009, pp. 11–12). Indicative of Csordas' claims, recent years have witnessed a rapid upsurge in academic engagement of the interface between globalization and religion (Altglas, 2011; Beyer and Beaman, 2007; Esposito, Fasching and Lewis, T., 2008; Geertz, A. and Warburg, 2008).

Exemplified by Berger's aforementioned reference to religious vitality across the contemporary world (1999, pp. 1–18), discussions of religion and globalization have tended to address the secularization debate in a way which treats global events as evidence of secularization theory's Eurocentric and conceptual limitations. As Csordas maintains:

> the present global situation calls into question an understanding that the world is undergoing a progressive and irreversible secularization . . . or disenchantment . . . The sleeping giant of religion, whose perpetual dream is our collective dream as a species, has never died, and it is now in the process of at least rolling over and at most leaping to its feet. (2009, p. 1)

Not unrelated to this approach, discussions of religion and globalization have also revolved around the emergence of religious fundamentalism. As Altglas asserts:

> Fundamentalism appears to be at the heart of the analysis of religious responses to globalization. Fundamentalism has increasingly been understood as a defensive reaction to globalization, an attempt to return to cultural or religious purity in response to what is perceived as a universalizing global culture. (2011, p. 14)

In the same vein, Beckford argues that 'ideas about fundamentalism tend to exercise a disproportionately heavy influence over theoretical writings about religion and globalization' (2003, p. 136).

As both secularization debates and religious fundamentalism have been treated at length elsewhere (see Chapters 4, 5 and 9), the remainder of this chapter engages the relationship between religion and globalization from other angles. First, a general sociological understanding of some of the most important aspects of globalization is established. Building upon this general understanding, the next two sections of the chapter comprise two interrelated, but analytically distinguishable, approaches to the interface of religion and globalization. The first of these sections explores academic treatments of religion as an increasingly globalized phenomenon. In so doing we engage the implications of the international reach and global spread of particular religions for the belief and practice of their individual members, organizational repertoires and overarching societal contexts. The following section explores the implications for religious belief and practice of globalizing dynamics as they relate to the typically modern processes of, for example, urban-industrialization, structural differentiation and socio-cultural plurality. The chapter concludes with some general remarks about the impact of globalization upon the contemporary religious landscape.

Globalization defined

One of the earliest scholars to give serious attention to the relationship of religion and globalization, Roland Robertson holds the concept of globalization to refer 'both to the compression of the world and the intensification of consciousness of the world as a whole' (1992, p. 8). Understood as the 'objective' aspect of globalization, the compression of the world comprises a 'concrete global interdependence' born of the 'increasing unicity' of contemporary existence. Such unicity has arisen, for example, from the establishment of international organizations and movements (such as the United Nations and environmentalism), the global transport of people and goods (migration, travel, trade) and emergence of worldwide networks such as the internet (1992, pp. 183–8). Conceived as a 'consciousness of the global whole', the 'subjective' aspect of globalization ('globality') involves an awareness that oneself, one's community (neighbourhood, ethnicity, religion) and one's society must now be understood as part of a greater, global whole. For a globalized consciousness, individual and collective identities are now understood and constructed against the all-encompassing backdrop of a global horizon. Robertson maintains that an important consequence of this globalizing dynamic is the 'relativization of basic reference points' by which individual and collective identity have traditionally been orientated.

> By relativization we mean a process involving the placing of socio-cultural or psychic entities in larger categorical contexts, such that the relativized entities are constrained to be more self-reflexive relative to other entities in the larger context. (Robertson and Chiciro, 1985, p. 234)

When situated within a globalized horizon populated by myriad options and alternative perspectives, local practices, values and beliefs – formerly experienced as fixed and indisputable – are (à la Berger and Luckmann) rendered unstable and ultimately provisional (1992, pp. 27, 176).

'Modernity is', according to Giddens, 'inherently globalizing' (1990, p. 63). Seeing globalization as a new way of ordering social life across time and space, Giddens identifies 'time-space distanciation' as a central dynamic:

> In the modern era, the level of time-space distanciation is much higher than in any previous period, and the relations between local and distant social forms and events become correspondingly 'stretched'. Globalization refers essentially to that stretching process, in so far as the modes of connection between different social contexts or regions become networked across the earth's surface as a whole. (1990, p. 64)

Globalization stretches the distance between time and space because where one is (and what time it is) in the globalized world becomes increasingly irrelevant to one's ability to interact with other parts (and time zones) of the world. Known also as 'delocalization', 'deterritorialization' or 'supraterritoriality', the stretching of time–space relations engendered by globalization decouples the 'here' from the 'now' in a way which fundamentally relativizes the traditional limitations of humankind's spatio-temporal existence (Harvey, 1990; Scholte, 2000). Underwritten by a network of advanced technologies, late-modern existence involves for Giddens the globalization of causal relations such that 'local happenings' in any one part of the world 'are shaped by events occurring many miles away and vice versa' (1990, p. 64).

The 'vice versa' is important here. It is important because Giddens stresses the reciprocal nature of globalized relations. As with his theory of 'structuration' and its representation of self–society relations (1984), Giddens' understanding of globalization involves a structural reciprocity in which the duality of 'local' and 'global' are locked in a 'recursive' relationship of mutual causation (1991, p. 2). Consequently, any 'local transformation' wrought by globalization is best conceptualized as resulting from the intermingling of regional and transnational dynamics whose outcomes may well comprise local developments at variance with globalizing trends (1990, p. 64). The processes of globalization, then, are neither all one-way nor uniform in outcome. A similar point is made by Robertson who had earlier coined the term 'glocalization' by combining the words 'global' and 'local'. For Robertson, regional variation (glocalization) exists within a globalized world through the local appropriation and subsequent modification of erstwhile global phenomena (1995, pp. 25–44). As with Giddens, Robertson rejects the view that globalization necessarily entails the wholesale homogenization of formerly different (because separate) sociocultural systems. Understood as a two-way process, globalization comprises both the 'universalization' of the particular and the 'particularization' of the universal (Robertson, 1992, pp. 97–114).

The themes of 'unicity' (Robertson) and 'network' (Giddens) which articulate the notion of connectedness so dear to many globalization theories is further emphasized by Waters' identification of the 'accelerated and increasingly effective cultural flows' made possible by the processes of globalization (2001, p. 25; see also Appadurai, 1996). Alongside his analysis of the economic and political trends stimulated by globalization, Waters treats the cultural arena which, he believes, is 'becoming more activated and energetic'. In its now globalized form, the cultural sphere embodies 'a continuous flow of ideas, information, commitment, values and tastes mediated through mobile individuals, symbolic tokens and electronic simulations' (2001, p. 196). As a result of globalization, Waters maintains:

> cultural products become more fluid and can be perceived as flows of preference, taste and information that can sweep the globe in unpredictable and uncontrolled ways. Even the most casual inspection of such preference issues as environmental concerns, Pokemon games, investment in high-tech shares, skirt lengths, roller blading and the Aids panic can confirm this development. (2001, pp. 24–5)

By virtue of these flows, the contemporary cultural arena is characterized by the rapid and large-scale transfer of practices, values and concepts between various parts of the globe. For Waters, the character and extent of these flows makes globalization a significant contributor to ongoing processes of socio-cultural diversity.

The structures and dynamics which combine to constitute the contemporary realities of globalization are perhaps best conceptualized as forming a worldwide and rapidly evolving network. On the one hand, globalization unfolds through the establishment of economic, legal, political, ethical and aesthetic structures and institutions which connect localities and regions to a seemingly limitless number of otherwise disparate locations. On the other hand, these global connections enable the flow of people, goods, information, power, tastes and values whose transmission occurs at a scale and speed best described as vertiginous. In combination, the global connections and the worldwide flows they enable embody practical and symbolic implications for human existence in all of its private and social dimensions.

Globalized religion

Like so many processes connected with the contemporary dynamics of globalization, the international spread of particular religious traditions and movements is by no means a recent historical phenomenon. The early-modern expansion of successive European colonial enterprises, for example, ensured the spread of Roman Catholic, Anglican and Protestant forms of Christianity to many regions of the globe. Not unrelated to the colonial enterprise, modern missionary endeavours ensured the continued presence and spread of Christianity subsequent to its initial global distribution. Likewise connected with imperial growth and related modes of wealth extraction, the forced transport of slave labour – principally, but not solely, from Africa – further contributed to the internationalization of previously regional forms of religious belief and practice. While the particular conditions of the US plantations undermined the persistence of inherited African religious traditions, for example, Latin American contexts proved conducive to the perdurance of certain homeland beliefs and practices as manifest in contemporary belief systems such as Candomblé (Brazil), Santería (Cuba) and Vodou (Haiti). At the same time, successive migratory flows such as the Muslim diaspora emanating from the Middle East and spreading across northern Africa and south-eastern Asia have been long-standing contributors to the global spread of particular religious traditions. As with the hybrid spiritual repertoires born of the mixture of European, Latin American and African components, the internationalization of Islam has spawned numerous forms of innovative religious expressions resulting from the mixing of local and imported beliefs and practices (Mandaville, 2007).

While the internationalizing processes of mission and migration are well established, as with so many individual elements of globalization, what is historically new is their intensification at the hands of the large-scale connectedness and accelerated flows typical of contemporary globalizing dynamics. Indicative of recent and exponential increases in international mobility and global networking, the relative ease, scale and rapidity by which people, goods, ideas and beliefs are diffused throughout the world constitutes the kind of transformation which is more than a simple difference of degree in respect of what has gone before. In addition to fundamentally altering the established patterns of already internationalized religious traditions, the contemporary dynamics of globalization have engendered a range of novel developments which are combining to reshape the late-modern religious landscape.

Global Christianities

Although of long-standing character, the international networks of Catholic and Protestant Christianity have been subject to innovative developments in the light of late-modern globalizing trends. Encouraged by the devolutionary aspirations articulated by the Second Vatican Council (1962–65), for example, Roman Catholic bishops in Latin America set about forging a version of the Christian faith which was grounded in and spoke directly to the conditions of poverty and injustice endemic across their continent. Spurred on by the success of the first Latin American Council of Bishops at Medellín, Colombia, in 1968, continent-wide networks were formed and foreign support mobilized in the cause of an emergent Roman Catholic regionalism. Popularized through print, radio and televisual media, the base ecclesial communities and liberation theology movement, for example, articulated a Latin American Catholicism which both galvanized the poor and challenged dominant economic-political arrangements (Dawson, A., 1999). In so doing, however, these Latin American regionalist movements were perceived by the Rome-based administrative centre as both potentially compromising institutional interests and comprising a dubious theological worldview. Commencing in the mid-1970s with Pope Paul VI (1963–78), and spearheaded by Cardinal Ratzinger (now Pope Benedict XVI), the Roman hierarchy set about re-establishing central bureaucratic control and thereby checking any regionalist challenge to Vatican (and de facto European) institutional dominance. Further reinforced under the papacy of John Paul II (1978–2005), the recentralization of administrative authority in Rome serves to minimize potential challenges from and strategic networking between nascent regional movements beyond the Church's European power base.

As Jenkins points out, the overwhelming majority of Christians now reside in the 'global South' (2007). Furthermore, whereas 80 per cent of Christians in 1900 were white, by the turn of the new millennium this figure had halved to 40 per cent (Freston, 2008, pp. 24–51). In addition to the obvious socio-cultural differences between 'North' and 'South', the popularity of conservative Christianity in Africa, for example, provides further contrast with the more liberal European and North American contexts (Hanciles, 2008, pp. 71–90). Both reflecting their newfound significance and articulating a growing theological confidence, conservative Christians in Africa are progressively challenging what they perceive as breaches of doctrinal and ecclesial orthodoxy undertaken by their European and North American counterparts. Recent meetings of both the Lutheran World Federation and Anglican Communion, for example, have been accompanied by forceful African-led critiques of the 'unchristian' practice of homosexuality which, it is argued, is being inappropriately tolerated by ecclesiastical authorities in the North.

The contemporary global profile of conservative Christianity is closely related to the rapid and widespread growth of Pentecostal and charismatic missionary churches (Coleman, 2000; Martin, 2002). As Freston notes:

> One of the key religious changes of the late twentieth century was the transformation of Pentecostalism into a global religion and the shift in its centre of numerical growth and missionary initiative to the Third World. This growth and transnational expansion have been largely independent of the churches of the developed West, stressing the polycentric nature of current Christian globalization. (2005, p. 34)

Freston's mention of the 'polycentric' (many-centred) character of globalization highlights the fact that the contemporary global spread of Christianity is no longer expressed through the movement of missionaries and religious resources from the urban-industrial North to the global South. Rather, the globalization of Christianity is today being driven by multiple flows of physical and material resources from and between a variety of locations, a great many of which are situated outside of the traditional Western heartlands of Christianity.[1] Although estimates vary, adherence to contemporary modes of conservative Christianity stands in the hundreds of millions, with a growth rate of anything up to ten million individual conversions a year – virtually all of which occur in the global South.

Csordas maintains that the ability of a religion to spread across geographical and socio-cultural boundaries is determined by two aspects: portability and transposability. Referring principally to the practical aspects of a religious repertoire, the notion of 'portable practice' refers to 'rites that can be easily learned', which require little by way of specialist 'knowledge or paraphernalia', are not 'necessarily linked to a specific cultural context', and may be 'performed without commitment to an elaborate ideological or institutional apparatus'. Treating the narrative aspects of the religious repertoire, the concept of 'transposable message' relates to 'the basis of appeal contained in religious tenets, premises, or promises' which 'can find footing across diverse linguistic and cultural settings'. Ultimately, the transposability of a 'religious message' depends upon its ability to mould to local settings ('plasticity') or relate the local context to an overarching message of global or cosmic significance ('universality') (2009, pp. 4–5). Although Csordas' notions of portability and transposability lend themselves to illuminating the global spread of Pentecostal and charismatic Christianity, they by no means provide an exhaustive explanation. As Robbins' discussion of academic treatments of the globalization of Pentecostal and charismatic Christianity points out, the particular modes of institutional formation and social organization related with these conservative religious phenomena make an important contribution to their ongoing global success (2004, pp. 117–43).

New religious globalities

Similar strains and stresses to those experienced by established world religions such as Christianity are increasingly felt by new religious movements as their growth and spread likewise engenders a global institutional reach. Now international in scope, NRMs such as the Unification Church, Jehovah's Witnesses, Latter-day Saints, Soka Gakkai and Scientology, for example, employ strategies and processes through which personnel (such as leadership selection and training), assets (such as ownership and remittances) and local initiatives (such as editorial censorship) are carefully managed to ensure central control, organizational cohesion and identity maintenance. Treating the Universal Church of the Kingdom of God

(UCKG), Freston explores a number of the implications of what he terms 'the growing transnationalization of Third World evangelical religion' (2005, pp. 33–65). Founded in Brazil in 1977, the neo-Pentecostal UCKG quickly spread abroad and today has over 1,000 churches in roughly 80 countries throughout the world. Benefitting from a 'centrally planned' transnational expansion, the UCKG employs an 'integrated . . . ecclesiastical strategy' to maintain bureaucratic control and uniformity of doctrine across its increasingly global and culturally diverse networks. Key to this control is the maintenance of a clerically centred authority structure through which 'congregational participation in decision-making is eliminated and strong horizontal ties among members are de-emphasized'. At the same time, 'the emergence of personal loyalties and local power bases' among the clergy are prevented through their regular transfer both within and outwith national territories. As Freston notes, for example, the then Bishop of Kenya 'is a Brazilian of 34 years of age, who has already been a pastor in at least 11 churches in different countries' (2005, p. 41).

Arising from the early twentieth-century healing ministry of Simon Kimbangu, the now internationalized Congolese Kimbanguist church faces similar issues to those of the UCKG. Officially founded in 1959, the Church of Christ on Earth by His Special Envoy Simon Kimbangu spread initially to parts of Africa before rapidly expanding across Europe and other regions through Congolese migration in the late twentieth century. Faced with the Church's rapid spread across increasingly diverse socio-cultural contexts, the Kimbanguist leadership set about reinforcing central administrative control by measures both practical and symbolic. Such practical measures, for example, included the issuing in 2002 of institutional regulations to which all Kimbanguist congregations were expected to adhere. As Garbin shows in his treatment of unofficial 'spiritual manifestations' occurring in London, these regulations (*Les Résolutions*) were used by the leadership to quell what amounted to a 'challenge to the ongoing concentration of spiritual power' (2011, p. 50). Symbolically, charismatic power was concentrated around the Congo-based leadership through the discursive representation of the Church's spiritual birthplace (Nkamba) as the 'Holy City' and 'New Jerusalem'. Complementing practical regulatory obligations, symbolic ties with Nkamba are furthered through its promotion as a site of pilgrimage along with the global circulation of earth and water collected from the Holy City which is widely distributed for use in Kimbanguist rituals of healing and cleansing (Garbin, 2011, pp. 40–57).

Migratory dynamics

In addition to their implications for institutional integrity and movement identity, the globalizing processes of mission, migration and mobility impact also upon migrant communities and their host nations. Intensified by contemporary globalizing dynamics, recent increases in international migratory flows have given rise to a range of innovative approaches to their impact upon the religious field. Drawing upon the geography of religion and diaspora and transnational studies, for example, academic engagement with migratory communities throws light upon transformations in belief and practice wrought by the processes of territorial upheaval and subsequent resettlement (Johnson, 2007; Levitt, 2007). Commencing with the processes of 'deterritorialization', the dynamics of migration conclude with an ongoing act of 'reterritorialization' through which the practices, beliefs and symbols of the migrants' religion are transposed to a new socio-cultural terrain. Such migratory transposition involves the practical and symbolic reconfiguration of religious repertoires as the received traditions and inherited rituals of the 'homeland' are adapted to meet the opportunities, challenges and demands of a new and perhaps radically different socio-cultural context. Aided by the contemporary global condition, transnational networks and international flows facilitate the formation of 'translocal' religious identities which are formed through literal and imagined movements between a native spiritual homeland and a newly adopted locale. Moving between preservation, adaptation and creativity, migrant communities celebrate, refashion and formulate religious repertoires which both recapitulate received traditions and speak to novel experiences.

Studies of migrant Hindu communities in South Africa and England, for example, evidence ritual reformulation and symbolic innovation expressed through the growth of female ritual responsibilities, the decreasing importance of caste as a determinant of spiritual status and the increasing irrelevance of traditional ethnic-linguistic distinctions (David, 2011, pp. 74–89; Kumar, 2000). Now functioning beyond the traditional context of south Asia, the religious repertoire of diaspora Hinduism has decreasing need to call upon the inherited divisions of sex, caste and ethnicity which stand increasingly out of place in the socially mobile and culturally plural context of modern, urban-industrial society. In the same vein, studies of the practical and symbolic adaptations made by Japanese new religions in Brazil underline their importance to the subsequent success of these migratory religious movements. Whether through unconscious refashioning or strategic modification, the 'Brazilianization' of Japanese new religious repertoires enabled movements such as the Church of World Messianity, Perfect Liberty Kyodan and Seicho-no-Ie to move beyond their migrant Japanese base and establish themselves as significant components of the Brazilian religious landscape. Along with the adoption of the Portuguese language, such Brazilianization included the alignment of traditional healing rituals with the prevailing therapeutic concerns of popular religion, the drawing of parallels between traditional Japanese deities and dominant Christian figures (Jesus and Mary) and the appropriation of Catholic prayers and terminology such as the 'Our Father', 'church' and 'mass' (Clarke, 2000; Dawson, A., 2007, pp. 29–34).

Macro-structural implications

As well impacting upon the flesh and blood practitioners of transnational religious repertoires, the globalizing dynamics of migration and mobility impact also upon the macro-structural processes of national and regional contexts. In the United Kingdom, for example, the growing presence of Hinduism and Islam has contributed to the reformulation of traditional legal protections (such as blasphemy laws) formerly applicable only to the established denominations of Christianity. Across the Channel in France, the growing presence of traditional Islamic dress has sparked debates in respect of the secular nature of French civic identity and the contemporary viability of traditional public–private distinctions. At the same time, the arrival in Europe of NRMs such as Scientology has provoked debates about received legal definitions – and their attendant juridical protections and socio-economic privileges – in respect of religion. Most recent of all, arrests in Australasia, Europe and the United States have publicized the now global spread of religious repertoires which use psychotropic substances such as ayahuasca as an integral component of their spiritual regimes (Dawson, A., forthcoming).[2] As with Christianity in China and Scientology in Germany, for example, a potentially hostile politico-legal environment has meant that ayahuasca religions such as Santo Daime and the Vegetable Union have functioned clandestinely for the vast majority of their existence outside of their native home of Brazil (where these religions are legal).[3] Whereas recent landmark rulings by Dutch and US courts have afforded Santo Daime and the Vegetable Union a certain degree of legality, in many other parts of the world their religious repertoires remain illegal or exist in an ill-defined juridical limbo which continues to leave their practitioners open to prosecution. In addition to engendering debate about state understandings of what constitutes religion, the ritual use of ayahuasca problematizes established juridical definitions of 'drugs' as either therapeutic or recreational. Understood and employed as a sacrament of healing and spiritual development, ayahuasca fits neither of these categories and thereby questions the ability of prevailing legislation to treat matters such as this appropriately.

Virtually global

By way of concluding this section, such is the progressive symbiosis between globalizing dynamics and technological innovation that some mention should be made of the relationship between religion and the internet. The successor to a long line of networking media (post, telegraph, telephone, radio, television), the immediacy, utility and interfacial potential of the worldwide web stands to make a significant contribution to the transformation of religious belief and practice in our nascent digital age.[4] At present, less than twenty per cent of the global population has access to the internet. At the same time, provision of and access to virtually mediated religious goods (that is 'cyber-religion') is somewhat minimal (Cowan and Dawson, L., 2004; Larsson, 2007). Nevertheless, religious use of the internet is already a significant contributor to the global flow of faith-related ideas, beliefs and practices (Hadden and Cowan, 2000; Højsgaard and Warburg, 2005).

In respect of research questions relating to religious interface with the internet, the manner and extent to which virtually mediated religious participation impacts upon the character of contemporary belief and ritual practice is worthy of consideration. Potentially highly rewarding in respect of cost–benefit returns, the mobilization of digitally mediated resources by religious organizations is likewise a fruitful area of study. In the same vein, and exemplified by the use of Wikipedia, home sites and designated domains, virtual image management by religious groups and movements promises to be a worthwhile topic of enquiry. Finally, individual and collective use of internetworking (chat-rooms, forums, blogs, discussion posts) for religious purposes is a growing phenomenon worthy of further investigation.

Globalizing modernity

Aforementioned arguments (see Chapter 5) that secularization theories formulated in Europe do not necessarily apply to other modern societies reflect the view that the social processes and structural dynamics collectively labelled 'modernity' do not play out in a uniform manner across different parts of the world (Berger, Davie and Fokas, 2008).[5] It is now commonplace for sociologists of religion to cite the concept of 'multiple modernities' as a means to arguing for the continued variegation of societal contexts regardless of contemporary increases in global connectedness and transnational flows (Davie, 2007).

Multiple modernities

Popularized by Shmuel Eisenstadt, the 'multiple modernities' thesis rejects what it regards as the argument for 'the convergence of industrial societies' implicit within 'classical theories of modernization' and 'sociological analysis' (2000, pp. 1–29). According to Eisenstadt, classical sociological approaches:

> all assumed, even if implicitly, that the cultural program of modernity as it developed in modern Europe and the basic institutional constellation

that emerged there would ultimately take over in all modernizing and modern societies; with the expansion of modernity, they would prevail throughout the world. (2000, p. 1)

Subsequent to the mid-twentieth century, however, the globalization of modern processes and dynamics has engendered 'multiple institutional and ideological patterns' in a manner which refutes 'the homogenizing and hegemonic assumptions' of classical approaches along with their theoretical association of modernization with Westernization. Consequently, while Western modes of modernity both 'enjoy historical precedence and continue to be a basic reference point for others . . . One of the most important implications of the term "multiple modernities" is that modernity and Westernization are not identical'. In sum, 'Western patterns of modernity are not the only "authentic" modernities' available for concrete societal expression.

Eisenstadt grounds the multiple modernity thesis upon the socio-cultural variegation generated by 'the ongoing dialogue' between the globalizing forces of 'modern reconstruction' and local 'cultural resources' embodied by 'respective civilizational traditions'. As a result of this ongoing interaction:

> Not only do multiple modernities continue to emerge . . . but within all societies, new questionings and reinterpretations of different dimensions of modernity are emerging. The undeniable trend . . . is the growing diversification of the understanding of modernity, of the basic cultural agendas of different modern societies . . . While the common starting point was once the cultural program of modernity as it developed in the West, more recent developments have seen a multiplicity of cultural and social formations going far beyond the very homogenizing aspects of the original version. All these developments do indeed attest to the continual development of multiple modernities, or of multiple interpretations of modernity — and, above all, to attempts at 'de-Westernization', depriving the West of its monopoly on modernity. (2000, p. 24)

In a tone reminiscent of Robertson's notion of 'glocalization', Eisenstadt sees the 'trends of globalization' as 'a story of continual constitution and reconstitution of a multiplicity of cultural programs' born of the interface of the 'cultural program of modernity' and the 'specific cultural patterns, traditions, and historical experiences' of any given locale.

Latin American mixed modernity

Prior to its actual formulation, the generic thrust of Eisenstadt's multiple modernities thesis was being explored and debated in various regions of the globe. In Latin America, for example, scholars have articulated understandings of their continent as a socio-cultural terrain characterized by the multifaceted mixture of the modern and the traditional (Canclini, 1995; Ortiz, 1994). As Canclini notes, 'we conceive of Latin America as a more complex articulation of traditions and modernities (diverse and unequal), a heterogeneous continent consisting of countries in each of which coexist multiple logics of development' (1995, p. 9). Not only in comparison with the North, Latin American modernity comprises multiple dimensions which contrast both across continental national boundaries and from region to region within a single country. Sociologically speaking, then, the specificity of Latin American modernity 'prevents the mechanical importation of explanatory schemes elaborated in response to other processes such as those of Europe' (Wanderley, 2007, p. 65).

Resistance to the uncritical application of explanatory schemes articulated outwith the Latin American continent is expressed also by sociologists of religion. Treating the relationship between neo-Pentecostalism and modernity in Brazil, for example, João Passos argues that the 'historical contradictions and cultural peculiarities' of the Brazilian context render irrelevant northern hemispheric debates pertaining to the secularization or re-enchantment of urban-industrial society. Passos rejects the relevance of this debate on the grounds that Brazil is an ex-colonial nation whose particular historical trajectory gives rise to a 'dependent modernization' characterized by different dynamics and processes than those experienced by the more powerful countries of the North. As a result of its peculiar modernizing trajectory, Brazil experienced the transition from pre-modernity to contemporary modernity in a fundamentally different way from the USA or Europe. In contrast to the 'rupture' between traditional and modern society experienced by the North, Passos maintains, Brazilian modernization exhibits a greater degree of continuity and overlap between pre-modern and contemporary societal forms. Consequently, sociological theories of religious development formulated in light of the northern hemispheric experience of modernity fail adequately to address a Brazilian context born of a different set of modernizing dynamics. For Passos, then, the rise and spread of Brazilian neo-Pentecostalism should not be understood through the application of an 'extrinsic' analytical continuum of enchantment–disenchantment–re-enchantment (2006). Rather than being seen as a revitalization of waning religious influence, the rise of neo-Pentecostalism in Brazil is more fruitfully viewed as a modern expression of traditional religious dynamics.

Likewise engaging Brazilian neo-Pentecostalism, Roger Roca rejects the naive application of 'foreign' models which attempt to explicate the relationship of money and religion within this historically novel religious phenomenon. Formulated in view of the dominant neo-liberal economic paradigm and ongoing commodification of modern Western society, Roca argues, foreign explanatory models dismiss the 'health and wealth' prosperity gospel of neo-Pentecostal groups such as the UCKG as a form of

'commodity fetishism' engendered by the capitalistic processes of globalization. In contrast, however, Roca maintains that alien models such as
these fail adequately to appreciate the actual processes at play in neo-Pentecostalism's attitude to wealth. Such is the case because these models do
not pay attention to the role traditionally played by money in the internal
dynamics of the Brazilian religious landscape. Were this role to be properly
appreciated, organizations such as the UCKG would not be dismissed as
'simply practising money fetishism' à la Western neo-liberal commodification. Viewed instead as recapitulating long-standing dynamics intrinsic to
the Brazilian religious field, the prosperity-orientated activities of groups
like the UCKG can be regarded as re-appropriating money in a way which
is understood to transform it 'into an instrument of Divine agency'. Rather
than exemplifying Western notions of 'money fetishism', when situated relative to the established dynamics of the Brazilian religious landscape, such
practices are best understood as a modern form of domestic 'money-magic'
(2007, pp. 319–39).

Treating the Latin American continent as a whole, the Mexican sociologist of religion Roberto Blancarte highlights the limitations of the 'modernity
paradigm, as outlined by Max Weber and Ernst Troeltsch' for understanding
the place of Protestant Christianity across the continent.[6] Blancarte argues
that any 'analysis of the religious life of Latin America' must engage the relationship between 'popular religion, Catholicism and religious dissent' (here,
Protestantism). In respect of Protestantism, however, Blancarte asserts that
'there is nothing to prove the existence of something similar to what Weber
talked about, a social group imbued by "worldly asceticism" and economic
development, or the emergence of a middle class influenced by religious individualism' (2000, p. 593). Consequently, notions of the 'Protestant ethic'
and understandings of 'religious evolution' formulated by Weber and Troeltsch respectively (see Chapters 3 and 7) articulate a Eurocentric perspective which simply does not apply to Latin America. Rejecting established
associations between 'Classic Protestantism' and 'the secularization process'
(here, 'the individualization of beliefs' and 'the separation of the political
and religious spheres'), Blancarte instead calls for a 'geography of religious
dissent' which does justice to the particularities of the Latin American context. In so doing, Blancarte analyses Protestant dissent by understanding it
relative to long-standing 'deficiencies in the Catholic ecclesiastic structure'
across the continent and the peculiar nature of Latin American popular religiosity (2000, pp. 591–603).

By way of concluding his piece, Blancarte remarks that Latin America
is today characterized by 'a great deal of mobility' which is both 'highly
dynamic and increasingly pluralistic'. At the same time, he calls for the application of 'tolerance' which, he admits, has not readily featured among the
'principal values' of the continent's 'civil or religious history'. As noted in
Chapter 1, these characteristics are typical of modernity and their increasing

presence in Latin America reflects the progressive influence of modern processes and dynamics akin to those already well established across the urban-industrial North. Blancarte's point, then, is not that Latin America should be excluded from consideration as modern. Rather, his argument is that the kind of modernity unfolding in Latin America is sufficiently different from that occurring in Europe and North America to render inapplicable the classic 'modernity paradigm' employed by the likes of Durkheim, Weber and Troeltsch in their discussions of religious development in an urban-industrializing context. Latin America is modern, but modern in its own way.

Theorizing modernity

How modernity is theoretically construed impacts directly upon academic understandings of social transformation and religious change. Eisenstadt's notion of 'multiple modernities', for example, builds upon the understanding of modernity as a 'cultural program' defined principally in relation to particular conceptualizations of 'human agency' and 'the possibility of different interpretations of core transcendental visions and . . . the institutional patterns related to them'. Among the most important of these typically modern conceptions are:

- 'the awareness of a great variety of roles existing beyond narrow, fixed, local, and familial ones';
- 'the possibility of belonging to wider translocal, possibly changing, communities';
- 'an emphasis on the autonomy of man' and 'his or her . . . emancipation from the fetters of traditional political and cultural authority';
- 'belief in the possibility that society could be actively formed by conscious human activity'.

In combination, these conceptions give rise to 'the modern program' of 'radical transformation' from which a new 'political order' emerges (2000, pp. 3–5).

The important thing about Eisenstadt's understanding of modernity as a 'cultural program' is its prioritization of human agency and its 'reflexive' intellectual project. Here, the cultural and political programme of modernity emerges from 'new self-conceptions and new forms of collective consciousness'. Born of 'arguments', 'premises' and 'interpretations', modernity is mobilized as an idea which is ultimately shaped through its discursive representation as a new mode of being in the world. What Eisenstadt does not do, however, is relate any of these developments to the kinds of concrete dynamics and material processes outlined in Chapter 1 as typical characteristics of modernity. In failing to do so, Eisenstadt represents modernity as a cultural programme whose relationship with the concrete macro-structural dynamics and material institutional processes of the last 200 years is at best ill-defined. Resulting from his prioritization of human agency and its novel self-conception, Eisenstadt offers a one-sided treatment of modernity which, in theoretical terms, falls foul of the sociological axiom that all good social theory does justice to both aspects of the self–society, agency–structure relationship.

By focusing solely upon individual agency and the self-conceptions which direct it, Eisenstadt defines modernity in isolation from the structural dynamics and material processes which gave rise to modern society as we know it. As shown throughout the preceding chapters, these structural dynamics and material processes have direct implications for religion. This is so because they set the overarching conditions of possibility within which religious belief and practice exist. Sociologically speaking, modernity is defined by the presence of a range of concrete characteristics, of which urban-industrialization, societal integration, structural differentiation, socio-cultural plurality, continual transformation, and individualization were treated in Chapter 1.[7]

One way or another, all of the matters engaged by this book reflect the impact of these processes upon the religious sphere. In no order of priority, for example, the dynamics of modernity have engendered the distancing of the state from religion (structural secularization), the waning influence of practices and beliefs inherited from prior generations (detraditionalization) and the growing diversity of the religious landscape (pluralization). Modern processes have also given rise to increased self-determination in matters religious (subjectivization), the growing presence of an innovative and flexible religiosity beyond traditional institutional confines (spiritualization) and the decreasing relevance of fixed or inherited categories such as sex or caste as determinants of spiritual status (mobilization).

When discussing the manner or extent to which a society may be considered modern, we must also consider in what way, if at all, the particular modernity in question instantiates the macro-structural dynamics, mid-range processes and micro-social practices which are, by definition, associated with modernity. In the same vein, when reflecting sociologically upon religion, the impact or otherwise of these characteristically modern developments upon belief and practice should likewise be treated. On the one hand, the pluralizing dynamics of contemporary globalizing processes entail the continued spread of modernity as a multiple phenomenon born of the 'glocalizing' interface of the global and the local. Such multiplicity entails variety and this variety entails difference. In respect of religion, this difference is manifested by both the variegation in modern belief and practice and the diversity of theoretical approaches formulated to engage such variegation. Consequently, and as noted above, the relevance of sociological theories of religion formulated within the academic communities of the North cannot be automatically assumed when treating modernizing societies of the global South.

On the other hand, however, the globalization of modernity means also the spread of dynamics and processes which, in some way or another, involves the replication of structural forces, institutional practices and associational patterns. Such replication entails similarity and this similarity entails comparability. As it pertains to religion, this comparability is expressed through shared developmental trajectories and, where appropriate, the justifiable application of concepts and theories which – though directly relevant to local events – may have been formulated in a different region of the globe. In view of modernizing processes at work in Brazil, for example, Antônio Pierucci and Reginaldo Prandi argue for the applicability of traditional secularization theories for understanding ongoing changes to the Brazilian religious landscape (1996). In the same vein, Bernado Sorj outlines the 'constitution of new collective identities' in Brazil which are formed in relation to the same structural processes of marketization and commodification already in play across the neo-liberalized North (2006, p. 91).

Conclusion

The impact of globalization upon the contemporary religious landscape involves for the sociology of religion elements of continuity, revision and rupture. Because the dynamics of globalization are embroiled with the processes of modernity, structural parallels, institutional comparisons and associational equivalences are in evidence between otherwise disparate geographical and socio-cultural contexts. This degree of continuity between the multiple modernities established and emerging across the globe affirms the ongoing relevance of much existing sociological theory both in respect of modern society in general and contemporary religion in particular. Where conditions allow – and irrespective of their Western provenance – theories of detraditionalization, mobilization, pluralization, secularization, sacralization, spiritualization and subjectivization are potentially relevant means of engaging the religious terrain of any modern context.

The relevance of these theories, however, is conditional upon a contextual sensitivity which remains alive to their revision or irrelevance in view of local conditions on the ground. Irrespective of the kind or location of the dynamics at play, modernity does not unfold in a vacuum, just as its constitutive processes do not take shape independently of a locality's established patterns of socio-cultural reproduction. Inherited structures and traditional ways of life supply a vibrant and, at times, resistant set of ingredients which impact upon the character ultimately assumed by all forms of modern society. At the same time, we should not forget that the globalized character of our own modern societies involves transformation at home as much as it connotes social change elsewhere. Not simply happening 'there', globalization is also occurring 'here'. The fact that these theories were coined in the West does not entail their automatic relevance to explaining what is now happening in the West. Whether at home or abroad, the insensitive and unreflexive application of sociological theories of religion should always be resisted.

Finally, the rapidity and scale of social transformation characteristic of globalizing modernity brings with it the constant possibility that religious change on the ground outruns our theoretical grasp of events. Ongoing debates about the relevance or otherwise of existing theories to one context or another should not blind us to the continued need for openness to new ways of understanding our rapidly changing world. From micro-social interactions, through mid-range processes to macro-structural dynamics, the rapid and far-reaching transformation inherent in globalizing modernity challenges the academic community to innovative theorizing upon every dimension of contemporary belief and practice. In addition to this and the other challenges issued, the theoretical opportunities engendered by globalizing modernity make the discipline of the sociology of religion a vibrant and, at times, exhilarating place to be.

Further reading

Altglas, V. (ed.), 2011, *Religion and Globalization: Religion and Space in Global Context*, London: Routledge.

Beyer, P. and Beaman, L. (eds), 2007, *Religion, Globalization, and Culture*, Boston: Brill.

Esposito, J. L., Fasching, D. and Lewis, T., 2008, *Religion and Globalization: World Religions in Historical Perspective*, Oxford: Oxford University Press.

Geertz, A. W. and Warburg, M. (eds), 2008, *New Religions and Globalization: Empirical, Theoretical and Methodological Perspectives*, Aarhus: Aarhus University Press.

Notes

1 As Kalu and others have noted, such is the polycentric nature of contemporary globalizing dynamics that Christian missionaries are increasingly being sent from the global South to undertake evangelistic ministries in the religious wilderness of the 'secular' North (2008, pp. 3–23).

2 The active agent of ayahuasca is dimethyltryptamine (DMT), which is treated by many legal frameworks as akin to cocaine and heroin. The form of ayahuasca most consumed in non-indigenous religious contexts is a beverage made from the boiled-down mixture of a vine (*Banisteriopsis caapi*) and shrub-leaves (*Psychotria viridis*).

3 An introductory overview of Brazil's ayahuasca religions is provided by Dawson, A., 2007, pp. 67–98.

4 Houtman and Aupers, for example, see the contemporary 'sacralization of digital technology' as contributing to the broader refutation of classical theories of secularization and disenchantment (2010, pp. 15–23).

5 An integral part of Weber's understanding of the emergence and development of modern society, the multilinear perspective nevertheless leaves room for disagreement as to the character and extent of variegation engendered by modernization.

6 Eloísa Martín rightly criticizes Blancarte for failing to recognize the heterogeneous character of Latin America, whose regional and national variations problematize the blanket application of continent-wide theories (2009, pp. 273–85).

7 As Chapter 1 also notes, the concept of late modernity assumes both the radicalization of these processes and the emergence of other dynamics such as marketization and globalization.

Bibliography

Abercrombie, N., Hill, S. and Turner, B. S., 1980, *The Dominant Ideology Thesis*, London: Allen & Unwin.

——. 1984, 'Ideology', in N. Abercrombie, S. Hill and B. S. Turner (eds), *The Penguin Dictionary of Sociology*, London: Penguin, pp. 118–19.

Ahmed, L., 1992, *Women and Gender in Islam: Historical Roots of a Modern Debate*, New Haven: Yale University Press.

Almond, G. A., Sivan, E. and Appleby, R. S., 1995a, 'Examining the Cases', in M. E. Marty and R. S. Appleby (eds), *Fundamentalisms Comprehended. The Fundamentalism Project*, vol. 5, Chicago: University of Chicago Press, pp. 445–82.

——. 1995b, 'Explaining Fundamentalisms', in M. E. Marty and R. S. Appleby (eds), *Fundamentalisms Comprehended*, pp. 425–44.

——. 1995c, 'Fundamentalism: Genus and Species', in M. E. Marty and R. S. Appleby (eds), *Fundamentalisms Comprehended*, pp. 399–424.

Almond, G. A., Appleby, R. S. and Sivan, E., 2003, *Strong Religion: The Rise of Fundamentalisms around the World*, Chicago: University of Chicago Press.

Alston, W. P., 1967, 'Religion', in P. Edwards (ed.), *Encyclopedia of Philosophy*, vol. 7, Macmillan and Free Press, pp. 140–7.

Altglas, V. (ed.), 2011, *Religion and Globalization: Religion and Space in Global Context*, London: Routledge.

Althaus-Reid, M., 2003, *The Queer God*, London: Routledge.

Althusser, L., 1971, 'Ideology and Ideological State Apparatuses: Notes Towards an Investigation', in L. Althusser (ed.), *Lenin and Philosophy, and Other Essays*, London: New Left Books, pp. 127–86.

Amaral, L., 2000, *Carnaval da Alma: Comunidade, Essência e Sincretismo na Nova Era*, Petrópolis: Editôra Vozes.

Ammerman, N. T., 1987, *Bible Believers: Fundamentalists in the Modern World*, New Brunswick: Rutgers University Press.

——. 1991, 'North American Protestant Fundamentalism', in M. E. Marty and R. S. Appleby (eds), *Fundamentalisms Observed. The Fundamentalism Project*, vol. 1, Chicago: University of Chicago Press, pp. 1–65.

——. 1997, *Congregation and Community*, New Brunswick: Rutgers University Press.

——. (ed.), 2007, *Everyday Religion: Observing Modern Religious Lives*, Oxford: Oxford University Press.

Antoun, R. T., 2008, *Understanding Fundamentalism: Christian, Islamic, and Jewish Movements*, 2nd edn, New York: Rowman & Littlefield.

Appadurai, A., 1996, *Modernity at Large: Cultural Dimensions of Globalization*, Minneapolis: University of Minnesota Press.

Archer, M. S., 1996, *Culture and Agency: The Place of Culture in Social Theory*, revised edn, Cambridge: Cambridge University Press.

——. 2008, *Being Human: The Problem of Agency*, Cambridge: Cambridge University Press.

Arjomand, S. A., 1995, 'Unity and Diversity in Islamic Fundamentalism', in M. E. Marty and R. S. Appleby (eds), *Fundamentalisms Comprehended*, pp. 179–98.

Assmann, H., 1981, 'The Power of Christ in History, Conflicting Christologies and Discernment', in R. Gibellini (ed.), *Frontiers of Theology in Latin America*, London: SCM Press, pp. 134–45.

Bailey, E. I., 1997, *Implicit Religion in Contemporary Society*, Den Haag: Kok Pharos.

Bainbridge, W. S., 1997, *The Sociology of Religious Movements*, London: Routledge.

Barker, E., 1999, 'New Religious Movements: Their Incidence and Significance', in B. Wilson and J. Cresswell (eds), *New Religious Movements: Challenge and Response*, London and New York Routledge, pp. 15–31.

——. 2008, 'The Church Without and the God Within: Religiosity and/or Spirituality?', in E. Barker (ed.), *The Centrality of Religion in Social Life: Essays in Honour of James A. Beckford*, Aldershot: Ashgate, pp. 187–202.

Bauman, Z., 1989, 'Hermeneutics and Modern Social Theory', in D. Held and J. B. Thompson (eds), *Social Theory of Modern Societies: Anthony Giddens and His Critics*, Cambridge: Cambridge University Press, pp. 34–55.

——. 2005, *Liquid Life*, Cambridge: Polity Press.

——. 2007, *Consuming Life*, Cambridge: Polity Press.

Beck, U., 1992, *Risk Society: Towards a New Modernity*, London: Newbury Park.

——. 2010, *A God of One's Own: Religion's Capacity for Peace and Potential for Violence*, Cambridge: Polity Press.

Beck, U. and Beck-Gernsheim, E., 2002, *Individualization: Institutionalized Individualism and its Social and Political Consequences*, London: Sage.

Beck, U., Giddens, A. and Lash, S. (eds), 1994, *Reflexive Modernization: Politics, Tradition and Aesthetics in the Modern Social Order*, Cambridge: Polity Press.

Beckford, J. A., 1980, *Scientology, Social Science and the Definition of Religion*, Los Angeles: Freedom Publishing.

——. 2003, *Social Theory and Religion*, Cambridge: Cambridge University Press.

Bellah, R. N., 1970, *Beyond Belief: Essays on Religion in a Post-Traditionalist World*, Berkeley: University of California Press.

——. 2005, 'Civil religion in America', *Daedalus* 134.4, pp. 40–55. [Originally published in 1967, *Daedalus* 96.1, pp. 1–21.]

Bendix, R., 1992, *Max Weber: An Intellectual Portrait*, Berkeley: University of California Press.

Berger, P. L., 1963, 'A market model for the analysis of ecumenicity', *Social Research* 30.2, pp. 75–90.

——. 1966, *Invitation to Sociology*, London: Pelican.

——. 1967, *The Sacred Canopy: Elements of a Sociological Theory of Religion* New York: Anchor Books.

——. 1969, *A Rumor of Angels: Modern Society and the Rediscovery of the Supernatural*, New York: Doubleday.

——. 1980, *The Heretical Imperative: Contemporary Possibilities of Religious Affirmation*, London: Collins.

——. 1999, 'The Desecularization of the World: A Global Overview', in P. Berger (ed.), *The Desecularization of the World: Resurgent Religion and World Politics*, Grand Rapids: Ethics and Public Policy Center, pp. 1–18.

Berger, P. L., Berger, B. and Kellner, H., 1974, *The Homeless Mind: Modernization and Consciousness*, Harmondsworth: Penguin.

Berger, P. L., Davie, G. and Fokas, E., 2008, 'Introduction', in P. Berger, G. Davie and E. Fokas (eds), *Religious America, Secular Europe? A Theme and Variations*, Aldershot: Ashgate, pp. 1–7.

Berger, P. L. and Luckmann, T., 1966, *The Social Construction of Reality: A Treatise in the Sociology of Knowledge*, London: Pelican.

Beyer, P., 1994, *Religion and Globalization*, London: Sage.

Beyer, P. and Beaman, L. (eds), 2007, *Religion, Globalization, and Culture*, Boston: Brill.

Bilton, T., Bonnett, K. and Jones, P., 2002, *Introductory Sociology*, 4th edn, Basingstoke: Palgrave Macmillan.

Blancarte, R. J., 2000, 'Popular religion, Catholicism and socioreligious dissent in Latin America: facing the modernity paradigm', *International Sociology* 15.4, pp. 591–603.

Boddy, J., 1989, *Wombs and Alien Spirits: Women, Men, and the Zar Cult in Northern Sudan*, Wisconsin: University of Wisconsin Press.

Boff, L., 1986, *E a Igreja se Fez Povo: Eclesiogênese a Igreja que Nasce da Fé do Povo*, Petrópolis: Editôra Vozes.

Bonino, J. M. (ed.), 1984, *Faces of Jesus: Latin American Christologies*, New York: Orbis.

Bourdieu, P., 1984, *Distinction: A Social Critique of the Judgement of Taste*, London: Routledge & Keegan Paul.

——. 1991a, 'Genesis and structure of the religious field', *Comparative Social Research* 13.1, pp. 1–44.

——. 1991b, *Language and Symbolic Power*, Cambridge: Polity Press.

——. 1993, *Sociology in Question*, London: Sage.

——. 1998, *Practical Reason: On the Theory of Action*, Cambridge: Polity Press.

Bourdieu, P. and Wacquant, L. J. D., 1992, *An Invitation to Reflexive Sociology*, Cambridge: Polity Press.

Boyd, S. B., Longwood, W. M. and Meusse, M. W. (eds), 1996, *Redeeming Men: Religion and Masculinities*, Louisville: Westminster John Knox Press.

Brasher, B., 1998, *Godly Women: Fundamentalism and Godly Power*, New Brunswick: Rutgers University Press.

Brenner, S., 1998, *The Domestication of Desire: Women, Wealth, and Modernity in Java*, Princeton: Princeton University Press.

Brink, T. L., 1995. 'Quantitative and/or qualitative methods in the scientific study of religion', *Zygon* 30.3, pp. 461–75.

Bromley, D. G., 2006, 'Affiliation and Disaffiliation Careers in New Religious Movements', in E. V. Gallagher and W. M. Ashcroft (eds), *Introduction to New and Alternative Religious Movements in America*, vol. 1, Westport: Praeger Press, pp. 42–64.

Brown, A. (ed.), 2004, *Mentsh: On Being Jewish and Queer*, New York: Alyson Books.

Browne, K., Munt S. R. and Yip. A. K. T. (eds), 2010, *Queer Spiritual Spaces: Sexuality and Sacred Spaces*, Aldershot: Ashgate.

Bruce, S., 1992, 'Introduction', in S. Bruce (ed.), *Religion and Modernization: Sociologists and Historians Debate the Secularization Thesis*, Oxford: Oxford University Press, pp. 1–7.

——. 1996, *Religion in the Modern World: From Cathedrals to Cults*, Oxford: Oxford University Press.

——. 1999, *Choice and Religion: A Critique of Rational Choice Theory*, Oxford: Oxford University Press.

——. 2000, *Fundamentalism*, Cambridge: Polity Press.

——. 2001, 'The Social Process of Secularization', in R. K. Fenn (ed.), *The Blackwell Companion to Sociology of Religion*, Oxford: Blackwell, pp. 249–63.

——. 2002, *God is Dead: Secularization in the West*, Oxford: Blackwell.

——. 2006, 'Secularization and the impotence of individualized religion', *The Hedgehog Review* 8.1/2, pp. 35–45.

——. 2009, 'The importance of social science in the study of religion', *Fieldwork in Religion* 4.1, pp. 7–28.

Bruce, S. and Glendinning, T., 2010, 'When was secularization? dating the decline of the British churches and locating its cause', *British Journal of Sociology* 16.1, pp. 107–26.

Bruce, S. and Voas, D., 2007, 'The Spiritual Revolution: Another False Dawn for the Sacred', in K. Flanagan and P. C. Jupp (eds), *A Sociology of Spirituality*, Aldershot: Ashgate, pp. 43–61.

——. 2010, 'Vicarious religion: an examination and critique', *Journal of Contemporary Religion* 25.2, pp. 243–59.

Bryman, A., 2004, *Social Research Methods*, 2nd edn, Oxford: Oxford University Press.

Burity, J. A., 2003, 'Mídia e religião: regimes do real entre o mistério, o aparente e o virtual', *Religião e Sociedade* 23.2, pp. 77–91.

Burr, V., 2003, *Social Constructionism*, 2nd edn, London: Routledge.

Butler, T. and Watt, P., 2007, *Understanding Social Inequality*, London: Sage.

Cabinet Office Strategy Unit, 2003, *Ethnic Minorities and the Labour Market: Final Report*, London: Cabinet Office Strategy Unit.

Campbell, C., 1987, *The Romantic Ethic and the Spirit of Modern Consumerism*, Oxford: Blackwell.

Campos, L. S., 2004, 'Protestantismo Brasileiro e Mudança Social', in B. M. de Souza and L. M. S. Martino (eds), *Sociologia da Religião e Mudança Social: Católicos, Protestantes e Novos Movimentos Religiosos no Brasil*, São Paulo: Paulus, pp. 106–36.

Canclini, N. G., 1995, *Hybrid Cultures: Strategies for Entering and Leaving Modernity*, Minneapolis: University of Minnesota Press.

Caplan, L. (ed.), 1987, *Studies in Religious Fundamentalism*, Basingstoke: Palgrave Macmillan.

Carrette, J. R. (ed.), 1999, *Religion and Culture: Michel Foucault*, Manchester: Manchester University Press.

Carrette, J. and King, R., 2005, *Selling Spirituality: The Silent Takeover of Religion*, London: Routledge.

Casanova, J., 1994, *Public Religions in the Modern World*, Chicago: University of Chicago Press.

——. 2006, 'Rethinking secularization: a global comparative perspective', *The Hedgehog Review* 8.1/2, pp. 7–22.

Chesnut, R. A., 2003, *Competitive Spirits: Latin America's New Religious Economy*, Oxford: Oxford University Press.

Chryssides, G., 1999, *Exploring New Religions*, London: Cassell.

Cipriani, R., 1984, 'Religion and politics. The Italian case: diffused religion', *Archives de Sciences Sociales des Religions* 58.1, pp. 29–51.

Clarke, P. B., 2000, *Japanese New Religions in Global Perspective*, London: Curzon Press.

——. 2005, *New Religious Movements in Global Perspective*, London: Routledge.

Cohen, R. and Kennedy, P., 2007, *Global Sociology*, 2nd edn, New York: NYU Press.

Coleman, S., 2000, *The Globalisation of Charismatic Christianity: Spreading the Gospel of Prosperity*, Cambridge: Cambridge University Press.

Cone, J. H., 1970, *A Black Theology of Liberation*, New York: Orbis.

Cowan, D. E. and Dawson, L. L. (eds), 2004, *Religion Online: Finding Faith on the Internet*, London: Routledge.

Craib, I., 1992, *Modern Social Theory: From Parsons to Habermas*, London: Harvester/Wheatsheaf.

——. 1997, *Classical Social Theory: An Introduction to the Thought of Marx, Weber, Durkheim, and Simmel*, Oxford: Oxford University Press.

Craib, I. and Benton, T., 2001, *Philosophy of Social Science: The Philosophical Foundations of Social Thought*, Basingstoke: Palgrave.

Csordas, T. J., 2009, 'Modalities of Transnational Transcendence', in T. J. Csordas (ed.), *Transnational Transcendence: Essays on Religion and Globalization*, Berkeley: University of California Press, pp. 1–29.

Daly, M., 1968, *The Church and the Second Sex*, New York: Harper & Row.

——. 1973, *Beyond God the Father: Toward a Philosophy of Women's Liberation*, Boston: Beacon Press.

David, A. R., 2011, 'Gendered Dynamics of the Divine: Trance and Hindu Possession in Diaspora Hindu Sites in East London', in A. Dawson (ed.), *Summoning the Spirits: Possession and Invocation in Contemporary Religion*, London: I. B. Tauris, pp. 74–89.

Davidman, L., 1993, *Tradition in a Rootless World: Women Turn to Orthodox Judaism*, Berkeley: University of California Press.

Davie, G., 1994, *Religion in Britain since 1945: Believing without Belonging*, Oxford: Blackwell.

——. 2000, *Religion in Modern Europe: A Memory Mutates*, Oxford: Oxford University Press.

——. 2006, 'Is Europe an exceptional case?', *The Hedgehog Review* 8.1/2, pp. 23–34.

——. 2007, *The Sociology of Religion*, London: Sage.

——. 2010, 'Vicarious religion: a response', *Journal of Contemporary Religion* 25.2, pp. 261–6.

Dawson, A., 1999, *The Birth and Impact of the Base Ecclesial Community and Liberative Theological Discourse in Brazil*, San Francisco: Catholic Scholars Press.

——. 2005, 'The gnostic church of Brazil: contemporary neo-esotericism in late-modern perspective', *Interdisciplinary Journal of Research on Religion* vol. 1, art. 8, www.religjournal.com/.

——. 2007, *New Era – New Religions: Religious Transformation in Contemporary Brazil*, Aldershot: Ashgate.

——. 2011a, 'Consuming the self: new spirituality as "mystified consumption"', *Social Compass* 58.3.

——. (ed.), 2011b, *Summoning the Spirits: Possession and Invocation in Contemporary Religion*, London: I. B. Tauris.

——. forthcoming, *Santo Daime: A New World Religion*, London: Continuum.

Dawson, L. L., 1998, *Comprehending Cults: The Sociology of New Religious Movements*, Toronto: Oxford University Press.

——. 2010, 'Church–Sect–Cult: Constructing Typologies of Religious Groups', in P. B. Clarke (ed.), *The Oxford Handbook of the Sociology of Religion*, Oxford: Oxford University Press, pp. 525–44.

Day, A., 2009, 'Researching belief without asking religious questions', *Fieldwork in Religion* 4.1, pp. 86–104.

Della Porta, D. and Diani, M., 1999, *Social Movements: An Introduction*, Oxford: Blackwell.

Dobbelaere, K., 2000, 'From religious sociology to sociology: towards globalisation?', *Journal for the Scientific Study of Religion* 39.4, pp. 433–47.

——. 2002, *Secularization: An Analysis at Three Levels*, Brussels: P. I. E.-Peter Lang.

——. 2009, 'The Meaning and Scope of Secularization', in P. B. Clarke (ed.), *The Oxford Handbook of the Sociology of Religion*, pp. 599–615.

Droogers, A., 2008, 'Defining Religion: A Social Science Approach', in P. B. Clarke (ed.), *The Oxford Handbook of the Sociology of Religion*, pp. 263–79.

Durkheim, É., 1961, *Moral Education: A Study in the Theory and Application of the Sociology of Education*, New York: Free Press.

——. 1965, *Sociology and Philosophy*, London: Cohen and West.

——. 1982, *The Rules of Sociological Method*, New York: Free Press.

——. 1984, *The Division of Labour in Society*, London: Macmillan.

——. 2001, *The Elementary Forms of Religious Life*, Oxford: Oxford University Press.

——. 2006, *On Suicide*, London: Penguin.

Eagleton, T., 1990, *Ideology: An Introduction*, London: Verso.

Edles, L. D., 2002, *Cultural Sociology in Practice*, Oxford: Blackwell.

Einstein, M., 2008, *Brands of Faith: Marketing Religion in a Commercial Age*, London: Routledge.

Elias, N., 1978, *What is Sociology?* London: Hutchinson.

Eisenstadt, S. N., 1999, *Fundamentalism, Sectarianism and Revolutions: The Jacobin Dimension of Modernity*, Cambridge: Cambridge University Press.

——. 2000, 'Multiple modernities', *Daedalus* 129.1, pp. 1–29.

Esposito, J. L., Fasching, D. and Lewis T., 2008, *Religion and Globalization: World Religions in Historical Perspective*, Oxford: Oxford University Press.

Ezzy, D., 2001, 'The commodification of witchcraft', *Australian Religious Studies Review* 14.1, pp. 31–44.

Feagin, J. R. and Vera, H., 2008, *Liberation Sociology*, 2nd edn, Boulder: Paradigm Publishers.

Feuerbach, L., 1957, *The Essence of Christianity*, New York: Harper Torchbooks.

Finke, R., 1997, 'The Consequences of Religious Competition: Supply-Side Explanations for Religious Change', in L. A. Young (ed.), *Rational Choice Theory and Religion: Summary and Assessment*, London: Routledge, pp. 45–64.

Finke, R. and Stark, R., 1992, *The Churching of America, 1776–1990: Winners and Losers in Our Religious Economy*, New Brunswick: Rutgers University Press.

Fiorenza, E. S., 1983, *In Memory of Her: A Feminist Theological Reconstruction of Christian Origins*, London: SCM Press.

Flanagan, K., 2007, 'Spirituality: Some Disciplinary Perspectives', in K. Flanagan and P. C. Jupp (eds), *A Sociology of Spirituality*, Aldershot: Ashgate, pp. 1–21.

Flanagan, K. and Jupp, P. C., 2007, 'Conclusion', in K. Flanagan and P. C. Jupp (eds), *A Sociology of Spirituality*, pp. 251-61.

Flory, R. W. and Miller, D. E., 2007, 'The Embodied Spirituality of the Post-Boomer Generations', in K. Flanagan and P. C. Jupp (eds), *A Sociology of Spirituality*, pp. 201–18.

——. 2008, *Finding Faith: The Spiritual Quest of the Post-Boomer Generation*, New Jersey: Rutgers University Press.

Freston, P., 2005, 'The universal church of the kingdom of God: a Brazilian church finds success in southern Africa', *Journal of Religion in Africa* 35.1, pp. 33–65.

——. 2008, 'Globalization, Religion, and Evangelical Christianity: A Sociological Meditation from the Third World', in O. U. Kalu and A. M. Low (eds), *Interpreting Contemporary Christianity: Global Processes and Local Identities*, Grand Rapids: Eerdmans, pp. 24–51.

Frigerio, A., 1996, *Scientology and Contemporary Definitions of Religion in the Social Sciences*, Los Angeles: Freedom Publishing.

Frykenberg, R. E., 1993, 'Hindu Fundamentalism and the Structural Stability of India', in M. E. Marty and R. S. Appleby (eds), *Fundamentalisms and the State. The Fundamentalism Project*, vol. 3, Chicago: University of Chicago Press, pp. 233–55.

Fuller, R. C., 2001, *Spiritual but not Religious: Understanding Unchurched America*, New York: Oxford University Press.

Galindo, D., 2004, 'Religião, mídia e entretenimento: o culto "tecnofun"', *Estudos de Religião* 26, pp. 24–52.

Garbin, D., 2011, 'Embodied Spirit(s) and Charismatic Power among Congolese Migrants in London', in A. Dawson (ed.), *Summoning the Spirits*, pp. 40–57.

Gardell, M., 1996, *Countdown to Armageddon: Louis Farrakhan and the Nation of Islam*, London: Hurst and Company.

Garvey, J. H., 1993, 'Introduction: Fundamentalism and Politics', in M. E. Marty and R. S. Appleby (eds), *Fundamentalisms and the State*, pp. 13–27.

Geertz, A. W. and Warburg, M. (eds), 2008, *New Religions and Globalization: Empirical, Theoretical and Methodological Perspectives*, Aarhus: Aarhus University Press.

Geertz, C., 1973, *The Interpretation of Cultures*, New York: Basic Books.

Giddens, A., 1971, *Capitalism and Modern Social Theory: An Analysis of the Writings of Marx, Durkheim and Max Weber*, Cambridge: Cambridge University Press.

——. 1979, *Central Problems in Social Theory: Action, Structure and Contradiction in Social Analysis*, Berkeley: University of California Press.

——. 1984, *The Constitution of Society: Outline of the Theory of Structuration*, Cambridge: Polity Press.

——. 1990, *The Consequences of Modernity*, Stanford: Stanford University Press.

——. 1991, *Modernity and Self-Identity: Self and Society in the Late Modern Age*, Cambridge: Polity Press.

——. 1994, 'Living in a Post-Traditional Society', in U. Beck, A. Giddens and S. Lash (eds), *Reflexive Modernization*, pp. 56–109.

——. 1998, *Conversations with Anthony Giddens: Making Sense of Modernity*, Stanford: Stanford University Press.

Gilbert, D., 2008, *The American Class Structure in an Age of Growing Inequality*, 7th edn, Newbury Park: Pine Forge Press.

Gill, R., Hadaway, C. K. and Marler, P. L., 1998, 'Is religious belief declining in Britain?', *Journal for the Scientific Study of Religion* 37.3, pp. 507–16.

Goldman, M. S., 1999, *Passionate Journeys: Why Successful Women Joined a Cult*, Ann Arbor: University of Michigan Press.

Göle, N., 1996, *The Forbidden Modern: Civilization and Veiling*, Ann Arbor: University of Michigan Press.

Gramsci, A., 1971, *Selections from the Prison Notebooks*, New York: International Press.

Griffiths, R. M., 1997, *God's Daughters: Evangelical Women and the Power of Submission*, Berkeley: University of California Press.

Guerra, L. D., 2003, *Mercado Religioso no Brasil: Competição, Demanda e a Dinâmica da Esfera da Religião*, João Pessoa: Idéia.

Gunew, S., 1990, 'Feminist Knowledge: Critique and Construct', in S. Gunew (ed.), *Feminist Knowledge: Critique and Construct*, London: Routledge, pp. 13–35.

Gutiérrez, G., 1974, *A Theology of Liberation*, London: SCM Press.

Habermas, J., 2002, *Religion and Rationality: Essays on Reason, God and Modernity*, Cambridge: MIT Press.

——. 2008, *Between Naturalism and Religion: Philosophical Essays*, Cambridge: Polity Press.

Hadden, J. K. and Cowan, D. E. (eds), 2000, *Religion on the Internet: Research Prospects and Promises*, New York: Elsevier Science.

Hall, D. (ed.), 1997, *Lived Religion in America*, Princeton: Princeton University Press.

Hall, S. et al., 1978, *On Ideology*, London: Hutchinson.

Hammond, P. E., 1992, *Religion and Personal Autonomy: The Third Disestablishment in America*, Columbia: University of South Carolina Press.

Hanciles, J. J., 2008, 'African Christianity, Globalization and Mission: Marginalizing the Center', in O. U. Kalu and A. M. Low (eds), *Interpreting Contemporary Christianity*, pp. 71–90.

Hanegraaff, W., 1999, 'New age spiritualities as secular religion: a historian's perspective', *Social Compass* 46.2, pp. 145–60.

Harding, S., 1996, 'Standpoint Epistemology (a Feminist Version)', in S. P. Turner (ed.), *Social Theory and Sociology: The Classics and Beyond*, Oxford: Blackwell, pp. 146–60.

Harvey, D., 1990, *The Condition of Postmodernity: An Enquiry into the Origins of Cultural Change*, Oxford: Blackwell.

Heald, G., 2000, *The Soul of Britain*, London: Opinion Research Business.

Heelas, P., 1996, *The New Age Movement: The Celebration of the Self and the Sacralization of Modernity*, Oxford: Blackwell.

——. 2006, 'Challenging secularization Theory. The growth of "new age" spiritualities of life', *The Hedgehog Review* 8.1/2, pp. 46–58.

——. 2007, 'The Holistic Milieu and Spirituality: Reflections on Voas and Bruce', in K. Flanagan and P. C. Jupp (eds), *A Sociology of Spirituality*, pp. 63–80.

——. 2008, *Spiritualities of Life: New Age Romanticism and Consumptive Capitalism*, Oxford: Blackwell.

——. 2009, 'Spiritualities of Life', in P. B. Clarke (ed.), *The Oxford Handbook of the Sociology of Religion*, pp. 758–82.

Heelas, P. and Woodhead, L., 2005, *The Spiritual Revolution: Why Religion is Giving Way to Spirituality*, Oxford: Blackwell.

Heilbron, J., 1995, *The Rise of Social Theory*, Cambridge: Polity Press.

Hervieu-Léger, D., 2000, *Religion as a Chain of Memory*, Cambridge: Polity Press.

Højsgaard, M. T. and Warburg, M. (eds), 2005, *Religion and Cyberspace*, London: Routledge.

Hood, R., 2005, 'Mystical, Spiritual, and Religious Experiences', in R. F. Paloutzian and C. L. Park (eds), *Handbook of the Psychology of Religion and Spirituality*, London: Guildford Press, pp. 348–64.

Houtart, F. and Rousseau, A., 1971, *The Church and Revolution*, New York: Orbis.

Houtman, D. and Aupers, S., 2010, 'Religions of Modernity: Relocating the Sacred to the Self and the Digital', in S. Aupers and D. Houtman (eds), *Religions of Modernity: Relocating the Sacred to the Self and the Digital*, Leiden: Brill, pp. 1–29.

Hunt, S., 2004, *The Alpha Enterprise: Evangelism in a Post-Christian Era*, Aldershot: Ashgate.

Iannaccone, L. R., 1992, 'Sacrifice and stigma: reducing free-riding in cults, communes, and other collectives', *Journal of Political Economy* 100.2, pp. 271–91.

——. 1997, 'Rational Choice: Framework for the Scientific Study of Religion', in L. A. Young (ed.), *Rational Choice Theory and Religion*, pp. 25–45.

——. 2002, 'A Marriage Made in Heaven? Economic Theory and Religious Studies', in S. Grossbard-Schechtman and C. Clague (eds), *The Expansion of Economics: Towards a More Inclusive Social Science*, New York: M. E. Sharpe, pp. 203–23.

Jenkins, P., 2007, *The Next Christendom: The Coming of Global Christianity*, revised edn, New York: Oxford University Press.

Jenkins, R., 1996, *Social Identity*, London: Routledge.

Johnson, P. C., 2007, *Diaspora Conversions: Black Carib Religion and the Recovery of Africa*, Berkeley: California University Press.

Juergensmeyer, M., 1993, *The New Cold War? Religious Nationalism Confronts the Secular State*, Berkeley: University of California Press.

Kalu, O. U., 2008, 'Changing Tides: Some Currents in World Christianity at the Opening of the Twenty-First Century', in O. U. Kalu and A. M. Low (eds), *Interpreting Contemporary Christianity*, pp. 3–23.

Kaplan, L. (ed.), 1992, *Fundamentalism in Comparative Perspective*, Amherst: University of Massachusetts Press.

Kaufman, D. R., 1991, *Rachel's Daughters: Newly Orthodox Jewish Women*, New Brunswick: Rutgers University Press.

Keller, M., 2002, *The Hammer and the Flute: Women, Power and Spirit Possession*, Baltimore: Johns Hopkins University Press.

Kritzman, L. D. (ed.), 1988, *Michel Foucault: Politics, Philosophy and Culture*, New York: Routledge.

Krondorfer, B. (ed.), 2009, *Men and Masculinities in Christianity and Judaism*, London: SCM Press.

Kuhn, T. S., 1962, *The Structure of Scientific Revolutions*, Chicago: University of Chicago Press.

Kumar, P. P., 2000, *Hindus in South Africa: Their Traditions and Beliefs*, Durban: University of Durban-Westville.

Larsson, G. (ed.), 2007, *Religious Communities on the Internet*, Stockholm: Swedish Science Press.

Lawrence, B. B., 1989, *Defenders of God: The Fundamentalist Revolt against the Modern Age*, San Francisco: Harper & Row.

Layder, D., 1994, *Understanding Social Theory*, London: Sage.

Lévi-Strauss, C., 1966, *The Savage Mind*, Chicago: University of Chicago Press.

Levitt, P., 2007, *God Needs No Passport: Immigrants and the Changing American Religious Landscape*, New York: New Press.

Lewis, I. M., 1986, *Religion in Context: Cults and Charisma*, Cambridge: Cambridge University Press.

——. 2003, *Ecstatic Religion: A Study of Spirit Possession and Shamanism*, 3rd edn, London: Routledge.

Lewis, J. R. (ed.), 2009, *Scientology*, Oxford: Oxford University Press.

Lewis, J. R. and Peterson, J. A. (eds), 2005, *Controversial New Religions*, Oxford: Oxford University Press.

Leyland, W. (ed.), 2000, *Queer Dharma: Voices of Gay Buddhists*, vol. 2, San Francisco: Gay Sunshine Books.

Liebman, C. S., 1993, 'Jewish Fundamentalism and the Israeli Polity', in M. E. Marty and R. S. Appleby (eds), *Fundamentalisms and the State*, pp. 68–87.

Lippy, C. H., 1994, *Being Religious, American Style: A History of Popular Religiosity in the United States*, Westport: Greenwood Press.

Lofland, J. and Skonovd, N., 1981, 'Conversion motifs', *Journal for the Scientific Study of Religion* 20.4, pp. 373–85.

Lofland, J. and Stark, R., 1965, 'Becoming a world-saver: a theory of conversion to a deviant perspective', *American Sociological Review* 30.6, pp. 862–75.

Loughlin, G., 2007, *Queer Theology: Rethinking the Western Body*, Oxford: Blackwell.

Luckmann, T., 1967, *The Invisible Religion: The Problem of Religion in Modern Society*, New York: Macmillan.

——. 1990, 'Shrinking transcendence, expanding religion?', *Sociological Analysis* 50.2, pp. 127–38.

Lukes, S., 1992, *Émile Durkheim, His Life and Work: A Historical and Critical Study*, London: Penguin.

Maduro, O., 1982, *Religion and Social Conflicts*, New York: Orbis.

Magnani, J. G. C., 2000, *O Brasil da Nova Era*, Rio de Janeiro: Jorge Zahar Editor.

Mahmood, S., 2005, *The Politics of Piety: The Islamic Revival and the Feminist Subject*, Princeton: Princeton University Press.

Mandaville, P., 2007, *Global Political Islam*, London: Routledge.

Marler, P. L. and Hadaway, C. K., 2002, '"Being religious" or "being spiritual" in America: a zero-sum proposition?', *Journal for the Scientific Study of Religion* 41.2, pp. 289–300.

Martin, D. A., 1965, 'Towards Eliminating the Concept of Secularization', in J. Gould (ed.), *Penguin Survey of the Social Sciences*, London: Penguin, pp. 169–82.

——. 1978, *A General Theory of Secularization*, London: Basil Blackwell.

——. 1990, *Tongues of Fire: The Explosion of Protestantism in Latin America*, Oxford: Blackwell.

——. 1996, *Forbidden Revolutions: Pentecostalism in Latin America and Catholicism in Eastern Europe*, London: SPCK.

——. 1997, *Does Christianity Cause War?* London: Clarendon Press.

——. 2002, *The World Their Parish: Pentecostalism as Cultural Revolution and Global Option*, Oxford: Blackwell.

——. 2005, *On Secularization: Towards a Revised General Theory*, Aldershot: Ashgate.

Martín, E., 2009, 'From popular religion to practices of sacralization: approaches for a conceptual discussion', *Social Compass* 56.2, pp. 273–85.

Marty, M. E. and Appleby, R. S., 1991, 'Conclusion: An Interim Report on a Hypothetical Family', in M. E. Marty and R. S. Appleby (eds), *Fundamentalisms Observed*, pp. 814–42.

Mathewes, C. T., 2006, 'An Interview with Peter Berger', *The Hedgehog Review* 8.1/2, pp. 152–61.

McCall, L., 2001, *Complex Inequality: Gender, Class and Race in the New Economy*, New York: Routledge.

McGuire, M. B., 2008a, *Lived Religion: Faith and Practice in Everyday Life*, Oxford: Oxford University Press.

——. 2008b, 'Toward a Sociology of Spirituality: Individual Religion in Social/ Historical Context', in E. Barker (ed.), *The Centrality of Religion in Social Life*, pp. 215–32.

McLellan, D., 1973, *Karl Marx: His Life and Thought*, New York: Harper & Row.

——. (ed.), 1977, *Karl Marx: Selected Writings*, Oxford: Oxford University Press.

——. 1995, *Ideology*, 2nd edn, Buckingham: Open University Press.

Melton, J. G., 2004, 'An Introduction to New Religions', in J. R. Lewis (ed.), *The Oxford Handbook of New Religious Movements*, Oxford: Oxford University Press, pp. 16–35.

Mendelsohn, E., 1993, 'Religious Fundamentalism and the Sciences', in M. E. Marty and R. S. Appleby (eds), *Fundamentalisms and Society. The Fundamentalism Project*, vol. 2, Chicago: University of Chicago Press, pp. 23–41.

Moberg, D. O., 1984, *The Church as a Social Institution: The Sociology of American Religion*, 2nd edn, Grand Rapids: Baker Book House.

Moore, R. L., 1994, *Selling God: American Religion in the Marketplace of Culture*, New York: Oxford University Press.

Niebuhr, H. R., 1957, *The Social Sources of Denominationalism*, New York: Meridian Books.

Oakley, A., 1972, *Sex, Gender and Society*, London: Maurice Temple Smith.

Ore, T., 2008, *The Social Construction of Difference and Inequality: Race, Class, Gender and Sexuality*, 4th edn, Columbus: McGraw-Hill.

Ortiz, R., 1994, *Mundialização e Cultura*, São Paulo: Editora Brasiliense.

Ouzgane, L. (ed.), 2006, *Islamic Masculinities*, New York: Zed Books.

Owen, A., 1989, *The Darkened Room: Women, Power, and Spiritualism in Late Victorian England*, London: Virago Press.

Palmer, S., 1994, *Moon Sisters, Krishna Mothers, Rajneesh Lovers*, Syracuse: Syracuse University Press.

Palmisano, S., 2010, 'Spirituality and Catholicism: the Italian experience', *Journal of Contemporary Religion* 25.2, pp. 221–41.

Parsons, S. F., 2002, *The Cambridge Companion to Feminist Theology*, Cambridge: Cambridge University Press.

Parsons, T., 1937, *The Structure of Social Action*, New York: McGraw-Hill.

——. 1951, *The Social System*, New York: Free Press.

——. 1960, *Structure and Process in Modern Society*, New York: Free Press.

——. 1963a, 'Christianity and Modern Industrial Society', in E. A. Tiryakian (ed.), *Sociological Theory, Values and Sociocultural Change*, New York: Free Press, pp. 33–70.

——. 1963b, 'Introduction to M. Weber', in Weber, M., *The Sociology of Religion*, Boston: Beacon Press, pp. xix–lxvii.

——. 1964, *Social Structure and Personality*, New York: Free Press.

——. 1966, 'Religion in a modern pluralistic society', *Review of Religious Research* 7.3, pp. 125–46.

——. 1968, 'Christianity', in D. L. Sills (ed.), *International Encyclopedia of the Social Sciences*, vol. 2, New York: Crowell, Collier & Macmillan, pp. 425–47.

——. 1979, 'Religious and economic symbolism in the western world', *Sociological Enquiry* 49.2/3, pp. 1–48.

Passos, J. D., 2006, 'Pentecostalismo e modernidade: conceitos sociológicos e religião popular metropolitana', *Revista Nures* 2.2, http://www.pucsp.br/revistanures/revista2/artigos_joao_decio.pdf.

Pierucci, A. F. and Prandi, R. (eds), 1996, *A Realidade Social das Religiões no Brasil: Religião, Sociedade e Política*, São Paulo: Editora Hucitec.

Redden, G., 2005, 'The new age: towards a market model', *Journal of Contemporary Religion* 20.2, pp. 231–46.

Riesebrodt, M., 1990, *Pious Passion: The Emergence of Modern Fundamentalism in the United States and Iran*, Berkeley: University of California Press.

Riis, O. P., 2008, 'Methodology in the Sociology of Religion', in P. B. Clarke (ed.), *The Oxford Handbook of the Sociology of Religion*, pp. 229–44.

Robbins, J., 2004, 'The globalization of Pentecostal and charismatic Christianity', *Annual Review of Anthropology* 33, pp. 117–43.

Robertson, R., 1992, *Globalization: Social Theory and Global Culture*, London: Sage.

——. 1995, 'Glocalization: Time–Space and Homogeneity–Heterogeneity', in M. Featherstone, S. Lash and R. Robertson (eds), *Global Modernities*, London: Sage, pp. 25–44.

Robertson, R. and Chiciro, J., 1985, 'Humanity, globalization, and worldwide religious resurgence: a theoretical exploration', *Sociological Analysis* 46.3, pp. 219–42.

Robson, C., 2002, *Real World Research*, 2nd edn, Oxford: Blackwell.

Roca, R. S., 2007, '"Dinheiro vivo": money and religion in Brazil', *Critique of Anthropology* 27.3, pp. 319–39.

Roof, W. C., 1993, *A Generation of Seekers: The Spiritual Journeys of the Baby Boom Generations*, New York: HarperCollins.

——. 1999, *Spiritual Marketplace: Baby Boomers and the Remaking of American Religion*, Princeton: Princeton University Press.

Rothenberg, P. S., 2006, *Race, Class and Gender in the United States*, 7th edn, New York: Worth Publishers.

Ruether, R. R., 1983, *Sexism and God-Talk: Toward a Feminist Theology*, London: SCM Press.

Ruthven, M., 2004, *Fundamentalism: The Search for Meaning*, Oxford: Oxford University Press.

Sanford, A. W., 2007, 'Pinned on karma rock: whitewater kayaking as religious experience', *Journal of the American Academy of Religion* 75.4, pp. 875–95.

Scholte, J. A., 2000, *Globalization: A Critical Introduction*, London: Macmillan.

Seidman, S., 2004, *Contested Knowledge: Social Theory Today*, 3rd edn, Oxford: Blackwell.

Sered, S. S., 1994, *Priestess, Mother, Sacred Sister: Religions Dominated by Women*, New York: Oxford University Press.

Sharma, A. and Young, K. K. (eds), 1999, *Feminism and World Religions*, Albany: SUNY Press.

Sharot, S., 1992, 'Religious Fundamentalism: Neo-Traditionalism in Modern Societies', in B. R. Wilson (ed.), *Religion: Contemporary Issues*, London: Bellew Publishing, pp. 24–45.

Sharpe, E. J., 1983, *Understanding Religion*, London: Duckworth.

Shaw, S. and Francis, A. (eds), 2008, *Deep Blue: Critical Reflections on Nature, Religion and Water*, London: Equinox.

Siqueira, D., 2003, *As Novas Religiosidades no Ocidente: Brasília, Cidade Mística*, Editora UnB/FINATEC.

Smart, N., 1973, *The Science of Religion and the Sociology of Knowledge*, Princeton: Princeton University Press.

——. 1996, *Dimensions of the Sacred: An Anatomy of the World's Beliefs*, London: HarperCollins.

Snow, D. A. and Machalek, R., 1984, 'The sociology of conversion', *Annual Review of Sociology* 10, pp. 167–90.

Snyder, S., 2007, 'New streams of religion: fly fishing as a lived religion of nature', *Journal of the American Academy of Religion* 75.4, pp. 896–922.

Sorj, B., 2006, *A Nova Sociedade Brasileira*, 3rd edn, Rio de Janeiro: Jorge Zahar Editor.

Southwold, M., 1978, 'Buddhism and the definition of religion', *Man* (new series) 13.3, pp. 362–79.

Spickard, J. V., 2004, 'Globalization and religious organizations: rethinking the relationship between church, culture, and market', *International Journal of Politics, Culture and Society* 18.1, pp. 47–63.

——. 2007, 'Micro Qualitative Approaches to the Sociology of Religion: Phenomenologies, Interviews, Narratives, and Ethnographies', in J. A. Beckford and N. J. Demereth III (eds), *The Sage Handbook of the Sociology of Religion*, London: Sage, pp. 121–43.

Stanczak, G. and Miller, D. E., 2002, *Engaged Spirituality: Spirituality and Social Transformation in Mainstream American Religious Traditions*, Los Angeles: University of South California.

Stanton, E. C., 2002, *The Woman's Bible: A Classic Feminist Perspective*, New York: Dover Publications.

Starhawk, 1979, *The Spiral Dance: A Rebirth of the Ancient Religion of the Great Goddess*, New York: HarperCollins.

Stark, R., 1971, 'Psychopathology and religious commitment', *Review of Religious Research* 12.3, pp. 165–76.

——. 1996, 'Why religious movements succeed or fail: a revised general model', *Journal of Contemporary Religion* 11.2, pp. 133–46.

——. 1999, 'Secularization RIP', *Sociology of Religion* 60.3, pp. 249–73.

Stark, R. and Bainbridge, W. S., 1985, *The Future of Religion: Secularization, Revival, and Cult Formation*, Berkeley: University of California Press.

——. 1987, *A Theory of Religion*, New York: Lang.

Stark, R. and Finke, R., 2000, *Acts of Faith: Explaining the Human Side of Religion*, Berkeley: University of California Press.

Stark, R. and Glock, C. Y., 1968, *American Piety: The Nature of Religious Commitment*, Berkeley: University of California Press.

Swatos, W. H., 1989, 'Religious Sociology and the Sociology of Religion in America at the turn of the Twentieth Century', *Sociological Analysis* 50.4, pp. 363–75.

Taylor, C., 2007, *A Secular Age*, Cambridge: Harvard University Press.

Thompson, J., 1984, *Studies in the Theory of Ideology*, Cambridge: Polity Press.

Thumma, S. and Gray, E. R. (eds), 2005, *Gay Religion*, Walnut Creek: AltaMira Press.

Tönnies, F., 1955, *Community and Association*, London: Routledge & Kegan Paul.

Troeltsch, E., 1931, *The Social Teaching of the Christian Churches*, vol. 1, London: George Allen & Unwin.

Turner, J., 1988, *A Theory of Social Interaction*, Cambridge: Polity Press.

Tylor, E. B., 1871, *Primitive Culture*, vol. 1, London: John Murray.

Urry, J., 2000, *Sociology Beyond Societies: Mobilities for the Twenty-First Century*, London: Routledge.

Voas, D., 2007, 'Surveys of Behaviour, Beliefs and Affiliation: Micro-Quantitative', in J. A. Beckford and N. J. Demereth III (eds), *The Sage Handbook of the Sociology of Religion*, pp. 144–66.

Voll, J. O., 1991, 'Fundamentalism in the Sunni Arab World: Egypt and the Sudan', in M. E. Marty and R. S. Appleby (eds), *Fundamentalisms Observed*, pp. 345–402.

Wallis, R., 1984, *The Elementary Forms of the New Religious Life*, London: Routledge & Kegan Paul.

Wanderley, L. E. W., 2007, 'Modernidade, Pós-modernidade e Implicações na Questão Social Latino-Americano', in T. Bernado and P. A. Resende (eds), *Ciências Sociais na Atualidade: Realidades e Imaginários*, São Paulo: Paulus, pp. 47–84.

Waters, M., 2001, *Globalization*, 2nd edn, London: Routledge.

Weber, M., 1949, '"Objectivity" in Social Science and Social Policy', in E. A. Shils and H. A. Finch (eds), *Max Weber: The Methodology of the Social Sciences*, New York: Free Press, pp. 50–112.

——. 1952, *Ancient Judaism*, London: Allen & Unwin.

——. 1963, *The Sociology of Religion*, Boston: Beacon Press.

——. 1967, *The Religion of India: The Sociology of Hinduism and Buddhism*, New York: Free Press.

——. 1968a, *Economy and Society*, New York: Bedminster Press.

——. 1968b, *The Religion of China: Confucianism and Taoism*, New York: Free Press.

——. 1991a, 'Class, Status, Party', in H. H. Gerth and C. Wright Mills (eds), *From Max Weber: Essays in Sociology*, new edn, London: Routledge, pp. 180–95.

——. 1991b, 'Religious Rejections of the World and Their Directions', in H. H. Gerth and C. Wright Mills (eds), *From Max Weber*, pp. 323–59.

——. 1991c, 'Science as a Vocation', in H. H. Gerth and C. Wright Mills (eds), *From Max Weber*, pp. 129–56.

——. 1991d, 'The Social Psychology of the World Religions', in H. H. Gerth and C. Wright Mills (eds), *From Max Weber*, pp. 129–56.

——. 1992, *The Protestant Ethic and the Spirit of Capitalism*, London: Routledge.

Wilcox, W. B., 2004, *Soft Patriarchs, New Men: How Christianity Shapes Fathers and Husbands*, Chicago: University of Chicago Press.

Williams, H., 1988, *Concepts of Ideology*, Brighton: Wheatsheaf.

Williams, R. M., 1951, *American Society: A Sociological Interpretation*, New York: Knopf.

Willig, C., 2001, *Introducing Qualitative Research in Psychology*, Buckingham: Open University Press.

Wilson, B. R., 1966, *Religion in Secular Society*, London: Penguin.

——. 1967, *Patterns of Sectarianism: Organisation and Ideology in Social and Religious Movements*, London: Heinemann.

——. 1970, *Religious Sects: A Sociological Study*, London: Weidenfeld & Nicolson.

——. 1976, *Contemporary Transformations of Religion*, London: Oxford University Press.

——. 1982, *Religion in Sociological Perspective*, Oxford: Oxford University Press.

——. 1985, 'Secularization: The Inherited Model', in P. Hammond (ed.), *The Sacred in a Secular Age: Toward Revision in the Scientific Study of Religion*, Berkeley: University of California Press, pp. 9–20.

——. 1998, 'The Secularization Thesis: Criticisms and Rebuttals', in R. Laermans, B. Wilson and J. Billiet (eds), *Secularization and Social Integration: Papers in Honor of Karel Dobbelaere*, Leuven: Leuven University Press, pp. 45–66.

Wittgenstein, L., 1980, *Culture and Value*, Oxford: Blackwell.

Wood, M., 2010, 'The Sociology of Spirituality: Reflections on a Problematic Endeavor', in B. S. Turner (ed.), *The New Blackwell Companion to the Sociology of Religion*, Oxford: Wiley-Blackwell, pp. 267–85.

Wuthnow, R., 1998, *After Heaven: Spirituality in America Since the 1950s*, Berkeley: University of California Press.

——. 2001, *Creative Spirituality: The Way of the Artist*, Berkeley: University of California Press.

Yinger, J. M., 1957, *Religion, Society, and the Individual: An Introduction to the Sociology of Religion*, New York: Macmillan.

——. 1970, *The Scientific Study of Religion*, New York: Macmillan.

Zinnbauer, B. J., Pargament, K. I. et al., 1997, 'Religion and spirituality: unfuzzying the fuzzy', *Journal for the Scientific Study of Religion* 36.4, pp. 549–64.

Index

Printed in November 2021
by Rotomail Italia S.p.A., Vignate (MI) - Italy